SOCRATES' SECOND SAILING

SOCRATES'
Second Sailing
On Plato's
Republic

SETH BENARDETE

THE UNIVERSITY OF CHICAGO PRESS
CHICAGO AND LONDON

Seth Benardete is Professor of Classics at New York University. Among his earlier translations and commentaries are Sophocles' *Antigone; The Aristeia of Diomedes and the Iliad; Herodotean Inquiries;* and *The Being of the Beautiful,* this last published by the University of Chicago Press in 1984.

The University of Chicago Press, Chicago 60637
The University of Chicago Press, Ltd., London
© 1989 by The University of Chicago
All rights reserved. Published 1989
Printed in the United States of America
98 97 96 95 94 93 92 91 90 89   5 4 3 2 1

Library of Congress Cataloging-in-Publication Data

Benardete, Seth.
    Socrates' second sailing.

    Includes index.
    1. Plato. Republic. I. Title.
JC71.P6B47   1989   321'.07   88-27909
ISBN 0-226-04242-1

∞ The paper used in this publication meets the minimum requirements of the American National Standard for Information Sciences—Permanence of Paper for Printed Library Materials, ANSI Z39.48-1984.

"All there is to thinking," he said, "is seeing something noticeable which makes you see something you weren't noticing which makes you see something that isn't even visible."

Norman F. Maclean, *A River Runs Through It*

CONTENTS

ACKNOWLEDGMENTS

This book began as a review of Leo Strauss's *The City and Man* (*The Political Science Reviewer* 1978, 1–20). Professor Reiner Schürmann gave me the opportunity to teach the *Republic* over three semesters in the Philosophy Department of the Graduate Faculty of the New School.

I also wish to thank Robert Berman, Ronna Burger, and Michael Davis for reading and discussing the manuscript with me; Julie Farr for helping to make it clearer; and Barbara Witucki for typing and correcting it.

INTRODUCTION

The title of this book alludes to the phrase Plato has Socrates use in his intellectual autobiography in the *Phaedo* (96a6–100b3).[1] Socrates tells his story as a preface to his reply to Cebes' counterargument to the proof Socrates has given about the deathlessness of soul. Cebes grants that if the soul never took on body, it might never wear out, but he wonders how continual reincarnations of soul could be shown to have no end. He is particularly distressed by the apparent conflict between the soul's own good, to be separate from body, and the necessity for soul to be conjoined with body. Why, he asks, is there becoming and not just being? Cebes' question launches Socrates into a discussion of causality, and, in light of the issue the soul's own good raises, of material and efficient causation in relation to teleology.

Socrates distinguishes between the kinds of causal questions he asked when he began to philosophize and the kinds of causal answers he could give prephilosophically. His prephilosophical answers, however, could not stand up to the broadest possible reflection on the minimal conditions to be satisfied by any causal account. Every causal account that Socrates could conceive of had at its base the character of the arithmetical operation of either addition or division, and he knew that one could not have a causal account if opposite causes yielded the same effect; but any mechanical representation of the sum of one and one cannot be distinguished from any mechanical representation of the division of something into two. The drawing near of two ones made for two no less than did the drawing apart; and the union of two ones made for one no less than did their separation. If body and soul together are one, they are also two; and if body and soul apart are two, each is one. So death as the separation of a one yields two, and life as the union of two yields one, but then life no less than death is both one and two.

Socrates then realized that these absurdities could vanish only if union and division were operations of the mind. Anaxagorean mind,

---

1. For a more detailed analysis of this passage, see R. Burger, *The Phaedo: A Platonic Labyrinth* (New Haven, 1984), 135–60.

1

however, was inadequate for two reasons. Anaxagoras had allowed all things to be together prior to mind. Mind was solely a separating power; but since mind had also to be a uniting power, there could never have been a time when things were either together or apart except insofar as mind had united or divided them. Anaxagoras had tried to combine a mechanical causation, in which there was no action at a distance, with a principle of understanding that would articulate the conglomerate that the unimpeded work of mechanical causation must bring about. Once, however, nearness is no less an operational effect of mind than distance is, things are together and apart simultaneously. The ordering power of mind then yields a causal arithmetic; but it is at a price. Mind now orders things, but it does not order them for the good. Mind is now the sole cause, but it is not rational. The original difficulty of how body and soul are together as both one and two recurs within mind itself, which splits between purposive and configurative rationality. The pattern of things is not the same as the goodness of things, and any attempt to combine them must confront the impossibility of causal sums. If some element were to convey the good of something to that something, the additive operation involved would no more produce the unity than the disunion of the being. So the desired union of the two aspects of rationality cannot be devised by either: one would fail because it would put together and keep apart order and good, and the other would fail because the good does not order things mechanically. The good can be neither the sum of things nor one of the things.

When the winds fail, the sailor turns to oars. He relies no longer on any help outside himself. Socratic philosophy, as we know it from Plato, is the practice of this so-called second sailing. Socrates tells Cebes that he was disappointed to find, after he had figured out what he expected to find in Anaxagoras' book, that Anaxagoras did not have recourse to mind as the cause of good. Socrates knew how the presence of mind could be detected infallibly, but he did not know how Anaxagoras would go about proving the presence of mind in both each thing and all things, for any good that was assigned to one thing might prove to be bad for it and another thing; and any good assigned to them together but not apart might prove in turn to be bad for them and another thing. Teleology must be architectonic; but if the good is at the end of a series because it depends on nothing else, the series might fall away with no loss to the good; and if the good is distributed along the series, it is necessary to know the entire series before the good can be ascribed to anything in the series. Final cause seems to be a necessary principle whose application is impossible.

Socrates illustrates its necessity with his own case. One cannot say that Socrates does all that he does by mind and then, in giving the causes for each of the things he does, say that Socrates sits in prison because his muscles and bones are arranged in a certain way and with certain capacities, and he converses with Cebes because of the vibrations in the ear and movements of sound in the air. Socrates has no objection to the citing of these kinds of causes as long as one does not neglect to speak of what truly causes his imprisonment and their conversation; and he certainly objects to any attempt to put together the mechanical and the true causes prior to a resolution of the difficulty that any causal arithmetic must face. The true causes are twofold: the Athenians conceived the opinion that it was better to condemn Socrates, and Socrates in turn on account of this maintained the opinion that it was better to sit in prison, and it was more just to submit to any penalty they ordained than to run away. Socrates drops the operation of Anaxagorean mind and replaces it with two opinions about the good, one of which holds that Socrates is unjust and one that he is just. If Socrates does what he does by mind, the Athenians cannot have done what they did by mind, for otherwise mind would be wholly irrational in reaching the same conclusion through opposite routes. The Athenians hold that death is an evil and life a good, and Socrates ought to suffer an evil; but Socrates told them that he did not know whether death is an evil, and he has maintained throughout the *Phaedo* that for him now it is a good. If Socrates had been arrested at the moment of the indictment and kept under such close guard that his friends could not have smuggled him out, it would have made no difference what Socrates' opinion was, and his condemnation and death would exemplify strangely the operation of mind. The irrationality of reason differs no doubt from the randomness of chance and the necessity in causal chains, but it would be hard to fault Anaxagoras for neglecting such a cause in his claim for the prevalence of mind.

The grounds for Socrates' being in prison seem to be over-determined and incoherent. Either his own opinion had no effect or his opinion supervened on the Athenians' opinion and contradicted it in principle and confirmed it in its conclusion; or what the Athenians interpret as an execution was in fact a suicide, and Socrates took a public occasion to cover his private interest. His interlocutors at any rate assume from the start that it is suicide, and in the absence of any political considerations in the *Phaedo,* it is not easy to say whether they believe differently at the end. Socrates himself remarks that under any ordinary understanding of teleology, his muscles and bones would have long since been haunting Megara or Boeotia, "conveyed by the opinion of the best" (99a2), since the good for Socrates, the living individual of body and soul, must be the maintenance of life. No teleology is possible if the good cannot be assigned to the union of necessary and sufficient conditions; and Socrates had come to the puzzle of the Socratic turn through his acknowledgment that he found it impossible to account for the required union. Socrates points to the way out in his rephrasing of the cause of his refusal to escape from prison. He believed it more just and more noble (or more beautiful) to stay (99a2–3). Socrates begins with the good and then splits it into the just, the noble, and the good. The good is now a complex of three things whose unity is as puzzling as its fragmentation. It thus becomes possible to begin to understand the false opinion of the Athenians and the true opinion of Socrates as both consequences of the operation of mind. The bits and pieces of the good that show up in opinion are not as bits and pieces what they are in the whole truly articulated by mind. These bits and pieces are the speeches or opinions of things to which Socrates has recourse after the possibility of looking at things directly has foundered on the problem of causality. These fragmentary speeches parade as wholes or *eidē* (*Statesman* 262a5–263b11), and Socrates saw it as the proper task of philosophy to proceed from them to the true *eidē.* I call this procedure eidetic analysis. It is designed to replace teleology without giving up on either mind or good.

Eidetic analysis does not lend itself to a presentation apart from its dialogic practice. It is therefore more fitting in an introduction to say something about Platonic arguments. Generally speaking, Plato has Socrates give us two kinds of arguments. They are either burstlike or filamentlike. On occasion, Socrates gives an example that is so clear and telling that the reader, no less than the interlocutor, must concede its force at once. Socrates' counterexample to Cephalus is such a burstlike argument (331c1–d1). A burstlike argument, however, rarely decides an issue. Most of the time, Socrates offers arguments that seem to be deductive, and yet we sense that in the course of the argument new premises are being smuggled in or terms are being continually deformed until, as Adimantus complains,

4

we feel trapped rather than convinced (487b1–c4). Filamentlike arguments tend to be periagogic or conversive (518d4). They turn us around to face something that we would not have seen unless Socrates had been not quite straight with us. In his connecting something with something else or disconnecting something from something else, we are forced suddenly to ascend merely to catch up. The *Republic* is an eidetic analysis of the beautiful, the good, and the just insofar as they contribute to the understanding of the just. Its procedure is twofold: to set the just alongside other things and to set the just apart from other things. It isolates and associates. Parting and pairing, however, make it impossible for any argument to run smoothly, for it is the unexpected break and the unexpected join in arguments that constitute the way of eidetic analysis.

PART ONE

BOOK I

1

SOCRATES

(327a1–328c4)

Symbolism is shorthand for an argument. The *Republic* begins as a story of a thwarted ascent. Socrates is its narrator. It seems to be a matter of chance that Socrates was thwarted and took the occasion to discuss justice. His plan was to go down to the Piraeus, pray to the Thracian goddess Bendis, watch the first celebration of her festival, and return home. His companion was Glaucon, the brother of Adimantus and Plato. The difference between Socrates' prayer and his seeing seem to point to the difference between the best city in speech, the conditions for whose realization cannot be established by human means (450d1, 456b12, 499c4), and the discovery of the nature of political things that accompanies the elaboration of Utopia (Cicero *de re publica* 2.30[52]). The two forms of the title in our manuscript tradition accidentally preserve this difference, *Politeia* and *Politeiai*, *Regime* and *Regimes*. Regardless of whether it is of necessity imaginary or not, the one best regime comprehends the manifold of all inferior regimes. It guides one's understanding of political life even if it never shapes one's actions.

The function of the one best regime is not unlike the narrative form of the *Republic* itself. Socrates is himself and plays all other parts. We see everything as he sees it, and we do not hear what he decides to omit (342d2–3, 350c12–d1). He introduces us to Polemarchus as if he had been present when Polemarchus caught sight of Socrates' and Glaucon's imminent departure and ordered his slave to run and ask them to wait up for his master (327b2–4). Socrates cancels in his narration the reasoning that went into it (cf. 328c2). He does not start with the sudden pull on his himation and the slave's request which made him turn around and ask where Polemarchus was. He drops the inference he drew from what he experienced and gives us instead a perfectly smooth description. If they still have to wait for Polemarchus to catch up with them, the slave must have run; but that Polemarchus told him to run—he did not tell him to grab

Socrates' himation—Socrates could have figured out only from his acquaintance with Polemarchus' peremptory nature. Socrates' certainty stands in immediate contrast with Polemarchus' own guesswork, which Socrates says was not bad, as to the plans of Socrates and Glaucon (327c4–6); but its larger import bears on Socrates' self-effacement on the level of narration. Since we see and hear everything through him, we tend to overlook the effect his actual presence might have had in the setting he conjures before us. We follow the argument and do not stand back to attend to Socrates' agency apart from the argument. Socrates indeed takes a backseat to the others from the moment Polemarchus' slave comes up to him to the moment he starts the discussion with Cephalus. Glaucon decides they will wait for Polemarchus (327b7–8); Glaucon again declares that if Polemarchus will not listen he cannot be persuaded (327c13); Adimantus, who has come along with Polemarchus, offers a way out of the impasse (328a1–2); and Socrates defers to Glaucon's decision to stay (328b2–3). Socrates keeps on talking and arranges nothing. He seems to be wholly involved in speeches and without the power to rule.

Polemarchus believes it follows from Socrates' seeing the number of his gang that Socrates and Glaucon must either prove to be stronger or stay. The word he uses for stronger (*kreittōn*) is Thrasymachus' word too, when he defines justice as the advantage of the stronger; but the word is ambiguous, and once Thrasymachus admits that he does not mean by "stronger" Poulydamas the pancratiast (338c5–d4), it recovers its broader meaning of "better," and raises the issue whether Socrates does not argue the same thesis as Thrasymachus. Polemarchus in any case threatens compulsion and resolves to turn a deaf ear to Socrates' alternative of persuasion. Neither Polemarchus' threat nor his resolve is serious. Would Adimantus lay hands on his own brother? And since Polemarchus could not have prevented everyone else from hearing Socrates out, would he not have found himself in the end outnumbered?

Polemarchus first urges the absolute right of majority rule, but then, after Glaucon confirms his view that speech is the only mode of persuasion, admits the possibility that the majority could be swayed. Polemarchus asks Socrates whether he could get around the obstacle of the will that refuses for no reason to listen to reason. The *Republic* is Socrates' answer to that question which Glaucon's intervention now prevents him from giving; but unless Glaucon had intervened, we would never have heard the answer. The discussion of justice occurs because a compromise is reached between the threat of force, which if executed would have led to criminal charges, and the alternative of persuasion, which if effective would have allowed Socrates and Glaucon to continue on their way back to town. Adimantus arranges for the compromise by asking whether Socrates and Glaucon do not know about the torch race from horseback scheduled for that night. He holds out the hope that a spectacle of rivalry might unite the divergent wills of Socrates and Polemarchus. Socrates once more expresses his interest in novelty and thus offers Polemarchus a chance to save face. Polemarchus now reveals that his representation of will as power concealed his friendly invitation to dinner and a show; and he throws in for good measure the chance of Socrates' talking with the many young who will be there. A pleasant enough evening is planned and replaces the disagreeable histrionics of Polemarchus; but Socrates starts something with Cephalus that sets aside that entertainment; and though the threat of force does not return, there is still talk till late in the *Republic* as if Socrates were under some constraint (472a8, 504e6, 509c3). Socrates can resist Polemarchus with the help of Glaucon and Adimantus; but he cannot resist a consensus that includes Thrasymachus (450a4–5). Socrates' narrative control certainly makes it seem that that consensus developed against his will and behind his back. It might still have been, however, against the grain and yet for his own good; and who can say, with a philosopher whose most notorious traits are irony and self-knowledge, that he was not promoting his own good from the start?

A series of frustrations initiates the *Republic* and marks its course throughout. Socrates and Glaucon do not get to go home; and they do not get to eat at Polemarchus' house and later to see the relay race. Once the discussion starts, Socrates believes he is quit of it after he expresses his disappointment at the insubstantial fare he accepted too greedily from Thrasymachus (354a10–c3). Afterwards, when he is proposing to give an account of corrupt regimes, rebellion among the auditors diverts him again, and he has to introduce the notion of the philosopher-king. The philosopher-king brings in its train "the idea of the good"; and here Socrates seems to have his revenge, for he refuses point blank to tell Glaucon his opinion about it (533a1–5). The constraints under which an understanding of justice becomes possible seem to be the same as the constraints that limit the understanding of the good. The *Republic*, it seems, cannot make up for the thwarted ascent of Socrates.

2

C E P H A L U S

(328c5–331d3)

Now that Cephalus confesses that the desires and pleasures of speeches are increasingly important to him, since the capacity for pleasures of the body—though not its desires—has diminished, Socrates asks him how he finds old age, for it is something that he too might have to endure. He cites the poets—"on the threshold of old age"—for the time of life to which Cephalus has come. The expression is ambiguous, for it does not say whether one is leaving the house of life or entering the house of Hades. Cephalus' contemporaries certainly believe that with old age everything is over and they only look back with regret, but Cephalus himself seems to look forward to another life of reward or punishment. He does not, however, bring in Hades immediately, but through Socrates' gentle probing it emerges once the question of moderation is replaced by that of justice. Old age, Cephalus says, is not itself the cause of the misery of old age; but he at once contradicts himself by saying that his contemporaries long for the pleasures of their youth for which they no longer have the capacity, and so for them old age is the culprit. Cephalus arraigns them not on the grounds that sexual and other pleasures should never be one's standard but that they refuse to acknowledge the serenity that old age alone makes possible. They refuse to heed the old Sophocles, whose indignation at an inquiry about his sexual capacity implies that he led a disorderly youth from which he is now glad to be free but for which apparently he is not responsible. Temperament (*tropos*) for Cephalus, though he allows decency and serenity to hold for one's youth as well, seems to mean in old age resignation. Resignation, however, seems superfluous, for according to Cephalus the desires in old age cease to strain, and there is then the release from many savage and insane masters. But since Cephalus' contemporaries must still be subject to desires in their imagination, he seems to identify "temperament" with belief in the sayings of the poets, from whom one can learn the truth about those desires. Poetry supplies the images in which old age finds in

12

speeches its pleasurable compensation and the proper way to express its resentment. Cephalus, however, takes his bearings by poetry without the poetry. Not only does he multiply Sophocles' singular master, but he drops his "as it were (*hōsper*)." His savage and insane masters are fully real.

Socrates does not try to unravel Cephalus' tangled account, in which old age and temperament compete as the single cause of serenity; but rather he adopts the vulgar view that Cephalus bears old age easily on account of his wealth: "The rich, they say, have many consolations." Money introduces justice; and perhaps nothing illustrates better the Thomistic characterization of the difference between pagan and Christian morality than that Cephalus does not count the sexual excesses of his youth as a moral matter for which he should fear punishment in the afterlife. (Thomas *Summa Theologica* 12^{ae} CIII, 4, 3^m). He began with pleasures and desires precisely because money has allayed his fears, and the pleasure of hope has replaced bodily desires. Cephalus admits that wealth is a condition, and that possibly his contemporaries are right about the decent but poor. Old age is very hard, but he still says that wealth cannot by itself do away with peevishness. Cephalus once more finds an authority for his views; but now it is a statesman and not a poet.

A man from the island of Seriphos was once abusing Themistocles, and asserted that his reputation was due to the city and not himself; Themistocles replied that if he had been a Seriphian he would not have become renowned, and neither would the Seriphian had he been an Athenian. Themistocles' greatness is to Athens' greatness as Cephalus' serenity is to his wealth. Cephalus has no qualms about magnifying his decent modesty. He implies that the following four resemblances hold: (1) Themistocles in Seriphos is like Cephalus without money; (2) Themistocles in Athens is like Cephalus with money; (3) a Seriphian in Seriphos is like the peevish without money; (4) a Seriphian in Athens is like the peevish with money. Cephalus does not reckon with the possibility that the poor but peevish man is peevish because he is poor, just as the Seriphian was abusive because he came from Seriphos. Socrates therefore wonders whether "old money" is not the condition for serenity, and Cephalus' indifference to moneymaking has made him easier to live with. Cephalus admits as much when he indignantly asks Socrates how he could imagine he was a moneymaker; his grandfather really made money; he just dabbled, for his temperament worked against his increasing his inheritance to cover the needs of three sons. He could not have made money and still be agreeable.

Socrates knew that Cephalus had inherited his money because he did not regard it as the equivalent of Themistocles' fame. He says that poets, fathers, and self-made millionaires are all alike: they are fond of their own products apart from their usefulness simply because they made them themselves. Socrates manages to get rid of poets and fathers in his communistic city, but he does not get rid of moneymakers. The city cannot do without them, even though what they make stands in the way of their loving the city wholeheartedly. Its auxiliaries and guardians owe their existence to the class of artisan-moneymakers whom their education teaches them to despise. An ignorance about one's own conditions is sometimes good. But can the city really do without poets and fathers? Socrates after all is the maker of his own city, and perhaps he is too fond of it. Themistocles had not made Athens or Athens him; and the same holds true of Socrates and Athens, whatever the personified laws of Athens may say (*Crito* 50d2–4). Themistocles' independence of Athens, as Alcibiades' after him, made it possible for him to be admired in Sparta and welcomed in Persia; for he was unlike Pausanias, whose absence from Sparta corrupted him and made him useless (Thucydides 1.77.6;95.3–5); but he was like Socrates, whose independence from Athens got him condemned. Will Socrates then never get free of the best city in speech just because it will never turn on him? Perhaps it is not good to live in conformity with a device of one's own imagination (592a5–b6). When the poets are finally banished in Book X, perhaps Socrates the poet goes into exile with them.

The link between Cephalus' moderation and Cephalus' justice is money; but whereas, according to Cephalus, money is a condition for moderation, it is almost everything for justice, for poverty may compel one to cheat and lie (331b2). Cephalus must again speak of temperament, for money can guarantee peace of mind only if one is subject to nightmares and susceptible to what stories about Hades report. Temperament is simply the way one interprets the poets. Cephalus says the stories twist the soul, and it makes no difference whether one's fear and anxiety are due to the weakness or to the greater insight of old age, for one's experiences, regardless of their cause, agree with the stories. Cephalus opposes stories and experience (*hoi te legomenoi muthoi . . . kai autos*). The once-ridiculed stories may be true—whoever did wrong must be punished in Hades—and in one's ignorance it would be well to be on the safe side; but the reckoning of one's justice or injustice brings with it hope or fear, and one lives one's old age in the imagination. Cephalus seems not unlike his contemporaries, whose memory fosters their dissatisfaction and who lack the advantage of knowing some poetry by heart. Poetry terrifies and consoles; but it can console only those it has thoroughly terrified. Cephalus seems to stand for everything with which the *Republic* must deal. The version of poetry proposed in Books II–III is intended to make Cephalus' nightmares impossible; but his account of the desires seems to be true in Book IX of the tyrant. The departure of Cephalus, though it allows Thrasymachus to speak frankly, does not dispose of Cephalus. His citation of Pindar introduces piety and joins it with justice (331a4); and though Socrates may drop it when he summarizes Cephalus' understanding of justice, the sacred may be not as easily dismissed as Cephalus dismisses his newfound pleasure in speeches. Socrates says it is his sacred duty to stand by Justice when she is reviled (368b7–c2).

If money is to have for justice as central a place as Cephalus gives it, he must identify justice with the possibility of compensation. There are no irreversible actions for which one cannot make up. There is perfect exchange and no unconditional conditions. Redemption is always possible. Gods and the immortality of the soul seem to be the minimal supports needed for such a view; and if justice could be absorbed completely into piety, Socrates' counterexample would lose its force. Cephalus, however, is not Euthyphro (*Euthyphro* 11e4–12d4). He plainly distinguishes between what one owes to gods and what one owes to men; and it certainly seems just, if a sane friend gives one a weapon on deposit, not to give it back and tell him the truth when he is crazed. The principle is weakly embodied in any law that regulates use (e.g., a driver's license) and strongly denied by any law that allows for unrestricted use (e.g., the right to bear arms). Socrates' principle, if formulated universally, would run: Knowledge alone determines right. Not only do prodigals thereby lose the right to use their own property, but anyone who does not know how to use anything he has—including his life— either has it taken away from him or handed over to another to manage. The principle is so terrifying that one must hope that either no one has this kind of knowledge, or, if anyone does have it, either he does not on its basis lay claim to rule, or he promises not to apply his knowledge too strictly. Thrasymachus indeed is so frightening at first because he speaks as if Socrates and Polemarchus ought to know better and must pay for their ignorance. Justice, then, seems to require that we all be ignorant, or truthfulness be acknowledged to be incompatible with justice. In Socrates' example, one could possibly refuse to give back the weapon but tell the truth and let the madman believe one is unjust, rather than, as Socrates proposes, have the madman believe one is just while being, in terms of his belief, unjust. Justice does not require that one explain oneself.

Socrates spoke not only of truthtelling but also of truth (331c8, d2). He seems to be alluding to Cephalus' account in which stories about Hades twist the soul when one is old lest they be true. If the stories are not true, and there is neither reward nor punishment in the afterlife, it would seem strange to deny that Cephalus is just because he paid what he owed on the possibility that they be true. The fear and anxiety Cephalus ascribes to the old do not make them out to be models of sobriety. Lying, then, would be just not only when there was ignorance of use but also when false opinions about the truth of things obtained. Socrates' best city in speech is based on falsehood. He implies that falsehood is ineradicably native to all cities; and we know that they are all armed. The city in itself seems to be a madman that puts in a claim for what is its own that ought not be satisfied. Is the city Socrates' friend?

3

P O L E M A R C H U S

(331d4–336a8)

Polemarchus comes to the defense of his father's definition but drops truth and cites a poet. Socrates has his defense submit to three different tests, the first of which examines the defense as a whole—justice is to benefit friends and harm enemies—while the second examines friends and enemies, and the third, benefit and harm. The first test concludes that justice is the art of theft; and insofar as Polemarchus' definition forces one to have recourse to a political interpretation of it—for only politically are there no neutrals and everyone not already a friend or enemy is potentially one or the other—the first test implies in its three successive phases that justice as an art of assignment and distribution is the knowledge of the fraternal and martial city, that as an art of production and acquisition justice is the knowledge of the imperialist city, and that as an art of security and protection justice is the knowledge of the defensive city (332c5–d1, d10–333a9, a10–334b9). All these implications, however, are below the surface argument in which Socrates distracts Polemarchus away from his own insight into the political character of his definition. The just man, he says, is most powerful when it comes to waging war and forming military alliances (332e5). In its political applicability, Polemarchus' definition, in pointing to patriotism as justice, points to a necessity that is indifferent to right because it is prior to right; and if that necessity is to be considered just, the city as such must first be proved to be good. Since it is not until Book IX that the word "fatherland (*patris*)" occurs, and the tyrant is there the first to have a fatherland he can set out to punish and enslave (575d3–9; cf. 592a8), one has in this the measure of the distance Socrates has to go before he can supply such a proof. That distance conveys as well the lesson of the *Republic*: in philosophy, the ideality of things must precede the reality of their good.

In Cephalus' definition, the debt was as neutral as the person to whom the debt was owed. In Polemarchus' defense, the debt becomes either good or bad, and the person either friend or enemy. Socrates' elaborate refutation, though it is of the same order as the one of Cephalus, shifts its viewpoint from recipient to agent, and from the recipient's sanity to the agent's knowledge. Polemarchus apparently does not see that the mutual relations of friend with friend and of enemy against enemy cannot be prior to the issue of justice: justice itself must determine the relation of those who act justly toward one another. Polemarchus does see, however, that if friends are not prior to just actions, then whomever one benefits is a friend, and almost everyone willy-nilly is just. As long as Polemarchus speaks exclusively of friends, he can speak of the obligation to benefit; but as soon as Socrates introduces enemies, he speaks besides of the appropriateness of harm. It is now not even for friends an obligation but a fact: friends do benefit and enemies do harm. The absence of obligation thus leads to Socrates' introducing justice as an art. Justice is not a question of character and will, for it operates once certain conditions are fulfilled; it is designed to enhance as a means an already existing situation. It must be a kind of knowledge. Socrates gives two examples, a genuine and a spurious art, and in both cases Polemarchus fails to generalize. If justice were like cookery, it would be something like sweet-talk or the coating of the pill, and justice would be the inducement of the belief in justice. If justice were like medicine, it would be concerned with souls, and either be a curing of injustice or an instilling of justice; and its means could be either, like medicines, corrective punishment or, like food, all the sciences. The word for medicines is *pharmaka*, which could equally be translated poisons; and justice as an art thus becomes neutral to kill or cure. If justice is to be an art and yet not be neutral, what passes for will or intention must be an automatic consequence of it as an art. Can justice as cognitive be good through its being cognitive? Is there any knowledge that can never be bad? If one's immediate answer is "self-knowledge," the answer itself shows the difficulty, if justice must be social, of showing in justice a coincidence of goodness and knowledge. A combination of self-knowledge with a medicinal justice plus a sweetener seems impossible.

Socrates proves that if justice is knowledge it is morally neutral; and since Polemarchus is willing to abandon his definition entirely, he drops knowledge and lets the just man be mistaken as to who his true friends and enemies are. If we restore knowledge, the just man has either a diagnostic knowledge he does not act on or a knowledge that would possibly in its effects be always out of phase with what his seeming friends and enemies expect from him. Knowledge of this kind would have to be shared among true friends at least; but it still would be ineffective unless everyone else, including false friends and true enemies, were in on it too; otherwise the situation of Glaucon's comparison-test would arise, and the just man would, apparently unjustly, be benefiting false enemies and harming false friends. There is only one situation, it seems, in which such knowledge could be useful and yet would not have to be shared, and that is in dialogue. When Adimantus numbers Thrasymachus among the many listeners who would resist Socrates' recommendations for a city-sponsored education for philosophy, Socrates says: "Don't set Thrasymachus and me at odds; we have just become friends and were not even before enemies" (498c9–d1). Thrasymachus' enmity is apparent even while Socrates is arguing with Polemarchus; it then yields, according to Glaucon, to his unfair bewitchment at the hands of Socrates, only to be revealed to have never been real and to have been changed by then into true friendship. This is surely due to Socrates' justice as knowledge; but it is hard to imagine how Socrates could be so effective anywhere else than in the *Republic*, since here he has no enemies he cannot avoid harming (cf. 335e7, 10).

Polemarchus finds the argument no good (*ponēros*) that it is just to harm the not unjust. He could mean that either Socrates' argument is poor or the conclusion wicked. He proposes accordingly to alter the way in which "friend" and "enemy" were posited. There is neither anyone nor anything to stop him from making a new arrangement (*thesis*). In the first test of Polemarchus' definition, the just man proved to be a useless partner for the arrangement and placement (*thesis*) of bricks, game-pieces, and notes (333b1–9); but it now seems that the just man might be the best partner for the placement of speeches in argument. As such a dialectical partner, however, Socrates' justice is always suspect, since he is also the most skilled in cheating and theft; but suspicion of Socrates does not vanish because one is confident of his good will but because he is ignorant (*Charmides* 166c7–d6). Having nothing of his own at stake, he has everything to gain if the pieces of the argument can be shown to stand up to his assault. Socrates can rob his partner only of a counterfeit deposit; but he cannot always convince him that he is better off without it (*Theaetetus* 151c5–d3).

In the third test of Polemarchus' definition, justice as knowledge returns; but now it is not morally neutral and it is incapable of doing anyone harm. Socrates arranges for this conclusion by shifting from the arts in their capacity to make or alter something to the arts in their capacity to teach themselves. Whereas the horseman is indifferently good at either training or ruining a horse, the horseman cannot by horsemanship make a non-horseman a non-horseman; he can only teach him, if he employs his art, how to train or ruin a horse. Polemarchus now agrees that justice is human virtue and by implication is either a knowledge or a capacity to transmit human virtue. The further question is left open: could justice, in making human beings human, be the perfection of a neutral instrument for good or evil? It is possible that what we are good for is no good, or we are only good for service (to gods, for example, as dogs and horses are to us) or self-sacrifice for the sake of the city or something else equally ideal.

4

THRASYMACHUS I

(336a9–347a6)

The dialogic partnership of Socrates and Polemarchus was not unsupported; a silent alliance of those who were sitting alongside Thrasymachus forcibly restrained him from barging in, for they wanted to hear the argument through. Thrasymachus' intrusion is the intrusion of insult, an attack on the very dignity of the speakers, and compensation for the harm of which does not seem to be readily assessable. Socrates likens the launching of his attack to that of a wild beast; and he later alludes to the story that if a man does not see a wolf first he becomes speechless. A bestiality of which man alone is capable is the basis for an assault to which man alone is susceptible. We seem to be as far removed as possible from that justice which, as the human virtue, Socrates apparently wanted to identify with some kind of knowledge; but Socrates himself now seems almost helpless before a threatening denial of his even being human. The unrealistic insistence on Socrates' part that will has nothing to do with justice seems to have provoked Thrasymachus into implying that Socrates willfully erred; but his realism, in turn, in taking the form Socrates gives it in his representation, seems to vindicate Socrates: if man is not wholly rational, he is inhuman. Thrasymachus, however, is not really a beast; not only is he playacting, but his leonine roaring of abuse is peculiar to man. Thrasymachus begins with insults but ends with blushes. The irrationality of shame and pride no less than the rationality of knowledge belongs to man as man; and its bursting in as it does suggests that the price one pays for the departure of Cephalus, which freed the discussion from the hold of the sacred, is the unleashing of Thrasymachus. Philosophy needs the brutal frankness of Thrasymachus, who says what everyone is thinking, more than the indifferent laughter of Cephalus.

Socrates' superiority to his interlocutors comes from his ability to refute by questioning any answer; but where, Thrasymachus asks, does Socrates get the right to question? His irony, by which he keeps to himself what he knows, shows that he is unjust, for he has no friends before whom he can be sincere. That justice is the art of lying for the benefit of one's true friends seems to be the combined conclusion of the arguments with Cephalus and Polemarchus; but, as Socrates himself argues in his "theology," "true friends" seems to mean those before whom one does not have to lie (382d11–e5). Socrates therefore cannot say what justice is without exposing it as his irony, having his true friends believe that he is lying about justice. Thrasymachus, however, believes that he can declare publicly what justice is without exposing himself to the charge of injustice. He is mistaken. Socrates soon forces him to face the difficulty that he cannot win for himself any pupils if they believe his sole consideration is his own advantage. Thrasymachus therefore can only defend his definition if he denies its applicability to himself. He is made to be just in defense of his knowledge and contradict what he says he knows. The distinction Socrates made use of in the argument with Polemarchus, between the neutrality of art as productive and its non-neutrality as educative, now returns in the form of Thrasymachus' having to be the just teacher of injustice (cf. 344d4). Socratic irony, on the other hand, is no obstacle to the discovery of the truth. His own ignorance may be feigned, but his interlocutors' is real enough even if if appears to them as knowledge; and perhaps the only way they can learn of their ignorance is through his. Lying may be just and fully in the service of truth.

Thrasymachus tries to enact his definition of justice. His superiority to Socrates gives him the right to lay down the law. Socrates is ordered to tell the truth. Thrasymachus demands obedience and lack of error. He denies the possibility of philosophy and prohibits it. He says there is no resemblance between his own prohibition of certain answers to the question of what justice is and Socrates' example of a prohibition in which no factors of twelve may be given as an answer to the question how much twelve is. Socrates says it makes no difference whether Thrasymachus is right to deny or Socrates is right to assert the resemblance. Socrates vindicates the appearance of things over against the truth of things as the starting point for thinking (cf. 349a6–8). If there is in fact no difference between Thrasymachus' prohibition and Socrates' example, then Thrasymachus is prohibiting the truth from being spoken; and if in fact there is a difference but there appears not to be, then Thrasymachus is still in appearance prohibiting the truth from being spoken. The truth can no more be ordered than the false forbidden (Herodotus 1.136.2–138.1). Socrates thus anticipates the contradiction in Thrasymachus' definition of justice. He assigns to the ruler in any regime a knowledge of his own advantage and yet has him embody in the law the principle of the regime; but he does not ask whether the regime could even survive, let alone be of profit to its ruler, if its principle were not diluted. Athens is a democracy without all its laws being democratic. Thrasymachus sees no difficulty in combining law and knowledge; but we are made to wonder whether his savagery is not due to his belief in their perfect combinability.

The first of Socrates' two arguments with Thrasymachus consists of three parts. The first concerns the definition of justice and its political meaning (338c1–340c9); the second starts from the distinction between precise speech and ordinary speech (340d1–342e11); and the third starts from the notion of the true or genuine ruler (343b1–346e2).

Thrasymachus sees clearly that any comprehensive definition of justice is open to some counterexample; only a formal definition that does not specify the content of justice is immune. The just, then, is whatever the law lays down anywhere at any time; but the ruling power lays down the law in light of its own advantage. These two propositions do not consist with one another. If the many poor of a democracy lay down a law, the law is to their advantage as a class over against the class of the few rich; but it is not to the advantage of any individual who is poor, since it already represents a compromise of his interest in light of his weakness. Thrasymachus does not recognize the need for justice within the ruling class. Only the tyrant could strictly conform with his definition; but the tyrant seems to be a degenerate case of the political. Why should the tyrant restrict today his advantage tomorrow by a law when, unlike other rulers, he has no need to settle for less than maximum gain? The true representative of Thrasymachus' definition thus denies the neutral insight into the regime-dependency of the just. Thrasymachus fails to distinguish between a regime-dependent law and a regime-advantaged law, and so between the principle of a regime, by means of which the rulers ground their right to rule, and whatever advantage the rulers might get from that right. The tyrant too might have to appeal to something that is not identical with himself. Thrasymachus does not mention among the tyrant's advantages that he can kill or sleep with whomever he wants (360c1–2); he thinks of advantage entirely in terms of money and therefore of something as conventional as he claims the just to be; but he thereby identifies the principle of oligarchy as the principle of every regime, and the variety of right once again vanishes. Thrasymachus, too, though his real desire is to shine and put Socrates down, pretends that his sole interest is cash

22

and not praise (338a5–c3). He is the seller of something of which he is very proud, and that is his knowledge. He is Socrates' superior because he knows the score. The just is the advantage of the superior knower.

Socrates forces Thrasymachus to choose between the justice of obedience and the justice of knowledge. Thrasymachus is concerned not with the advantage that would accrue to the rulers if their subjects believe it to be just to obey them but with the strict knowledge the rulers must have of their own interest (an interest, however, of which their subjects must be wholly ignorant if they are not to act justly in disobeying an erroneous law). Since Thrasymachus does not acknowledge the advantage of obedience, which would far outweigh in most cases any miscalculation of self-interest, he does not object to Socrates' unrealistic premise, that the subjects are ordered by law to see to the interests of their rulers. The difficulty he has to get out of is only in speech; it is not something that should trouble the realist Thrasymachus; but his distinction between precise and ordinary speech leaves reality behind. Clitophon, in defending him, says that Thrasymachus proposed it to be just to do what the rulers ordered; but Polemarchus, who must have noticed the resemblance of rulers mistaking their own interest to men mistaking their true friends, says Thrasymachus proposed the advantage of the stronger to be just. In Clitophon's reading, even if what the rulers order is to their own advantage, it is not for that reason just; and in Polemarchus' reading, it is just regardless of whether the rulers order it and whether the subjects perform it. Thrasymachus' solution requires that he borrow Clitophon's "to do" and Polemarchus' "the advantage of the stronger" (341a3–4); but though he now has the ruler unerring, the just has ceased to be lawful and becomes instead the secret spring of his rule. "Each artisan, to the extent that he is what we address him by, never makes a mistake" (340d7–e1). "Ruler," however, seems to be necessarily a word that cannot lose its ordinary sense, for "The king rules" cannot cease to be true when he makes a mistake and cancels his right to rule. By law he remains a king and by error he abdicates, but he still sits on his throne. Thrasymachus abandons reality when he abandons the law. He already is in need of the coincidence of knowledge and power.

Thrasymachus' notion of the error-free artisan not only has strange legal consequences—in a malpractice suit one is seeking damages from a layman—but it seems to deny there are any mistakes that only an artisan can make in his specialty; and of these the one most common to every art is to suppose its competence extends beyond the range it does (*Apology of Socrates* 22c9–e5). Thrasymachus must deny that there is either any subordination within a set of arts or any subordination of all the arts to one art, for in either case a complete and error-free art would be impossible. There is no art ruling the arts. If there were such an art, it would have to be self-regarding and consider the good of its practitioner, for otherwise there would be another art that was superior to the ruling art. The selflessness of each artisan in serving the autonomy of his art requires that he have another art for his own good, the moneymaking art; and in practice each artisan will work out some compromise between the demands of his art and his own needs. Under only one condition, then, can the artisan be devoted simply to one art—if that art is nothing but the moneymaking art itself, whose sole purpose is to benefit the artisan and whose sole function is to make money out of money without going through the intermediate step of making anything for sale. This art is as comprehensive as philosophy claims to be, but it does not rule. (Philosophy does not rule politically either; whether it rules anyway without ever exercising its rule is another question.) Thrasymachus could of course have avoided the need for each artisan to have two arts, if he had appealed to the pride he took in his knowledge, but he had already denied it to be a good for him when he demanded pay for his correct answer. Socrates exerts enough force on Thrasymachus for him to keep silent about his own interest; and he gives him the slip by equating the fact that an art does not need any other art to be an art with the claim that an art does not need anything else to be good. Thrasymachus cannot but believe in the goodness of knowledge.

Socrates establishes the equivalence of three propositions: (1) no art is defective; (2) no art rules another art; (3) no art is self-regarding. There are apparently no unsolved problems that belong to the scope of any art, for each art treats only what it knows; but it could not be certain that it is staying within its competence unless it makes everything it knows. The defectiveness of things (body, eyes, ears), to make up for which the several arts have been devised, has to be replaced by things that are perfect and fully in the control of the arts. The solid bodies of geometry and the true city in speech of Socrates both seem to be expressions of the principle Thrasymachus and Socrates here lay down. The true city too is made

24

at the start without a ruling element (for without soul there is neither the possibility of nor the necessity for rule); but its realization in deed would require the further step Timaeus took, the making from scratch of its citizens. Timaeus, however, was defeated by the recalcitrance of necessity, which could not be eliminated but only persuaded to cooperate. This necessity is not acknowledged by Thrasymachus. It is the necessity of soul, which is neither body nor mind, and but for the presence of which Timaeus allowed there could be a perfect cycle of corporeal transformations.[1] Thrasymachus has art make up for the defectiveness of body; but since he does not notice that the defectiveness is of living body, he cannot ask whether soul makes body defective and what arts make up for the defectiveness of soul. What body needs may be different not only from what soul needs but incompatible with it (cf. 591c5–d3). Thrasymachus will soon admit his bafflement before Socrates' stubbornness: "But how am I to persuade you? If you have not been persuaded by what I was just now saying, what am I still to do for you? Am I to spoon feed the argument into your soul?" (345b4–6) Thrasymachus knows how to manipulate the passions, but he lacks any knowledge of the fit of argument and soul (349a9–10; *Phaedrus* 270e1–271b6).

At one point in the argument there is a break in Socrates' report of the argument: "He agreed to this too finally, but he tried to dispute it, but after he had agreed . . . " (342d2–3) Although there is an equivocation in Socrates' use of the verbs "rule (*archein*)" and "prevail over (*kratein*)" to describe the relation between an art and its subject matter, Socrates assigns no reason for Thrasymachus' resistance to the drift of the argument and lets his auditors infer that it is due to mere willfulness; but insofar as there is a fault in the argument, the pressure on Thrasymachus to give in has a source other than the rational necessity of argument itself. Thrasymachus is made to experience the force of consent, the fact that to "everyone it was manifest that the argument about justice had veered around to the opposite quarter." (343a1–2) Having proposed the lawful as the just, he is made to live the equality of the law, from which he cannot exempt himself, surrounded as he is by the silent partisans of

---

1. *Timaeus* 31b4–32c4, in which the four elements are transformable into one another, precedes the account of soul, which begins at 34b10; but the second account of body, which begins at 53c4, does not allow earth to be part of the sequence (54b6–c5).

Socrates. He is made a reluctant subject and gives up the attempt to be a ruler. In his final outburst, he inserts the shepherd between the sheep and the shepherd's master, and thus admits that his knowledge of how to sheer the flock does not in itself yield him any profit (343b1–4). Thrasymachus' outburst covers up rather effectively the shift his subordination to the ruler entails. Without knowing that he does so, he replaces the criterion of precision with that of truth and reality (343b5, c4, 6; cf. 341c6): rulers who are truly rulers look on the ruled as those to be fleeced. The rulers now are not error-free but are endowed with a mental attitude (cf. 343b5–6); they are now unjust in the ordinary sense and do not hide their crimes behind the law. Whereas what is just in reality should, according to Thrasymachus, be the other's good and in appearance one's own, it turns out that the just man in the ordinary sense is really just (343c3–d3); and justice and injustice end up by being the same (344c7–8). Thrasymachus fails to distinguish between the praise the tyrant receives for getting away with injustice and the publicity of the lawful in the glare of which one gets away with murder. He thus prepares the second round of his argument with Socrates—whether justice is better than injustice; but he cannot radicalize the question and ask whether injustice is unavoidable (366c3–d3).

Polemarchus had at least looked outside the city and seen its enemies; but for Thrasymachus the law and the city within are all there is; there is no "nature" in light of which making and positing have to be understood. Not even his good lies outside the city. The identity of the real with the precise, which began with his presenting models of pure regimes as real regimes, and ends with his presenting real tyrants as rulers in the precise sense, conceals the issue of necessity from him. Thrasymachus is a conventional Platonist.

5

THRASYMACHUS II

(347a7–354c3)

Thrasymachus started out with a definition of justice that seemingly was neutral to the issue of its goodness; but compelled to make the tyrant the truth of his definition, he could only get out of the unreality of the selfless artisan by becoming the selfless spokesman for the real tyrant and his self-evident goods. In the second round, Thrasymachus does not face Socrates alone (348b8). He has not persuaded Glaucon either that the life of the unjust man is better, stronger, or more profitable; and Glaucon wants to persuade him that it is untrue. Seeing that the tide is against him, Thrasymachus decides to cut his losses and becomes less argumentative and more grudging. The argument once more is in three parts. The first discusses whether the just or the unjust man is good and wise; the second argues for the indispensability of justice in any common enterprise; and the third discusses whether the just or unjust man is happy. Only the second argument seems sound; it is a burstlike argument surrounded on either side by filamentlike arguments. Its persuasiveness, however, sacrifices the goodness of justice, which is central to the other two arguments; and since Socrates extends the obvious efficiency of justice in a group to the individual, he points again to the question his argument with Polemarchus raised, whether we are good when we are good for anything good. However that may be, Thrasymachus must certainly be bewildered by what is happening to him. The efficiency with which the first argument is conducted (Thrasymachus does not balk at any of Socrates' moves), seems to be a sparkling proof of justice as the lubricant of any joint effort; but the efficiency proves to be an illusion of narration, for Socrates tells us afterwards that Thrasymachus blushed and sweated profusely in the course of the actual conversation (350d1–3). Unless justice is punishment, Thrasymachus' experiences are not exactly evidence that cooperation requires justice; and if it is just to go along with Socrates (351d7), it is not obvious what common enterprise they are engaged in, since Socrates seems to be completely selfish in working the group for all it is worth. The spokesman for justice gains more than the spokesman for injustice, and so much so that Socrates complains at the end that his greediness left him unsatisfied. Thrasymachus' cooperation did Socrates no good; perhaps, however, it did the group good. If their common enterprise is to be the discovery of justice, perhaps it was necessary for Socrates to make a pig of himself, so that they could see how easily one's own apparent good can overwhelm one's real good and conceal the difference between the question what justice is and the question what good it is. To gratify is not to benefit one's true friends.

27

The hinge on which Socrates' first argument turns is the assumed equivalence of two propositions. One is weak and supplied by Thrasymachus: "He who is of a certain sort resembles those of that sort"; but Socrates' is far stronger: "Each of the two [just and unjust] is of the sort whom he resembles." It thus turns out that the just man, because he resembles any of the precision artisans, is wise and good, and the unjust man, who does not resemble them, is foolish and bad. In falling for so obvious a sophism, Thrasymachus is properly embarrassed; but it is not as obvious why he falls for it and how Socrates knew that he would. Thrasymachus is willing to attribute to the unjust man power or virtue, but he is unwilling to identify complete unjustice with wisdom or prudence (*phronēsis*). The will of the unjust man is to have more, and what Thrasymachus must mean is to have more than anybody else (349c6). His is a competitive will that, through its translatability into a cash equivalence, disguises itself as a built-in measure of good. Thrasymachus, however, cannot admit the social and political character of the will, for in the case of his own knowledge, which he must take in the strict sense, there is no place for any pride grounded in the will alone. He therefore cannot see it in the artisan either, whose will can likewise be engaged in surpassing his fellow craftsmen. The democratic equality of the arts follows only on the artificial isolation of the arts from their practitioners, whose will accordingly consists in a devotion to the attainment of the precision which the art itself, as it were, wills (341d10–11; cf. 370b10). Since the just man wills to conform to the just itself, without any regard to his own ambition or that of his fellow just men, his will becomes identified with his power through the resemblance that he has to all other artisans, whose will is identical with the meaning of art in the precise sense. Socrates has Thrasymachus sweating and blushing as he exhibits in him the political as a cross between knowledge and sociality. He represents what he initially claimed he knew how to rule. Socrates sweats Thrasymachus' pride out of him so that he becomes as empty of will as he willed the precision artisan to be. Glaucon says he was charmed like a snake (358b3).

For the second argument Socrates forgoes the conclusion of the first, since it would follow at once from it that justice is more powerful than unjustice if justice is wisdom and virtue; and he has to forgo it if he wants to show that some justice is always necessary even for those who are all thieves together, for otherwise they too are wise and good. There cannot be then complete injustice. Does it follow that there cannot be complete justice either? If it does, then justice can only have an ordinary sense and be incapable of the precision which Glaucon believes it can have and which he wants Socrates to praise. Socrates' proof of the necessity for justice makes justice out to be a means and not an end. Thrasymachus' mistake would then have been to assign to ministerial arts a precision that can belong only to arts if they are by nature theoretical (e.g., mathematics) or are treated as if they are theoretical insofar as they are done for their own sake (e.g., chess). Thrasymachus had surely hinted at the possibility of a precision ruler; and if he existed, he would seem to be in possession of a nonministerial art. Socrates suggests as much: the completely wise man is to be king in the best city. And yet he too must descend into the cave if he is to be king; and Socrates does not say that he then exercises his wisdom in the precise sense when he rules among the shadows of artifacts.

The acquiescence and compliance Thrasymachus now displays is perhaps the only evidence one needs for Socrates' assertion that injustice does not lose its power in the individual but brings about discord and paralysis in him too; but it is not so much the injustice in Thrasymachus that silences him as the very arguments he has on behalf of injustice. The selfishness these arguments advocate makes them politically indefensible; and if one is to say them, one must, as Glaucon realizes, disclaim them, or make them the basis for an appeal to a common venture. Thrasymachus would need to be far cleverer than he is to have forged such an alliance with Socrates; but it is not beyond Socrates to work Thrasymachus into the group and disarm him. Everything Thrasymachus stands for finds its way into the best city. The democratic feature of a class of artisans, each equipped equally with precision knowledge of some means, and the oligarchic feature of their collective devotion to the art of money-making are both preserved in all their contradictoriness in the best city, for Thrasymachus himself, it seems, can be refuted but what he represents cannot be overcome.

In the twelfth and final argument of Book I, Socrates gets his surfeit and confesses it is his own fault that he has not dined well. He implies that his injustice consists in his failure to answer the question of what justice is, and that virtue is happiness if virtue is to do nothing but ask what virtue and everything else is (*Apology of Socrates* 38a1–6). There might, however, still be something salvageable in this last argument if one leaves out the unknown "justice" and treats it as a formal examination of the relation between the function of something and its excellence or virtue. The argument now looks at soul, which is not clearly separable from or identifiable with the individual, who in the former argument was said to be incapable of functioning if injustice loses none of its power in him. "Soul" too, then, must be added to the unknowns of the argument, for Socrates is wholly silent about body, and we do not know what or who lives when soul is doing its job of living. The life of the just man for all his happiness is as unreal as the error-free artisan of Thrasymachus. There are no prior conditions to which he must conform and by which he is limited, and no obstacles he is fated to confront that can either diminish the efficiency of his soul's functioning or mar his own happiness. The last argument thus seems to be a promissory note that, we are led to believe, the rest of the *Republic,* once it has supplied the conditions and determined the obstacles, will pay in full. It presents schematically the terms and relations on which the *Republic* must make good.

Socrates distinguishes between two kinds of function, one which only a certain thing can do, and another which something can do best. Eyes and ears can each do something that nothing else can do; but though a sword and a cobbler's knife can cut off a vine branch, the pruning hook can do it best, for it has been made for the purpose. We are invited to apply this distinction to the *Republic.* Does the city have a function? Is it something only the city can do, or can the city do it better than the household, village, tribe, or nation? Can there be no philosophy without the city though philosophy is not the city's function? The city might be that without which the human itself cannot be, and the human itself might interfere with philosophy. These questions extend their import to the city in speech. Is the imaginary city that solely by means of which justice can be found, or is it the best way to find it? Socrates later says it is easier to start with the city than with the individual (368e8); and it turns out to be how philosophy too is found. Is the city, then, that without which philosophy cannot be found?

Socrates next introduces the virtues of the eyes and the ears, but he does not let Thrasymachus identify sight and hearing as their respective virtues, or blindness and deafness as their vices; all they have to agree on is that the eyes and ears, each with their proper virtue, will perform their function well, and if they are deprived of it will do it badly. Since the eyes still see when they do not see well, poor sight corresponds to the vinedresser's use of a surgical blade, and perfect sight is equivalent to a pruning hook. It seems, then, that virtue and vice are solely applicable to things without which something cannot be done, and in turn there is, in the case of those things which do something best, no virtue apart from function. To say that a pruning hook lacks virtue is to deny that it is a pruning hook; it has simply slipped into the larger class of cutting tools. As soon as a Forstner bit no longer drills a perfectly clean flat-bottomed hole, it makes sense to discard it, or, if one retains it, to reclassify it. Socrates seems to be proposing a correction and a refinement of Thrasymachus' distinction between the precise and the ordinary. The precise/ordinary difference might be applicable only to those cases where there are multiple means but not to things of the "that without which" class. Thrasymachus would then have been mistaken to say that if a doctor erred, he ceased to be a doctor; for if the doctor has a job no one else can do, he can either have the virtue of a doctor or else act badly as a doctor. It might then be that there is no pruning hook for philosophy, no method in short, but only more or less crude tools available to it. Man likewise might be capable of virtue and vice only insofar as he is that without which something cannot be done, and philosophy and the city might go together if man is not even man without the city. If, however, man were one of several beings which could philosophize, and one were designed for it and were not man, then it would not be man's function to philosophize. To know whether man was to philosophize would be to have a teleological physics, which it was part of Socrates' second sailing to renounce. Socrates then apparently does not know to which class man belongs, "that without which" or pruning hook; but he does know that if man belongs to "that without which," a teleological physics is impossible.

Socrates' application of this analysis to soul is not easy to make out, for soul turns out to belong to "that without which," but its functions are multiple. Soul then is capable of virtue and vice, but possibly it is capable of several things, though Socrates must assume for his conclusion that there is a coincidence of the virtue of living and the virtue of ruling and deliberating well. Socrates' too-easy triumph is also due to his failure to distinguish between the verbs of hearing and seeing that he used to characterize functions without specifying the class of their transitive objects, and a verb like cutting, on the other hand, which as soon as its object is specified restricts the kind of tool that does the job best. If 'to think' could be determined to mean for soul 'to think X', and 'X' itself were known, then soul would be a pruning hook, and there would be no virtue of soul that was not soul. If, however, soul cannot be determined in this way, then once more no teleological physics is possible. But since Socrates gave multiple functions to soul, he granted the possibility of interference if soul belongs to the class of "that without which," and the necessity of interference if soul belongs to the class of multiple means. Socrates therefore already knows that in either case a teleological physics is impossible, for the fact of the soul's multiple functions replaces the need to know whether there is any other being which by design philosophizes perfectly. In the myth of Er, philosophy is not a way of life that one can choose.

PART TWO

BOOKS II–IV:
THE BEAUTIFUL

6

GLAUCON
AND ADIMANTUS

(357a1–368c3)

Glaucon wants Socrates to praise justice. He wants him to show that justice is attractive and has the kind of charm seeing or thinking has; but he also wants to hear the truth about justice. Socrates, however, could not do better even in the praise of Eros than to select the most beautiful aspects of it and arrange them as becomingly as possible (and he said he knew that this condition applied to the praise of anything whatsoever [*Symposium* 198d3–7]); but Glaucon seems to want the truth about justice to be the unvarnished praise of justice. He recalls Simmias and Cebes who want Socrates to enchant them rationally in the face of death. Glaucon believes that a praise of justice "alone by itself" is the same as the account of the power it has "alone by itself" in the soul. The beauty of justice in speech is the same as the power of justice in soul. Socrates is to make fully manifest what is wholly immanifest without any distortion. Yet Glaucon seems to want still more than this. He wants to hear from Socrates what justice is as well as what power it has in the soul. These are two questions for Glaucon; they are one for Adimantus (366e5–367b5, e1–5). What justice becomes in soul is not necessarily the same as what it is. There could well be justice no less different from that which shows up in action than that which is present in soul but does not show up in action. Glaucon thus anticipates the distinction Socrates later makes between the being of justice itself and the becoming of the just man, who in his becoming must fall short of being (472b7–d2). Glaucon, it seems, would not be satisfied unless there were 'Ideas' and justice were one of them.

Glaucon's renovation of Thrasymachus' argument consists of three parts:

> First I shall say what sort of thing they say justice is and from what it has come to be, second that all who practice it practice it unwillingly as necessary but not as good, and third that they do so reasonably.

These three parts match the three issues that Socrates said at the end of Book I were still unresolved: what justice is, whether it is vice and folly or wisdom and virtue, and whether injustice is more profitable than justice (354b4–8). In each part Glaucon uses a different pair of terms that do not match up exactly with one another. The first is being (*ousia*) and becoming (*genesis*); the second, nature (*phusis*) and law or convention (*nomos*); and the third, reality (*einai*) and appearance (*dokein*). Glaucon tells a brief story in order to establish the first thesis, then conducts a thought-experiment in order to show the just and the unjust man are in principle indistinguishable, and, finally, for his comparison-test imagines that the appearance of injustice be in reality justice and vice versa. The second and third parts involve in their proofs something quite fantastical, the conferral of the power of invisibility, on the one hand, and the powerlessness of reality to appear, on the other; but the first seems to depend on the experience anyone can have of justice and injustice. This experience must be conceived as occurring whenever government has broken down completely, and those without the capacity to avoid injustice and get away with doing it contract among themselves not to inflict or submit to injustice. Glaucon implies that 'injustice' as the natural good is a negative term by law; without law it would have been positive, and 'justice' designated as incapacity (*adunamia*) or lack of strength (*arrōstia*). The being of justice is solely to be discovered in the becoming of justice; but the name of justice flatters the weak into believing that they have been forced to take less than they can. The law is a command that began as an agreement. What was initially in the interest of every defective human being looks as if it is against everyone's interest. Every nondefective being does what it can; every defective being wills what it cannot: everyone acknowledges the natural goodness of injustice. The sole constraints in nature are circumstantial; there are none built into any noncrippled nature. Glaucon identifies the one who would never make a contract with a 'real' man (*anēr*), but he must mean a god, for no matter how weak each defective being might be alone, together they can always surpass any individual's capacity. Justice is the advantage of the naturally weak, but though the naturally stronger is stronger prepolitically, he is weaker than the collective strength of the naturally weak. This collective strength is only by law; there is no collective strength by nature. The city cannot be by nature.

Glaucon needs the ring of Gyges in order to show that justice is practiced unwillingly, and if the just were strong, they would act as unjustly as the unjust; but he needs two rings so that the naturally strong can still be unjust in a political setting, for the city has forcibly diverted the strong from his nature, and he is more hampered by the law than the just are defective by nature. Invisibility alone can overcome the publicity inherent in any living together and without altering the nature of the weak compensate for it. The ring of Gyges enhances the strong no less than the weak and makes their natural differences irrelevant. It thus resembles Socrates' proposal of total communism, for if the education of the guardians fails to take in any individual case, the institution of communism insures that the defective will act as justly as any golden soul.

The story of Gyges is not necessary for Glaucon's thought-experiment, for which most of the circumstances are nothing but color; indeed, the story reads as if it were originally designed to present a usurpation as a providential dispensation. It is not a story of how the weak, given power, is as unjust as he always wants to be, but how a series of miracles—the ring being but one—arranged for the establishment of a new dynasty.

In its original intention the story allowed for but one ring; but Glaucon demythologizes the story and discovers nature. The meaning of the story is not in the divine apparatus that envelops it, but in the course of action Gyges adopts once he learns of the ring's power. The story, however, in Glaucon's revision, does not account for Gyges' success. The queen whom Gyges seduced must have believed that he was a god when he materialized before her (cf. 360c3; Herodotus 6.68–69). Gyges could have stolen as much as he wanted and got away with it, but he could not have gained the throne without appearing, and he could not have appeared unless he was seen to have the power to vanish. When he was invisible to his fellow shepherds he was as good as gone.

Gyges must have had more going for him than the ring. The ring suggests another way of understanding the origin of law. It was not the many who were weak but the one who was naturally strong who proposed the equality of law so as to conceal his usurpation of rule (Herodotus 1.96.2, 99). The ring stands for the veil the law wraps around the foundation of the city. Glaucon, however, separated the law from the foundation of the city—he did not mention the city in sketching the origin of law—and hence subverted the thrust of the Gyges story for the sake of making visible the universal belief in the advantage of injustice. He wants Socrates to ignore the surface conformity to justice on the part of most men and look into what lies hidden within: What effect does the belief in the superiority of injustice have on the soul? Prove, he tells Socrates, that justice in itself and not fear of punishment or retaliation informs or can inform the soul. Justice, he implies, loses its power once the sun has set (*Cratylus* 413b3–c1).

In the thought-experiment the will of the just man is exposed as powerlessness; but in the comparison-test, in which the unjust man is granted the skill to avoid detection as the real equivalent of the ring of Gyges, the just man is granted nothing but justice, which allows him to endure, without wavering, the most terrible tortures. Why, then, is the just man's will broken as soon as he is given power and remains unbroken when he has none? The thought-experiment implies that without the change in conditions the just man appears just and the unjust unjust; but in the real counterpart, the just man appears unjust and the unjust just. In the thought-experiment, fear of punishment motivates the just man; in the comparison-test, the hope for reward is denied him, since the real turns out to mean for him the 'idea.' The just man has nothing but the 'idea' and as such cannot alter or appear. The unjust man, then, should be a participant in the idea 'justice' and as such appear and only appear just but be unjust and necessarily so. Glaucon, however, waffles on the issue of whether he can be perfectly unjust. Insofar as he sticks to the possible, he is supposed to be as unerring as any other artisan; but insofar as he occasionally makes mistakes but still goes scot-free in the lawcourts and elsewhere, he is no longer the real equivalent to Gyges. The unjust man should seem not perfectly just but perfectly ordinary: he practices justice when he must and injustice when he can. His soul, however, never wavers in its injustice, for he never acts for the sake of justice, and the practice of justice has no effect on his soul. Glaucon grants him friends, force, and eloquence to make up for the imperfections in his pretense, but he does not grant the just man to be equally imperfect and to that extent protected by the appearance of justice. Glaucon does not notice the absurdity of the just man, whose opinion about what is just is the same as everyone else's, never coming to doubt his justice despite the opinion everyone has of him. He is stripped of everything except justice, to which neither he nor anyone else has any access. His justice is like Philoctetes' wound—a constant source of pain but about which nothing can be done: he stinks too much to have any friends, and all he can do is howl but not persuade. The strangeness of this disappears if Glaucon means without knowing it that the just man always lives in the light of opinion because there is no other way of relating to justice. Justice and opinion go together because they vanish together. The just man has will and the unjust man knowledge, for only injustice is real (cf. 362a4–5).

The thought-experiment is needed because without it law conceals nature; but the basis of the comparison-test is the real, which is not nature but 'idea.' The discovery of nature is bound up with the natural goods; but the distinction between appearance and reality is bound up with conventional goods. The really unjust man has his rewards assigned him because he seems just; and his seeming just can never obtain for him the natural goods. The thought-experiment requires the suspension of the possible; it turns out to mean the removal of appearance, which in turn looks like the removal of appearance in the comparison-test. The just man is invisible in both cases. In the first he does not appear at all, and that is the uncovering of nature; and in the second he does not appear as just, and that is the concealment of what is; and at the concealment of what is, the unjust man is adept. Glaucon seems to have stumbled on the Cave in which there are nothing but shadows of artifacts. Glaucon thus makes us raise two questions: Is the covering opinion of the city an invention of the unjust man, i.e., is the city by nature unjust? And does the covering opinion of the city necessarily have chinks through which what is shines, i.e., is the Cave always open to the light?

Glaucon is not only the first to introduce into the *Republic* the word for nature (*phusis*), but he is also the first to introduce a word for kind (*eidos*). He begins by speaking of three kinds of good (357c5), but he never connects that 'eidetic' analysis with his account of the nature of justice; and this failure of his foreshadows Socrates' own. How *eidos* and *phusis* are bound together and split apart in the course of the *Republic* determines exactly the degree to which what it succeeds in doing depends on what it fails to do. Now Glaucon's threefold classification of goods has a superficial clarity that dissolves on reflection. There are goods we would choose to have for their own sakes and not for their consequences (joy and harmless pleasure); goods we cherish for themselves and their consequences (thinking, seeing, and being healthy); and goods we would want for their consequences alone (toilsome effort that pays off in one way or another).

The first and third kinds of goods are distinguished by pleasure and pain; the second and third are connected through the notion of good consequences; but Glaucon does not explain what good are the consequences if they are not further pleasures, and he fails to give any example of the first kind. "To enjoy" seems to need a supplementary verb that designates some activity in which we take pleasure, like seeing; but among Glaucon's harmless pleasures he cannot include the smelling of a perfume, for we choose rarely if ever to have such pleasures, however much we might enjoy having them. Glaucon's second kind, to which as the most beautiful Socrates assigns justice, does not enter his speech in defense of injustice, for injustice seems to be chosen solely for its consequences. From Glaucon's saying that every nature is naturally geared to aggrandizement (359c5), and that no one who is truly a man ever contracts with anyone (359b2), one could no doubt winkle out the notion that injustice is a state of health for certain strong natures that are stunted and diseased under the constraints of the law. But Glaucon never mounts so Calliclean an argument, for injustice would then not be something just anyone could choose, and justice in turn would be a natural necessity for most. Injustice must be just for Glaucon and available to all. Glaucon therefore never puts point blank the question his second kind of good raises. Thinking, seeing, and being healthy are goods that plainly do not depend on justice, and if justice belongs to this kind, it must be either like health a good order of soul or like thinking a particular activity.

Glaucon thus seems to have hit upon at the start of the *Republic* the identification of justice and philosophy that Socrates comes finally round to (583b2), and at the same time to have suggested as an alternative that justice could be a strength of soul that was always good regardless of the use to which it was put. This suggestion also lurks in the third kind of good, in which Glaucon puts exercising but where he discounts the possibility that as in weights or jogging the greater the competence the greater the pleasure in its practice. Glaucon does not think of justice as something one does—in the comparison-test the just man suffers—and the gods are the first to be spoken of as doing just things when they punish (380b1); only later are men spoken of in the same way, when the analogue of justice is the restoration and preservation of health (444c2).

Adimantus complements Glaucon. He supplies an account of opinion to balance his brother's account of what is. If one does not believe Thrasymachus, one must heed the poets, who are makers and spokesmen of opinion; and for the poets, there are only the gods. The gods are essential to opinion; they are an acknowledgment on the part of opinion that opinion-based justice is not rewarded and opinion-based injustice not punished even though the gods are there to guarantee that opinion-based justice pays and opinion-based injustice must pay. That the expansion of rewards and punishments in this life through the gods and their extension into the next are done by the poets—not the gods but the poets bury sinners in mud and compel them to carry water in sieves (363d5–7)—reveals the spuriousness of opinion in this life. The poets could not have attached a theodicy to morality unless they were made for each other, and they would not have had to attach it unless the morality were untrue. If the gods are there to anchor morality to reality, one has only to look at their own unreality—an unreality that is besides self-contradictorily repugnant to morality—to realize that opinion encourages the practice of seeming that "does violence even to truth." The gods are the model for Gyges.

Glaucon wants to know what effect justice and injustice each in itself have on the soul; Adimantus reminds Socrates that "in itself" means that conscience, to the extent that it depends on the gods' omniscience and the consequent fear of punishment, must be discounted. The efficacy of opinion goes far beyond the range of its political enforcement. Glaucon had given the unjust man great resourcefulness, but Adimantus does not grant him the strength of soul to overcome or dispel the nightmares of divine punishment. Injustice is to damage the soul all by itself, and justice to make up for any deficiencies, whether of nature or knowledge (366c3–d1). Adimantus wants morality to be supplied with a necessary causal chain in nature. He wants the mud in which the poets bury sinners to be an image of the real presence of injustice in soul (*Gorgias* 493d5–494a1). He wants to know the nature of soul in itself; he does not yet know that according to Socrates the way to know the nature of justice precludes a precise knowledge of soul (435c9-d5).

The contradiction in the poets' presentation of the gods—they punish and reward in strict conformity with right and they can be bought off—parallels not only the contradiction between the encouragement to be just for the sake of pleasure and the pleasantness and ease of injustice but also the contradiction between Adimantus' identification of the natural goodness in injustice with pleasure and his admission that nothing great is easy (364a3–4, 365c7–d1). Are these contradictions of the same order? Clearly, pleasure cannot be an adequate motive for injustice if it is easier to be just; but neither can the nontroublesomeness of justice make it praiseworthy.

Socrates would then have to appeal to something great from which justice was inseparable. If only something political could have the proper magnitude, and the union of freedom and empire could be the only possible candidate, Adimantus would be asking why the individual should not imitate the core—at least the apparent core—of the political: to expand in power and to have no master. The answer not allowed is that the individual if successful would destroy the city; for the issue of justice is tied up with an individual's happiness for whom the city cannot be of any concern prior to the establishment of justice as the common good. The individual equivalent to the political, and combining pleasure and greatness, would thus seem to be necessarily criminal acts that strike at the foundations of the city. The crimes of Oedipus seem to be called for; and Socrates would have the task of showing the misery of a witting Oedipus. Oedipus himself, however, is a tragic figure, and Socrates banishes tragedy. Adimantus thus prepares the way for renewing the ancient quarrel between poetry and philosophy, even as Glaucon prepares the way for a confrontation between philosophy and the city.

Adimantus and Glaucon have between them caused Cephalus to disintegrate. His departure to take care of the sacrifices, which made the discussion of Book I possible, has now been argued for. Not only does he have no place, but what he stands for is indefensible. The two brothers of Plato have seen the connection between Socrates' questioning Cephalus about old age and the issue of justice. Cephalus' desires are not matched by his capacity, his money is a form of bribery, and the gods he trusts and fears are the fictions of the poets. In short, the weakness of old age is the truth about justice (366d2). Socrates is properly admiring of Glaucon and Adimantus:

> Though I had always admired the nature of Glaucon and Adimantus, I was then in particular very pleased and said: ". . . you have experienced something divine, if you have not been persuaded that injustice is better than justice, though you were so able to speak on its behalf. You seem to me truly not to have been persuaded; my evidence is from the rest of your temperament, since in light of the speeches themselves I would not now believe you."

Socrates takes pleasure in their resistance to their own persuasiveness. They surely seem to have been persuaded; and Glaucon had initiated the rest of the *Republic* by saying that Socrates seems to have persuaded them, but not truly persuaded them, that justice is better. Socrates now suggests that Glaucon had implied that they had been truly persuaded that injustice is better, but that in conformity with Glaucon's own distinction between seeming and being they adopted the seeming of the unjust man. Socrates tells them they are mistaken, that they truly have not been persuaded and that there is a truth about themselves they do not know. The differences between hypocrisy and inner conviction does not hold in their case, for their true inner conviction has its source in nature or the divine and is not equipped with arguments. In Glaucon's argument, "nature" had belonged to the thought-experiment and seeming/being to the comparison-test. Socrates casts doubt on this distinction. Their speeches show that they seem to be unjust, and since only the truly just man seems to be unjust (the unjust man never says anything unjust), they must be in reality just by nature. The truth of their justice shows up in their speeches that had no argument for it and could not defend it (cf. 363c3–d3). Their justice gave no external sign of its presence. They themselves then must be the representatives of seeming injustice and real justice. The *Republic* therefore has to answer their question as it applies to them. What effect does the presence of dumb justice have on themselves (cf. 367e1–3)? Socrates' education of them would thus be the coming into seeming of the truth of their justice. It would be an attempt to give their justice an argument and themselves self-knowledge.

Socrates distinguishes between what he tells the auditors and what he told Glaucon and Adimantus the day before. "Nature" now expresses what at the time he called "divine"; and "nature" brings along with it Socrates' pleasure. The verb "to be pleased (*hēdomai*)" never recurs in the Republic.[1] The anti-hedonistic cast of the *Republic* as a whole breaks down only here; everywhere else in the narrative Socrates speaks of the various kinds of compulsion he experienced to continue the discussion. Even the renewal of the argument at the beginning of Book II he ascribes wholly to Glaucon's manliness; but it is far more plausible to consider Socrates' declaration of his own dissatisfaction with the arguments of Book I as the chief cause of Glaucon's coming forward. One is forced to wonder then whether his ascription to their nature of Glaucon's and Adimantus' resistance to their own arguments does not likewise conceal his influence on them. What is no less holding them back

1. The compound *sunēdomai* occurs at 462e2.

from following Thrasymachus is Socrates (cf. 367d5–e1). His apparently giving voice to their justice is in fact the seeming of the reality of his own thinking. This is his justice. Only if justice is not what it is in opinion could Glaucon's comparison-test hold, and only Socrates thinks it possible that justice is what neither Thrasymachus nor Cephalus says it is.

7

THE TWO CITIES

(368c4–373e8)

Glaucon and Adimantus had kept the question of justice (what it is) linked with the issue of its goodness, and Socrates tells his audience that everyone begged him to examine both (368c4–7). His proposal, however, to look at justice writ large seems to be a way of separating them, for the city involves justice in the same way as a gang of robbers does without involving the issue of goodness. Socrates, in suspending for a time the issue of goodness, seems to be catering to his own interest in knowing and ignoring the reason for Glaucon's and Adimantus' willingness to keep on talking all night. If they were not still wanting their suspicion confirmed that justice was something noble and grand, Socrates' argument for the indispensability of justice in any common enterprise would have ended the discussion before they had entered it; but since their desire to know what justice is does not arise from a belief in the goodness of knowing but a belief in the goodness of justice, an answer in conformity with their belief would satisfy them and make the answer suspect. Disinterest will always take the first discovery for the final discovery; interest will shape the discovery itself. If the smugness of disinterest is to be avoided no less than the reinforcement of prejudice, discovery, it seems, must involve a displacement of what one starts out to discover. The discovery of the city on the way to the discovery of justice is such a displacement; and it is the perfect displacement because the city itself offers Glaucon and Adimantus something noble and grand that differs from the goodness they want to be

44

found in justice. Their becoming the joint founders of the city with Socrates has the effect of displacing both their interest and their question.

> If someone [i.e., Glaucon and the rest] had ordered those without very keen sight to read small letters far off, and then someone [i.e., Socrates] realized the same letters are larger somewhere else and in something larger, it would have proved I suspect a lucky find for them to read the larger letters first and then go on to examine whether the smaller letters are in fact the same.

Socrates' proposal is on the face of it absurd. If one knows that the same letters are both small and larger, then one has already read the smaller letters; but the following considerations make it less absurd and deepen the puzzle. Justice in man could be JST and more readable as JUST in the city; and since Socrates says the larger letters are in something larger, JUST in the city might be in a simple sentence of considerable length, but in the individual the sentence could be complex and very short. Further, JUST might be audible as the same but not legible in both, so that its elements would not be as clearly differentiable in both cases. Since, however, "just" is a word that is predicated of both city and individual, Socrates admits the possibility that the sound in both cases be the same but the spelling be different (for otherwise he could not propose a further examination of their sameness), and that there are silent elements present in one and absent from the other. It would not have to be a case of homophones, like "write" and "right," for justice to fail to be the same in man and city. The silent element could well be "happiness," which Socrates is to prove follows on justice, but which seems not to be equally predicable of city and man.

Socrates seems to make his example unnecessarily complicated. If the small letters are far off, it is superfluous for the readers to be not sharpsighted; and if the letters are of any size, they would appear small if they are far enough away. Socrates does not say where the larger letters are. Does he imply that they are always larger than the others regardless of how far away from them one stands? Since the small letters are the justice of the individual, the individual must always be at a greater distance than the city, and one cannot get any closer. No one is either well equipped or well stationed for self-knowledge. The city is to make up for defective vision, but perhaps it does not so much correct it as enlarge the range of the visible (cf. 368e7), so that the greater vividness of its justice depends on something not applicable to the individual. Socrates speaks of the justice of the individual and of the city as a whole, but whereas the larger letters are in the larger thing, he does not say in what the smaller letters are. If Socrates follows Glaucon's request, he must look at justice in the soul (358b5), if he follows two of Adimantus' three formulations, he must look at the effect justice has on the individual (366e8, 367b4, e3). If we suppose justice in soul corresponds to justice in city, what is the "soul" of the city in which it is found? We certainly get the impression that the class-structure of the city exhibits the city's justice. Since it takes Socrates two books to get there, the greater ease of Socrates' way has nothing to do with length, but with the fact that Socrates makes the city in which he finds justice. The alternative to Socrates' way would, it seems, be Timaeus', whose making of the individual, however, entails the prior making of the cosmos; and Socrates is clearly in doubt as to whether the letters of justice are in the cosmos, and, no matter their size, perhaps too faint for even the most sharpsighted.

The city has an inside and an outside no less that the individual has. Glaucon and Adimantus tell Socrates to disregard the individual's outside (what the just man receives from others for his seeming justice), and Socrates responds by proposing to look at the city's inside, for the city then surely does not get either rewarded or punished by other cities. The distinction, however, between appearance and reality seems to be irrelevant for a city. Can a city be just toward its neighbors and appear unjust, or be unjust and appear just? This difficulty points directly at what Socrates' proposal amounts to: the internality of the city is the externality of the individual. Socrates maps the external onto the internal of one entity (individual) through the internal of another entity (city). Socrates speaks of the *idea* of the individual (369a3), which presumably is not just a periphrasis for the individual. If it means the structure of the individual soul, Socrates will have broken the unity of the individual with which he began in such a way as never to allow for its reconstitution. Socrates' mapping, precisely because it passes from the inside of the city to the inside of the individual without passing through the individual by way of his outside, opens up another way of reading the small letters. The elements that make up justice in the individual might be the same without being in the same order as the city's. JST could still be paradigmatic for JTS and yet be misleading.

Socrates calls our attention to a simultaneous formation of two cities by formulating in two ways the way in which a city comes into

46

being. The first is at 369b5–c8, and the second begins at 369c9 and goes on continuously until "the true city" is completed. This double formulation is connected with the difference between the interlocutors' being spectators of a city coming into being in speech and their making a city in speech (369a5–6, c9). If they make the city, there is a transparency to it, for nothing goes into it which they do not put in knowingly; and justice should not be found there unless they put in either it itself or all its elements. If, however, they are going to watch a city coming into being, there is possibly an opacity to the seed of justice that will not let it be recognized even when it comes fully into the light. If the city is made, they do not have to start at the beginning with, for example, a man and a woman, a country, or a people with a past. Making in speech cuts out place and time, both of which are indispensable for becoming. When Timaeus undertakes to realize some version of Socrates' best city in speech, he is forced to become a cosmologist for it to be in place and in time. The city that is made in the *Republic* is the city of which Glaucon and Adimantus, no less than Socrates, are the founders. The city that becomes is the *Republic* itself, whose invisible founder is Socrates and in which are enrolled as citizens everyone present, including Thrasymachus (450a5–6). It is in this dialogic city that the justice of the city that can be mapped onto the individual is to be found. The dialogic city is the philosophic city in which Socrates is already king.

Socrates describes the dialogic city as follows: "A city comes to be since each of us is not self-sufficient but in need of many" (369b5–7). Socrates' "many" could be equally "many people" or "many things"; but in either case he starts out by denying Glaucon's distinction between defective and nondefective human beings. We are all needy. Socrates then goes on: "On this basis one enlists another, [one] for the need of one thing, another for the need of another thing, and [we], needing many, gather many into one dwelling as partners and helpers, and put the name 'city' on this keeping house together" (369c1–4). The translation tries to bring out the several peculiarities of this single sentence. By an anacoluthon less startling in Greek than in English, Socrates identifies the gathering he addresses first with needy individuals and then with those who give the name of city to a certain type of gathering without his ever asserting that they make the city they name. The phrase "one enlists another" could be translated as "different people enlist different people"; and we could picture a city (see fig. 1) in which A enlists

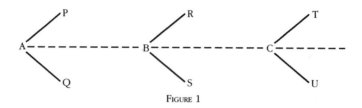

FIGURE 1

B, P, and Q; B enlists A, R, and S; etc. A far simpler picture (see fig. 2) would have been given had Socrates mentioned just one individual

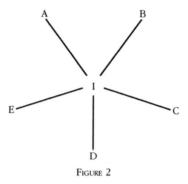

FIGURE 2

with the need of many others. It would have allowed another individual, e.g., D, to be placed at the center of his own circle, as in figure 3.

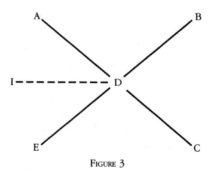

FIGURE 3

Socrates would then have had the advantage of restricting the gathering to those with the same needs; instead, his language allows for an unlooped

48

chain, as in the first figure, or, by his omission of *ton men* ("one"), it allows that differences of need might not entail differences of people. Each member of this city shares in give and take solely because he believes it is better for himself (369c6–7); he does not have to join in because he needs others as they need him in order to live (369d1). That is the basis for the city they make in speech; it is not the basis for the city they now belong to and in which they all go hungry for an entire night. The movement of the *Republic* culminates in Glaucon and Adimantus asking Socrates, without their realizing it, this question: Can the city of bodily needs become the dialogic city? If one looks back to Book I, this question is equivalent to their asking whether the arts on the level of production, in which they are all neutral, can be the arts on the level of transmission and education, in which they are all good. If one looks forward, it is equivalent to their asking whether soul or its analogue, the class-structure of the city, can be grafted onto the city of bodily needs without a seam. Closer to home, their question amounts to this: Can our disintegration of everything Cephalus stands for, which was a dialogic necessity, be incorporated into the best city in speech?

The needs that bring man together are conscious needs; they are not natural drives for association but rather they are any need anyone calculates to be better satisfied through association. It is a wholly selfish association and in principle does not require any living together except for the sake of the greatest efficiency of exchange and distribution. No one in the city of bodily needs would ever have to come face to face with anyone else; but the dialogic city is impossible unless its participants are together to a greater degree than commercial relations require. Although selfishness is common to the formative principle of both cities, the dialogic city needs people, the city of bodily needs needs only things, which may or may not require people. Socrates first makes a city out of four or five men, and then admits to Adimantus that a jack-of-all-trades, in minding his own business, has less trouble (370a3–4); but though he should have made this admission before he began to make the city, he could not, since his account of the city, in starting off with the dialogic city, started off with the need for other people and not things. That "minding one's own business," which turns out to be the comprehensive definition of justice, first shows up asocially is a sign of Socrates' merging the two cities; and that Adimantus reverses, in his response to the alternative of independence or cooperation, the ordinary usage of the adverbs "in this way" and "in that way," also suggests such a merging. If we take Adimantus at his word, he says

49

that the jack-of-all-trades has an easier time of it (370a5–6). Socrates' merging of the cities alerts us to the peculiarity that not even our conscious needs make the city but rather that knowledge determines the necessity for association. The division of labor is a division of arts, each one of which is so specialized that it cannot exist apart from all the other equally specialized arts. The dialogic city thus slides into the city of bodily needs without any awareness by members of either city that the needs of knowledge inform both cities. The arts have their own needs—of beauty, for example—that are not designed to improve the satisfaction of our needs but to conform with the partiality of our natures. The principle of one man/one art allies nature and knowledge; it does not alter our needs. If Socrates belonged to "the true city," he would have to take a pair of shoes he never needed; but there would be no one in it to make him a pair of slippers.

The jack-of-all-trades minds his own business asocially; the artisan does so socially, since the requirements of his art force him to pay attention to nothing else and yet be dependent on every other artisan. The original principle, that each man is good for just one product, soon yields to the principle of perfect artifice—the more limited the scope the more refined the result—and there is no suggestion that our nature keeps pace with the divisions of which the arts are capable. Socrates first expands the city through its toolmakers; and only then does he remark that the site of the city will in all probability be incapable of supporting the specialists he introduced. Imports bring in their train exports, for every new subdivision of an art insures an increase in productivity. There is then no reason why the city should not consist of toolmakers alone without any territory outside the city itself. The city of arts does not need any farmers; and their importance in Socrates' description of the true city's way of life serves only to underline the disproportion between the refinement of the arts and the simplicity of the life. A high-tech Eden is science fiction.

Retailers and money succeed merchants and barter. Despite Adimantus' contempt for them, they are the first inhabitants of the city who are out in the open and at its center. They are the first who do not make anything. They must decide on what a fair price is, for as long as the city is governed by the equality of needs, the exchange of one house for one cloak or one-fourth of the harvest for one pair of shoes will hold; but as soon as there is money, things equally useful must be fractioned into units that establish their exchangeability apart from use; and by a kind of providence, the minute divisions of the arts agree with the needs of exchange. In accordance with Socrates' argument with Thrasymachus, no artisan is a retailer or moneymaker; but, in contrast with the drift of his argument, the retailers are the heart of the city. They are the weakest (371c7). Socrates then introduces wage-earning manual laborers, who without any art join the city as servants to the other artisans. A vertical element of rule sneaks into the midst of the horizontal equality of the artisans. Their presence makes one aware that if the city is to last more than one generation, women must be introduced for the sake of an artless production, and the issue of subordination within the family would then have to be raised. The city now has the structure as shown in figure 4. The way of life Socrates ascribes to the city includes the women he did not mention and excludes the technical and financial core of the city.

Socrates calls this city the true, genuine, and healthy city (372e6–7, 373b3); and the city Glaucon demands he calls the city of fevered heat, but he does not call it the untrue or false city. He acknowledges, however, by his very procedure, that falsehood and disease are indispensable for the discovery of the truth about justice and everything else: the dialogic city is not possible in the true city. A sign of this is that a member of the dialogic city—Glaucon—forces Socrates to abandon the true city. His dissatisfaction with it focuses on two things: there is no meat-eating in the city of pigs, and there are no tables and couches. Tables and couches are the first items Socrates adds (373a2), and tables and couches are the examples Socrates uses in Book X in order to introduce a doctrine of "ideas" (596b1). In the vegetarian city there are no pigs—the only domestic animal whose use for food involves its slaughter—and in the true city there are no tables and couches. It is not easy to say what "meat" and "ideas" have to do with one another. Glaucon himself connects meat with tables and couches as simply examples of all the customary practices of Athens he misses in Socrates' city. Tables put meat off the ground, and couches put men off the ground (372b4–6); they separate man from pig by elevating him and delay the satisfaction of his desires. They are the first instruments that intervene between the consumer and his immediate consumption of things. Glaucon's objection thus leads Socrates to duplicate for the consumer the subdivision of arts that in the true city he had already done for

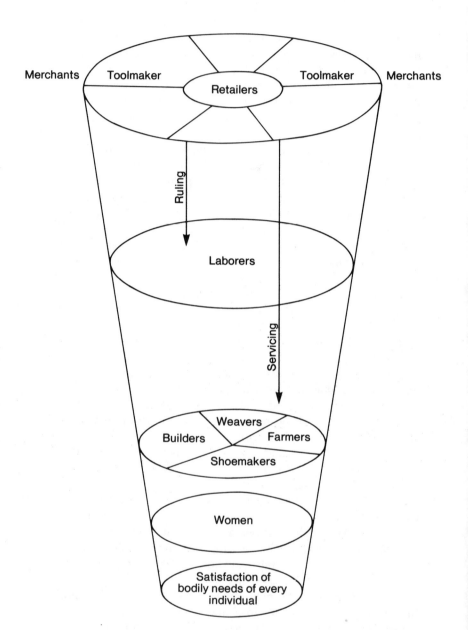

FIGURE 4

production (see fig. 5). The artful distancing of satisfaction goes along with the subdividing of desires, which, in no longer being

internal trade   external trade (surplus)

CONSUMERS − − − − − − − − −▶ FOOD ◀− − − − − − − − − TOOLMAKERS

arts of consumption   arts of production

FIGURE 5

bound to mere life, are no longer guided by reality to which they are ultimately indifferent. Along with beds and couches come their imitations (373b5). Glaucon's demand for meat therefore does not have to be satisfied so that Glaucon can be satisfied. His demand is symbolic. His contrafactual—"If you were arranging a city of pigs, Socrates, what else would you be feeding them?"—expresses his contempt for these men and his refusal to be one of them. His demand on behalf of human pride is expressed mediately. His expression puts what he really wants at a distance. In rejecting the healthy city, he rejects what he himself assigned to the highest kind of good (cf. 372b8). To be human is preferable to being good.

The arts that make for the city of fevered heat are not generated by anything within the city; and just as there is perfect harmony without rule in the healthy city, the city is suddenly unhealthy by the agency of Glaucon and Socrates. We do not know whether in fact expansion leads to luxury or the desire for luxury to expansion, since Glaucon's desires simply intrude on the healthy city dialogically. Glaucon does not want to be a spectator of something he cannot effect; and he compensates for the frustration he experiences in the asceticism of the dialogic city by stuffing the city in speech; but he is then forced to care for the city. The "we" of construction becomes the "we" of participation at the very moment, as Socrates puts it,

> We have to cut off a piece of our neighbors' land if we are going to have enough to graze and plough, or they in turn have to cut off a piece of ours if they too let themselves go to the infinite acquisition of goods and transgress the boundary of what is necessary. (373d7–10)

In the new situation, in which an "us" has been cogenerated with a "them," the healthy city too has no choice but to acquire an army. Glaucon is thus made to fight for the city he has corrupted so that he can realize another overwhelming necessity (373e1). The addition he makes to his country's territory for the sake of the superfluities he craved turns out to be the same as the addition the city needs to support the soldiers who, wholly nonproductive, are meant to fight for the entire substance of the city and its inhabitants against invaders (373e9–374a2). Glaucon and Socrates originally expanded the city dialogically (373d7), and now it is confronting invaders; but a moment's reflection shows that the army cannot be first formed now but it had to precede the original expansion; indeed, it had to precede the surplus the city created for export. The soldier must have been an original member of the true city. He is the fifth man (369d11).

The army takes over from the retailers as the bond of the city; and through it the city begins to shrink. Socrates' phrase for the healthy city, "the most necessary city," now gains a new sense. It is the city formed for the exclusive satisfaction of the warrior, for he alone lives the life confined to the satisfaction of natural needs. The healthy city lives on within the city of arts as the city to which the warriors belong; and they share in the city of arts through their need of the most advanced weapons the arts can devise. This resolution, how-ever, of the paradox of high technology united with the simple life is bought at a price. As the healthy city can now exist only if the rest of the city is not as healthy, so it can no longer be the true city, for it must recover through an education in lies what it lost once Glaucon made it violate the originally perfect coincidence between natural needs and productive knowledge. It must be kept in mind, however, that that perfect coincidence was possible only in speech.

8

PHILOSOPHER-DOGS

(373e9–376c6)

Socrates' strict application of the principle one man/one art to the city, so that all its artisans are disarmed and cannot defend what they produce, surprises Glaucon (374a3). He should have questioned Socrates at the start as to why neither the shepherd nor the huntsman could be an alternative to the farmer. Socrates needed to coop up the populace in one place and make it helpless in the face of predators, whether inside or outside the city, in order to force Glaucon to recognize the necessity for the education of the guardians, who are made watchdogs of the artisan-flock before it gets any shepherds (416a2–7). Education is a good that war forces on the city and distinguishes it from a gang of robbers; and war in turn dictates the kind of nature Glaucon and Socrates must recruit and educate. Weapons must not turn a people automatically into warriors, for in the hands of artisans who have become surreptitiously consumers they would of necessity foster and magnify the imperialism that, Socrates implies, is inherent in the arts which serve the body. The warriors are the first citizens said to have a soul, but theirs is not at first an exclusively human soul (375a11–b2,d10). Glaucon, who dismissed the artisans as pigs, does not object to guardians as dogs. Stirred by human pride he then spoke up, but now he is silent when Socrates models men on the most fawning of domestic animals (389e13). A people whose knowledge identifies them from the start as human are to be protected and restrained by those who have yet to become human.

Socrates characterizes the soul of the warrior as *thumoeidēs*. Xenophon tells us that *orgē* was by his time the human term for what in horses was still called *thumos* (Xenophon *de re equestri* ix.2); and in Thucydides *orgē* (almost forty instances) has almost driven off *thumos*, which occurs only three times and never of Athenians: a naval battle between Corinthians and Corcyraeans was fought more by *thumos* than by science (1.49.3); and Archidamus tells his troops on the occasion of the first assault on Attica that those who use calculation least are especially set for action by *thumos* (2.11.7, 5.80.2). It is of course a common word in Homer, whom Socrates first confronts by taking over from him this old-fashioned word. The word is as primitive as the warriors it characterizes are uncivilized. Socrates, it seems, goes out of his way to make it as difficult as possible to incorporate the warriors into the city; he could have, after all, left it at saying that they must be manly; there was no need for him to trace manliness any further back. Glaucon himself, in whose manliness there is no trace of Thrasymachaean fierceness, already exhibits apparently what Socrates says looks impossible, harshness and gentleness together; but Glaucon exhibits them dialogically, in his resistance to Socrates' silencing of Thrasymachus and his agree-ment not to shirk in cowardice—with all the power at his command—the important matter they have undertaken (374e10—

375a1). Socrates wants at this stage something wilder than Glaucon, and he sets Glaucon, the philosophic puppy, to find his untutored original.

Socrates speaks of *thumos* and the one who has it as *thumoeidēs*.[1] There is "heart" and the "hearty"; but *thumoeidēs* is a peculiar if not a unique formation, for the suffix *-eidēs*, which is cognate with *eidos*, means in all other such words in Plato "with the form of X," for example, *sphairoeidēs*, "with the form of a sphere" or "spherelike." What would it mean, then, to call someone "*thumos*like" or thumoe-idetic? "Have you not noticed," he asks Glaucon, "that *thumos* is unbeatable and unconquerable, and when it is present every soul is fearless and undefeatable in the face of everything?" *Thumos*, it seems, never shows itself as itself in anyone; its presence in soul makes the soul like it but not the same as it. The language is surely the language of the "ideas"; it seems in any case to make death no proof of its defeatability, since even when it informs soul it does not guarantee the individual's survival. To be *thumoeidēs* is to be ready for self-sacrifice. The *thumoeidēs* is bound not even to his body, or rather he does not recognize even his body as his own, let alone anyone else as his own. Socrates then says he is stumped; the guardians cannot be allowed to destroy those they have been chosen to guard. *Thumos* reproduces on the level of nature the argument Socrates developed with Polemarchus on the level of art. Art was neutral to kill or cure, steal or guard; and *thumos* is likewise neutral and indifferent; but Socrates then found the unity of banker and thief in the thief, who was at least not idle; and now Socrates needs their unity in the banker, who has plenty to do in the city. Socrates' solution to this problem in Book I was to shift to the level of the transmission of knowledge which could not fail to be good; his solution now will be an education through poetry that is to "culminate in the things conducive to the love of the beautiful" (403c6).

Socrates finds a way out of what seems impossible—the harsh but gentle guardian—by reflecting on what they have said. "It is just that we be perplexed," he tells Glaucon, "for we abandoned the image we set before ourselves." An image, which like any image puts together seemingly heterogeneous things, shows them a way to put together opposite natures (375c7–8). Socrates, however, does not

---

1. Cf. W. Jaeger, *Eranos*, XLIV 1946, 123-30 (=*Scripta Minora* II, Rome 1960, 309–16).

leave it at the fact that dogs exhibit the two traits they want in their guardians; he goes on to assert that the nature contrary to the thumoeidetic contains within itself the opposites of friendliness and enmity. The dog is a philosopher by nature, "because it is harsh towards anyone with whom it is unfamiliar, though it has not experienced a single evil beforehand, and it greets with affection anyone with whom it is familiar, even if it has not experienced any good at his hands"; and this is to be truly philosophic, to discriminate between a friendly and a hostile sight by no other distinction than knowledge of one and ignorance of the other.

It should seem, then, that Socrates ought to drop entirely the thumoeidetic and demand now that the guardians be philosophers; instead, he identifies the philosophic nature entirely with gentleness and thus avoids anticipating his own conclusion that the philosophers ought to be kings (376b11–c2). We are forced, then, to wonder whether Socrates is not presenting the thumoeidetic itself in the guise of the philosopher. To be truly philosophic would be to be open to everything one does not know and hostile to everything one takes for granted. The philosopher's best friends are his opponents. Socrates, however, identifies the philosophic with the love of learning (*to philomathes*), which he then takes perversely to be the equivalent of *mathein ta phila*, to know one's friends. The assumed identity between knowledge and familiarity assimilates the guardian to any other artisan, for they both have a know-how by nature; and again, like any other artisan in his devotion to his art, the guardian recognizes what is his own apart from his own good and what is alien to him apart from his own bad. The city as a whole becomes his specialty to which he is selflessly dedicated. The city is his artifact, for he is the precision craftsman of its freedom (395c1).

It seems that *thumos* itself, in its refusal to admit defeat, has taken part in this evidently forced solution, as if it claimed to remain itself in all its harshness only to discover itself in its opposite, which likewise still remains what it is. It has made the philosophic nature in its own image. The heart, says the heart, is the mind. How could this have happened? Glaucon wanted restored to him both his dinner and his pride; and Socrates, in order to satisfy the first, gave it to him in speech, and, to satisfy the second, gave him an image, in terms of which what is one's own was not something with which one becomes acquainted but something to be known. Glaucon's sudden attachment to the city he was looking at, which turned the dialogic "we" of production into the "us" against "them" of politics, gets re-presented in the argument as the identity of self-sacrifice with objectivity. Political philosophy has become political.

9

E D U C A T I O N
(376c7–378e3)

After Socrates has selected the nature of those who are to fight for the city, he outlines their education. The major part he calls "music," the smaller part gymnastic, and the last concerns the twofold form of the noble lie (376e6–403c8, 403c9–412b7, 412b8–415d6). The music part falls into three parts: *logos* (the content of speeches); *lexis* (the form of speaking); and music in the ordinary sense of sung speech, harmony, and rhythm (376e8–392c6, 392c7–398b9, 398c1–401d3). Both the *logos* and *lexis* sections are in three parts: the *logos* about gods, the *logos* about heroes, and the *logos* about men (377e6–383c7, 386a1–392a7, 392a8–c6); and the *lexis* of narration (*diēgēsis*), the *lexis* of imitation (*mimēsis*), and the *lexis* that mixes both. The purpose of all music things is to induce the love of the beautiful (403c6); and the barely stated problem is how to keep the soul open to the truth while habituating it by means of lies (377a1–2). The beautiful, it seems, is designed to negotiate between falsehood and truth; and Socrates accordingly ought to have selected at the start erotic and not thumoeidetic natures; but he had no choice. He had to find men fit to be soldiers, whom he then had to educate to keep from destroying their fellow citizens. He could not begin with those natures fit to be educated in the beautiful. Socrates outlines an education in which *thumos* apparently gets transformed into *erōs*, or at least an education that can assume their perfect compatibility. Socrates seems to have Glaucon in mind. His intrusion into the conversation is due to his great manliness; and later he is reminded that as being one himself he ought not forget what characterizes erotic men (474d4). The discussion of what in general should be the types of educative speech seems to be itself an individual education of Glaucon. The *Republic* is a story that slips into Glaucon in the form of a story about stories (376d9–10). Its *lexis* is in the mixed style of narration and imitation, in which Socrates speaks all the parts and repeats his own speeches. It is not something that will be allowed to be read in the best city in speech.

Although Adimantus and Socrates start out with the belief that music and gymnastic, the twofold form of education that has been discovered in the course of much time, are assigned respectively to soul and bodies, and they must begin with the thumoeidetic soul (which is a single nature with a double aspect), Glaucon and Socrates learn by the end that they are dealing with a pair of natures (410e6) that are meant to be fitted together by means of a double education, and, contrary to their initial belief, gymnastic has the exclusive education of the thumoeidetic and music of the philosophic nature (410b10–c6). In light of this discovery, Adimantus, Glaucon, and Socrates must be understood to have done one of two things. Either they started with music in the true sense and believed it to be music in the vulgar sense, or they started with a combined gymnastic and music in the vulgar sense and without knowing it treated the body and soul together. It seems, however, that both must be true: Glaucon and Adimantus were doing the latter while Socrates was doing the former by gradually leading Glaucon to replace the false with the true division.

The story about education in stories is itself an education that starts in falsehood and ends in truth. It begins with a formally true proposition—music deals with soul—whose content is false—music educates the thumoeidetic—and proceeds to recover its true content—music educates the philosophic—by way of a music education that cannot be wholly uncontaminated by the falsehood with which it began. Moderation and courage are the forms of virtue in which music education culminates; but to be competent in music is not possible, Socrates says, "before we get to recognize the species [eidē] of moderation and courage, liberality and magnificence, and all their cousins and their contraries, in their ubiquitous manifestations and perceive them as present in what [namely, soul and body] they are present, both themselves and their images, and despise them in neither small nor large things, but believe it belongs to the same art and practice in either case" (402b9–c8). Socrates says that neither they nor the guardians can have moderation and courage before they know moderation and courage. They are not what they are as habits, for then "they like all other so-called virtues of soul are pretty near to being virtues of the body" (518d9–10). At the peak of the *Republic*, Socrates asserts that the education outlined in Books

II–III was a form of gymnastic in the vulgar sense. Only in its dialogic form does it come close to being a music education. Since it would cease entirely to be music if it ever ceased to be about types, and poets were found to make up the proper stories, education in those stories would insure that no one would ever ascend from the Cave (367a1–4). If Homer, it seems, were as good as he should be he would be worse.

After he has surveyed the poets' stories about gods and heroes, Socrates says that the third kind of speeches would concern human beings, but at the moment they cannot deal with it since they would then be anticipating what they have to prove, viz., that the just are happy regardless of whether their justice is backed by opinion (392a8–c6). On the face of it, Socrates is being ridiculous. If the issue of the effective goodness of justice had not already been settled, Socrates would be allowing for the conclusion that Thrasymachus was right after all, but the stories about gods and heroes—he has suggested how they are to be reworked so as to be in conformity with justice—would still constitute the education of the soldiers while the poets would be free to say what they have always said about men. The third kind of speeches must be in strict agreement with the first and second kinds; and it is the necessity for their consistency that makes any discussion superfluous. The separation of the dialogic city from the city in speech has had the effect of getting the founders of the latter to embrace justice with pleasure, and, in their realizing its necessity for the city, to be indifferent to the experiencing of that necessity as necessity as a point against justice. They are not about to let the army destroy their city. Socrates makes Glaucon and Adimantus not only into the defenders of justice without their knowing what it is but he makes them act justly without their being just in themselves. As founders of the city they stand outside it. They are the founder-heroes of a city of human beings; and Socrates proposes to bypass human beings. If, however, the gods are only the cause of good, and the guardians are to be as godlike as possible (383c3–5), how will they not come to believe in their imperturbability that the greatest acts of savagery are all for the good? And if they are to be imperturbable, but they are always to tell the truth, will they not be punished if they say they are not perturbed when they are, and if they are truly not perturbed, how will they be able to distinguish between the death of a friend and the death of an enemy? The perspective of the dialogic city, in eliminating the human reluctance to accept justice, has eliminated the human.

Adimantus agrees at once that music precedes gymnastic education; but he does not know that this priority means nothing more than that education must begin almost entirely with false speeches or stories (377a9). Socrates seems to exaggerate. It would have been enough to say that the stories must be moral, and whether they are true depends on the cogency of his subsequent argument. Socrates would be demanding too much if moral stories could be true only if they came with a proof of the truth of morality. It would seem, then, that their falsity is due to their being stories. They are first made up or molded (*plasthentes*) and then, in turn, make up or mold (*plattein*) the souls of the young. The story slips into the young as a die (*tupos*) that stamps them with its own shape. What then is a die, and why must it be false? Surely, if Achilles once lived, his story would not cease to be false in Socrates' sense. The story of Achilles, in stamping another with the die of Achilles, does not reproduce the original Achilles but an Achilles-type, for the story of Achilles is itself a type. There is no living individual in any story. There is no body and no soul. If the die is cleanly struck into someone, he will be the living Achilles of the story. He will make fully real the unreal. Will he then be living a lie? Socrates' language certainly suggests that he becomes as fictionalized as the fiction, for either the type he becomes is not true to the type he is, or no nature runs true to type but persists as what it is inside the form it assumes. Socrates' way of proceeding insures in any case that there will be no matchup between nature and type. He does not work up from the thumoeidetic soul to the type or types it is or could be, but rather down from the type to the individual to be molded. He reconstructs a better Achilles according to the demands of morality, but he supplies no proof that the type is in conformity with the thumoeidetic nature. The linkage that exists in the type does not necessarily correspond to a natural nexus of cause and effect in soul.

The type itself is one source of falsehood; the plot of a story is another. Like the true city it too is put together and not generated. Horace interprets the Aristotelian principle that a story must have a beginning, middle, and end as involving of necessity falsehood. Homer, he says, starts in the middle of things, "just as if it were well-known, pulls the listener along, and what he despairs of being able to make shine if he handled it, he omits; and so he lies and mixes false with true in order that the middle may not be discordant with the beginning, and the end with the middle" (Horace *Ars*

Poetica 148–52). Homer has the beautiful determine the very sequence of events. He thus missed his chance to be the inculcator of the strictest morality, for the requisite coherence of a story's plot allows its beauty to represent the beauty of morality. The immoral will then appear as the impossible and the moral will be endowed with the inevitability of geometric demonstration (378c7–8, e1–3). The coherence of plot, however, can be the truth of things only if there is no becoming and no chance but everything is made perfect from the start. Until the art of poetry, then, has become productive in the full sense and ceased to be imitative, the soldiers will have to believe, Socrates says, that their experience of education was all a dream; but that in truth they were made up (*plattomenoi*) within the earth, and when they had been worked up completely, they came out of the land (414d4–e6). They will have to believe that the story of Athena's birth is true of them. Athena is the complete denial of becoming. Zeus swallowed Athena's mother Metis (Craft or Mind); Hephaestus, the god of all fabrication, split open the head of Zeus, and she sprang out fully grown and armed. Socrates' proposal thus amounts to making Athena into the single die with which all the soldiers are to be stamped as well as into the paradigm of the city of arts as a whole (*Critias* 110b5–c2). Socrates seems to fault the poets for not going far enough and, in letting Zeus' overthrow be a threat Zeus evaded, failing to put at the head of the gods the poets' own representative, Athena. The poets were too hampered by the need to tell lies like the truth to tell the complete lie.

10

T H E O L O G Y

(378e4–383c7)

Socrates offers two dies for the gods. The first concerns the gods as causes, the second their being. The gods are good and the cause of good; they are beautiful but are not the cause of anything beautiful (381c2). Socrates does not show that their goodness is consistent with their beauty. Should that consistency depend on the gods being only final causes, Socrates' theology would be remarkably similar to

Aristotle's, which likewise argues for the convergence of the beautiful and the good in the highest beings and cannot keep being together with causality except through final cause (*Metaphysics* 1072a26–b4). Socrates himself indicates the separability of the two dies by presenting the first almost entirely in nominal sentences (379b1, 15, c2), and only when he insists that a god must not be held responsible for evils does he say that a god *is* good (380b5). In working up the first die, moreover, Socrates reserves the singular "god" for what he wants and the plural for what he disapproves of (379d1, e5); but this distinction does not hold for the second die (381e8). The causality of the gods is the causality of a class to which as yet no member has been assigned. These gods cannot have any of the conventional names; whether they can be the so-called Platonic ideas is another question.

Even though there are for human beings far fewer goods than evils, education does not and cannot consist in any account of evil. It certainly cannot give any account of itself, for its origin is to be traced to war, and Socrates urged Glaucon not to say yet whether war produces any evil or any good (373e4–5). Homer, on the other hand, who has Achilles agree with Socrates that no man gets unmixed goods, makes Zeus the dispenser of war (*Iliad* 4.84; 19.224); and Socrates seems to allude to this when he cites a halfline our texts of Homer do not have in which Zeus is the dispenser of both good and evil (379e2). The good and evil of war do not admit of the neat separation which Socrates' theology requires. Warriors are to know nothing of war. Only immediate and unambiguous goods can be assigned to the gods, for if Socrates really allowed the poets to say that the gods benefited whomever they punished (380b4–6), every evil could be made a good if the poets were ingenious enough in their plotting. It is, moreover, one thing to say, as Socrates would put it, "The beating made him better," and it is quite another for a poet to represent the experience of beating as a course in self-improvement. "Understanding through suffering" is not to be the motto for this education. Socrates' rejection of immoral stories with or without "underthought (*huponoia*)" precludes such tragic wisdom. Children must not be given the opportunity to draw any inference from the action of a story (378d6). The stories must be transparent and not have to be "read"; they must be like the goods of which the gods are the cause and which are good not only in themselves but in their effect. These goods do not alter circumstantially but are in appearance what they are in reality. Socrates does not mention any good of this kind. If justice is the good we are meant to think of, the second die denies it. The gods may be good and beautiful; they cannot be just.

Two principles make up the second die of the gods. The gods neither alter in themselves nor, without altering in themselves, give us apparitional alterations of themselves. The first principle denies that either from the outside or on their own do the gods alter. The gods are as indifferent to friendship as they are to enmity. They are so much the models of self-sufficiency that they cease to be the models of care. Indeed, since Socrates assigns them hypothetically a will only to deny them the possibility of exercising it, it is not clear whether they are meant to be alive. Perhaps they are beautiful but invisible statues. They are in any case not allowed to be self-identical in the way in which Socrates once suggested it might be true of human beings. In the *Phaedo*, he reports that the same dream came to him constantly, "appearing at different times in different shapes, but saying the same, 'Socrates,' it said, 'make music and work at it'" (60e4–7; cf. 58a10). The self, he implies, could be a dream whose *logos* was the same; and, as he goes on to relate, the sameness of the *logos* does not preclude ambiguity in its meaning. The gods, on the other hand, cannot have a *logos*, for they do not admit of any difference between surface and depth that could possibly justify "underthoughts" on the poets' part. The poets are not to say that the gods appear among men disguised as strangers, for they are not policemen who come to discover which men are just and which not. (*Odyssey* 17.485-87; *Sophist* 216a5–b6). To start with music education rather than legislation is to refrain from the use of fear and postpone the need for sanctions. Gods cannot be said to look like strangers without inducing the belief that, with the mask thrown off, they would prove to be friends (*Odyssey* 7.199–206). Gods never look like strangers for they are forever strangers. The philosopher-dogs, it seems, must treat them as their permanent enemy.

Socrates' counterexample to Cephalus clearly makes Adimantus hesitate now as to whether the gods ever lie to us, for if we were always sane, we would not need any friends to save us from ourselves. The gods cannot dictate anything to the city, for Socrates does not allow them to translate anything they know or do not know into a form intelligible to men (382e10–11). Education is entirely a human concern, and there is no divine law. The founders of the city are now free to formulate the proper kind of lies for the city without any fear that the gods might override them with either truth or

64

falsehood. False prophets cannot arise in a city in which there are no true prophets (389d3). Socrates thus desanctifies the city in the name of the sanctity of the gods.

11

COURAGE AND MODERATION

(386a1–392c5)

There are altogether nine topics into which Socrates divides his discussion of Homeric poetry: (1) Hades (386a6–387b7); (2) terrifying names (387b8–c10); (3) grief (387d1–388e4); (4) laughter (388e5–389b1); (5) truth (389b2–d6); (6) obedience (389d7–390a7); (7) food and drink (390a8–b5); (8) sex (390b6–d6); (9) money (390d7–391c7). The bond between the first four topics (education for courage) and the last four (education for moderation) is truth (389d7). Courage is concerned with painful things and moderation with pleasant things; but Socrates never discusses pain, and though he talks about laughter he is silent about tears. Achilles never does or says anything that meets with his approval; Odysseus is praised once but anonymously. The number of lines Socrates excises from Homer is not very great, but they are decisive, and with them goes the *Iliad*. It comes as a shock to read that the poets must not portray heroes as no better than men (391d3–e2), for Socrates' theology makes it impossible for there to be any children of gods; and nothing he has said could ever be formulated in a die. To tell stories to children is to be self-contradictory. Socrates has made an attempt he cannot have made. If the heroes are nothing but men, he has Adimantus agree how men should be, and the best way of life is determined without the issue of justice being settled. Once moderation and courage are in place, justice is superfluous. Socrates proposes to replace justice with two other virtues, whose presence in the soldiers will promote their own well-being and dispose them to have no need of anyone else (387d11–e1). To be human is to be superior to everything human.

65

Warriors must not fear death; and Adimantus acknowledges that anyone who believes in the existence of Hades and the terrible things there will not be fearless in the face of death. Socrates, however, does not propose to get rid of Hades or change its name; instead, the poets are to praise whatever is in Hades. It is presumably the absence in Hades of body and mind, of whatever, in short, can be held to be one's own, that instills dread (386d5, 7, 9, 387a2). The poets, then, should still say, as they now do, that Hades is, but they must add that either body and mind are truly in Hades, or that the soldiers have neither a body nor a mind whose loss they can fear. The poets must either deny the soldiers any individuality or locate it in Hades. If they do the latter, they will identify Hades with the true city, where there was a perfect cooperation between body and mind without soul. If they do the former, they will establish a selflessness of the kind the noble lie proposes, when it has the soldiers molded to perfection within the earth. Socrates makes clear his own preference in Book VII, where Achilles' speech to Odysseus, which here in the discussion heads the list of the seven censored passages on Hades, is what a man liberated from the cave speaks of when he remembers his life there (516d5). The shadows flickering past the prisoners are the shadows of artifacts; they are the truth of Homer's souls (386d7). The true city, then, is not true because it is the locus of reality but rather because the city in its essence is false. Glaucon's contemptuous dismissal of it was the first step out of it. The true city is the true lie which all gods and men hate to possess in their soul (382b2); but beautiful falsehoods in speech, which are imitations of it, are designed to stamp the soul and protect it from the city.

In the review of poetry in Book X, Socrates recalls what he says now, that the decent man puts up most easily with calamities; but he makes up for an omission here by speaking in Book X of pain (603e3–8). Not the experience of pity and grief but their expression is to be canceled. The decent man would not grieve publicly for his dead comrade as if he had experienced something terrible, since he believes that death for a decent man is not terrible. The experience of things is the opinion of things. There are no tears of things. Names can cancel things. The shudder certain words inspire vanishes with the words (387b8–c10); and other words with the opposite tone can be invented to replace them. In time, to speak euphemistically is to call a spade a spade. The language of death is to cease to be affective and become neutral. Life is mere life. Tragic experience requires that

Priam wallow in dung and Achilles pour ashes on his head. The high must fall. Socrates proposes instead perfect consistency. Everyone is to stay where he is and always say the same. Tragedy should survive only as parody and Achilles as Thersites. Education in courage is education in contempt (388d3). One is too big for small things. Detachment is freedom. The city, therefore, in duplicating its own freedom and self-sufficiency in its warriors cannot help but detach them from itself. The city casehardens the warriors for its own protection and discovers it is making each of them into a city unto himself (cf. 400e6).

Laughter follows grief. It should, one might suppose, belong with the discussion of moderation and its control not be considered to promote courage. Why the soldiers must not be fond of laughter is explained obscurely: "Whenever anyone gives in to a violent laugh, an occasion of that sort seeks a violent change as well." Socrates seems to imply that after the laughter come the tears, or, to generalize, that after the comedy there is always a swing to tragedy (cf. 563e9–10). The two lines he quotes—"Unquenchable laughter arose among the blessed gods, when they saw Hephaestus bustling about through the halls"—occur at the end of the first book of the *Iliad*. Within fifteen lines of this quotation, Zeus sets in motion his plan that ends with the deaths of Patroclus and Hector and seals the fate of Achilles. If Socrates has this in mind, the connection between the gods' laughter and the rest of the *Iliad* seems to be merely symbolic; but such symbolism does remind us that in Plato, Socrates laughs only on the day of his death, and in the *Republic*, while Adimantus of course never laughts, Glaucon often does and speaks of laughable things, but he gives up laughing once Socrates has the Muses sing how the best city must perish. In the *Iliad* too, after the gods laughed at Hephaestus, the Muses sang in answer to Apollo's lyre.

The very placement of the discussion of truth implies that the issue of lying pertains more to moderation than to courage, for the rulers must now counteract the independence that courage has fostered in the soldiers and not just restrain them from expressing what they experience (they do not know one way or the other about Hades and death). The rulers must also prevent the soldiers from realizing the knowledge they have. Since Socrates introduces rulers into the city through the issue of lying but fails to indicate who the rulers are to be, he implies as strongly as possible that the soldiers must be trained to obey their rulers without any regard as to whether they deserve to be obeyed. Clitophon is simply right. Lying is a form of drug; but the rulers cannot apply it if their subjects do not tell them the truth about their condition, for the rulers have no independent access to the truth, inasmuch as the education in stories has already concealed the truth. Perhaps the rulers know the subjects are telling the truth when they do not tell them the lies they are taught. Socrates thus poses the issue of truth—not just of truthtelling (389c5)—in a way that cannot be solved right before he brings up moderation, which simply requires that it be solved in favor of lying. The first line of Homer that Socrates praises is Diomedes' rebuke of Sthenelus, who has just told Agamemnon not to lie; Sthenelus claims that they are better than their fathers and gives the evidence to provide it (*Iliad* 4.404–410). Socrates apparently cannot cite any passage from Homer in which there is punishment for or failure to punish lying; but he does quote as a grace note two lines from the *Odyssey* in order to suggest how extensive the prohibition against lying ought to be. He stops his quotation before Homer says "or a divinely speaking singer, who delights by singing" (17.385). By the omission of the line, the poets are forthwith expelled, though by the same token they are allowed to stay. The swineherd Eumaeus, who makes the speech in which these lines occur, is a former prince himself and is rebuking a false prince, Antinous, for telling a lie about a prince in disguise, Odysseus.

Socrates excises two passages in which the gods are overcome by sexual passion; he then cites a line from a speech Odysseus makes to himself as encapsulating the kind of self-control the soldiers should hear about: "He struck his chest and addressed his heart with a speech: 'Endure, heart. You put up once with even something else more doglike.'" Odysseus is lying down in the guest room of his own palace; the maidservants, who have been sleeping with the suitors, come out of the women's quarters "giving laughter and joy to one another," and Odysseus is torn for a moment between killing them on the spot or allowing them to sleep with the suitors one last time, "and his heart was barking within, just as a bitch, standing watch over her weak puppies, barks when she fails to recognize a man and is eager to fight, so was his howl within, indignant as he was at evil deeds" (20.1–16). Moderation is silent barking. The same harshness the philosopher-dogs had to display against the enemy is now directed against disloyal members of one's own city. Odysseus' self-control is merely calculation: after he kills the suitors he lets

Eumaeus and Telemachus hang the servants. His self-control is expressed as a self-inflicted beating accompanied by a speech in which, since he speaks to his heart as if it were all of himself and the same as his chest while he was some other, he must of necessity lie. Socrates later quotes this line as a confirmation of his view that the rational and the thumoeidetic are distinct (441b3–c1); but it is remarkable how perfectly reason serves the interests of anger. Odysseus in any case recalls here that the Cyclops once ate his comrades, but he endured until his wisdom (*mētis*) brought him out of the cave (20.19–21).

12

EMULATION
AND IMITATION

(392c6–398b9)

The education of Adimantus does not begin until the education of the warriors ends. Adimantus believes in the unlimited power of speech, and that the mere repetition of consistent stories would suffice to lay to rest the perplexities of the young (366d7–367a4). He is now told of the complex relation that obtains between forms of narration and education. That relation turns on the difference and sameness of emulation and imitation. In Greek, *mimēsis* means both (Aristotle *Poetics* 1448b4–19). The ambiguity of *mimēsis* forces Socrates to give a double account of narration, of which the first is wholly neutral and the second morally and politically determined. We can thus forecast the need he will have to discuss imitation again; but now he begins Adimantus' political education. The first account speaks of poetry, the second of poets. The first divides narration into simple narration, imitation, and the compound of them both; the second account divides poets into mixed or unmixed imitators. The political perspective forces Socrates to drop simple narration and reinterpret imitation. "Simple" loses its literary meaning of "without any admixture of imitation" and acquires the moral meaning of "a person who is all of a piece" (392d5, 397e1). It is precisely because moral simplicity is impossible without a large measure of imitation that Socrates must revise his account of poetry.

Socrates distinguishes between Homer's speaking as himself and his impersonating another. Homer does not make up or invent the priest Chryses; he lets us imagine that he is Chryses. Homer never ceases to be the narrator of the *Iliad*, but he is in turn Achilles and Agamemnon, Thetis and Zeus. Among several minor changes of language, Socrates, in putting Agamemnon's speech in Book I back into narrative form, drops two lines entirely. Line 31 is about Chryseïs: "She plies the loom and goes to my bed." The Greek expression for the latter phrase—*emon lekhos antioōsan*—is unique in Homer with regard to both its syntax and its meaning. It is a euphemism for sexual intercourse. By its omission Socrates shows the power of impersonation. Had he included it in his narration, he would have had to have been explicit—"and shares my bed"—and would have failed to tell what Agamemnon really said, or, had he been as euphemistic as Agamemnon, the phrase would have ceased to be Agamemnon's euphemism and would have become his own. For the same reason, Socrates omits line 25: "He dismissed him harshly and ordained a mighty speech." As an editorial comment it cannot be included unless the words themselves are quoted. Impersonation, then, makes possible two things that amount to the same thing: the separation of the poet's perspective from that of his characters. Simple narration is morally neutral. It cannot take sides without giving the evidence. The city therefore cannot let simple narration be a form of poetry, for simple narration is identical with the form of its legislation without the sanctions: "If a general dishonors a priest,..."[1] The formation of character requires the presentation of character; but the poet represents character without having the character. The poets do better at impersonation than others do at emulation. There is hardly any risk that a warrior will impersonate a blacksmith well or get the crashing of the sea exactly right; rather, the danger is that the poet will do both with ease and then do the warrior as well and show up the one who is to be "really beautiful and good" for a fake (396b11). The poets, then, must be wholly invisible and stand behind the parapet in the Cave, either carrying the artifacts whose shadows the prisoners see or making them for others to carry.

1. Cf. D. Daube, *Forms of Roman Legislation* (Oxford 1956), 6–8.

The principle of the city—one man/one job—is, according to Socrates, a principle of nature. There are no mimetic natures and therefore no undetectable forms of lying. Character is a second nature induced through emulation of the paradigm of one's own nature (395d1–3). The warriors become who they are through habituation. The poets are the evidence to the contrary. They never become anyone by habit. Only the poet could do Glaucon's unjust man. The poets then threaten to expose the warriors not only by appearing superior to them but by casting doubt on their consistency. If the poet shows one man courageous without moderation and another moderate without courage, the unity of the warrior's nature becomes suspect. Socrates therefore appeals to the fact that comic and tragic poets are not the same, despite the closeness of their imitative forms. He can then argue that poetic impersonation is always presentation of a single type which the poet himself is, and Antigone and Philoctetes belong together as much as the Paphlagonian and Dikaiopolis do, and courageous, moderate, holy, and free men are all one (395a3–d1). Comic poets may be comic, and tragic poets tragic, but it is not plausible to say that Homer is heroic, for he lets Odysseus sing only part of his *Odyssey*. Homer is the enemy. Socrates, in any case, has the warriors practice the Homeric style of mixed narration and imitation without ever saying who Homer himself is. He goes even further. He simultaneously denies that anyone can imitate more than one type well and asserts that the warriors are precision craftsmen of freedom (395c1). There is no art of imitation, but there is an art of freedom. "Freedom" sounds like an "idea," made not by a god but by those who have no knowledge of how to make anything. If the artful poets are around, they will show up the freedom-makers' incompetence and the spuriousness of their artifact. They must be banished from the tragedy they are making (*Laws* 817b1–5).

If we follow Socrates' example of Homer's impersonation of Chryses, whenever I say, "He said, 'Goodbye,'" the listener believes that I am he. Cephalus, then, it seems, was claiming to be both Sophocles and Sophocles' questioner when he quoted them directly but he was not claiming to be either Themistocles or the Seriphian. The warrior, on the other hand, is never to say "I" unless he is wholly that "I"; and this perfect sincerity is to be accomplished through lies. It follows, then, that complete communism is necessary, so that whenever a fellow citizen suffers an injury and I, a warrior, say, "He said, 'I'm hurt,'" I can rightly be believed to be he because I am he

(462b4–e3). In the best city in speech, simple narration and imitation collapse into one die. Education sets out to produce the integral self—no one can be anyone else—and ends up by producing the collective self: each one is everyone else. The city thus aspires to reproduce the anonymity of knowledge on the level of corporeality; and what seems true of knowledge—if two know the proof of a mathematical theorem, it makes no difference whether one of them says, "I know," or, "He says, 'I know,'"—is adopted in ignorance, for all the opinions of the city. The city impersonates wisdom. It is the sophist of all sophists (492a1–d1; *Statesman* 303b8–c5).

13

MUSIC AND GYMNASTIC

(398c1–412b7)

Harmony and rhythm are the two elements of music that are prerational and penetrate the deepest into the inside of the soul (401d5–402a6). It would seem, then, that Socrates got Adimantus to start at the wrong place in music. But they could not have started in any other way, for not only could they not have selected the proper scales unless they knew the virtues the stories were to instill (400d1–5), but Glaucon, who is trained in music, and Socrates, who does not know the scales, are equally ignorant of how the various meters match up with various temperaments. They do not yet know enough to be founders. They are on the way to being founders (cf. 388e3, 394d7–9, 416b5–9). As Socrates now remarks, unaware they have been purging the city of fevered heat; they have not been, as Adimantus believes, starting from scratch (399e5–7, 394d5–6). The education of Glaucon and Adimantus consists in the growing awareness of their own ignorance which works against the ostensible indoctrination of the guardians. In light of their joint ignorance, Socrates proposes that the beautiful be the standard of rhythm. The beautiful stands for what one loves but does not and cannot have and does not know (402d1–e2). Musical education is not just the incorporation of opinions but the incorporation of images as well, which, by being recognized as images (401b2, 5, 8), separate love of one's own (*philein*) from love of the beautiful (*eran*). The love of the beautiful is equivalent in the city in speech to philosophy in the dialogic city. Images of moderation and courage, each with its own scale, keep at a distance from ourselves and each other moderation and courage so that they do not mix together in an unattractive blandness. Aristotle may be right and Glaucon wrong—the Phrygian scale may not represent moderation (Aristotle *Politics* 1342a32–b3)—but it is more important that steadiness in the face of violence and war be kept distinct from orderliness in peaceful and voluntary actions (399a1–c6). The consonant difference between the Dorian and Phrygian modes lays the basis for the possibility of learning to discern the species of moderation and courage and finding their harmony in a human being lovable (402b9–d9). Socrates and Glaucon are done with philosopher-dogs.

The end of the music education is signaled by the coemergence of two themes, the love of the beautiful and the discovery of kinds (*eidē*). Philosophy has been at work in making the filamentlike argument of music education periagogic and therefore tied in with a reflection on itself. It has proceeded so modestly that the excessive harshness of the thumoeidetic nature, which music education was supposed to remove, has, as Socrates now reveals, vanished without music education's ever having confronted it. Music education is designed solely to breed in moderation. The thumoeidetic nature, then, still stands in the way of philosophy, the ease of whose triumph recalls how Socrates, by his omission of narrative interludes, displayed the submission of Thrasymachus without sweat or shame. Music has charmed the city of fevered heat too, for, unarmed and soft as it is, it could not offer any resistance. Marsyas' flute has been cast aside, but Marsyas himself has not been flayed (399e1–4), for the new theology has denied that the flaying ever occurred. Socrates has taken the Olympian order out of time and, in censoring the chaos and struggle which preceded it, censored the thumoeidetic itself. The chaste lover of the beloved with a perfect soul and not as perfect a form (*eidos*) has usurped its place (402d1–403c3). Socrates, it seems, has accepted Agathon's praise of Eros and denied that Necessity ever reigned (*Symposium* 195c1–6). When Socrates turns from music to gymnastic, he identifies soul with thought (403d7; cf. 400e3).

The proposed relation between gymnastic and music can be formulated as follows: whatever Homer speaks of in his own name in simple narration sets the standard for the warriors' way of life, but whatever Homer has said in the name of another must be removed (404b10–c7; cf. 468d7). Life in the true city is to life in the city of fevered heat as Homeric narration is to Homeric impersonation and as body is to soul. Socrates praises Homer for never having his heroes dine on fish: the two occasions on which the *Iliad* mentions fishing are in similes (16.406–410; 24.80–82). Without any show of reluctance Glaucon dismantles all the refinements he himself had introduced (404c6–e2). Now that he can contemplate a human kind of beauty, he does not mind. Health is once more a desirable good. Through health Socrates introduces justice as punishment and argues for it to recover the simplicity of Homeric medicine. The elaborate comparison Socrates makes between the arts of medicine and justice precedes his reassignment of gymnastic to the care of the thumoeidetic soul. It is accordingly unclear whether curative justice must not be reassigned too and be the court of last resort for defects in the thumoeidetic, or whether it should retain its place and correct the musical discordances of soul. That there should be one art of the judge regardless of the source of the vice but two virtues—each with its one art—seems to be due to a failure in division (*Sophist* 229b7–230d5). While Socrates' own refutative art is being shown at work, it seems to be lurking in an art it has not yet finished dividing. That too is a part of its being shown. The articulation of things always occurs against the background of the confusion of things.

Socrates first banishes the inaustere poet, then puts the city on a diet, and ends up by conducting a purge. There is to be no valetudinarianism of soul. Justice comes back with the sword. The beautiful has made injustice so repulsive that Glaucon fails to notice that justice too is tainted. It is good only insofar as it is necessary. Glaucon accepts even more than this: execution is the best thing that could happen to the incurable (410a3–6; *Laws* 627d11–628a3). Glaucon is led to this view through Socrates' showing him the difference between the doctor and the judge. At first, he believes that the judge should have a firsthand acquaintance with natures of every kind (408d2), for Socrates could, it seems, satisfy his original demand only if he exposed from the inside the misery of the unjust soul. Now, however, Socrates convinces him of the prurience of such an inquiry. Adimantus had allowed that one would not be drawn to

74

injustice in two cases: if either one knew that justice were best, or if by a natural disgust one refrained from injustice (366c3–d1). Socrates has gotten Glaucon to emulate the second type; and he now sets over him the judge with knowledge. Socrates distinguishes between experience and knowledge (409b8–c1). The bad judge has within himself a model drawn from his own experience of every criminal who comes before him, but he cannot recognize good men and must suspect them. The good judge begins with a noble simplicity and in time acquires knowledge of vice and virtue. This nonexperiential knowledge arises from "his practice of an injustice not his own in souls not his own" (409b7). Virtue comes to discern kinds (*eidē*), vice lives its own paradigms. Socrates admits that if Glaucon's perfectly unjust man were possible, he would and should be invisible to the good judge. Ignorance, which is inseparable from love of the beautiful, is likewise inseparable from aversion to the ugly. The judge is certainly not to denounce wickedness and urge the examination of conscience on the off chance that he might extract a confession. Moral indignation, Socrates suggests, results from a mixture of the gymnastic of the thumoeidetic soul with a punitive justice that can never make up for an original baseness (406a8–b1). He indicts the tragic poets. Their Asclepius holds out the hope of deathlessness along with the spectacle of unending punishment (408b7–c4). An eternal purgatory therefore seems to be precluded. Since, however, the myth of Er does apparently restore to Glaucon what is here denied him, Socrates might imply that without the reality of the best city, the art of justice can never be as vestigial as he now proposes. If a ruthless surgery is not available, the self-tormenting of soul, despite its loathsomeness, might have to be prolonged.

14

THE NOBLE LIE

(412b8–417b9)

To be perfectly musical is to know how to mix the gymnastic of the thumoeidetic nature with the music of the philosophic and apply it to the soul; but it is not the same as to be most competent at ruling and guarding the city (412a4–c10). The philosopher and the king are still apart. To keep the regime safe is not the same as to protect the city. Throughout Book III education in music has been advancing from a habit to an art, but the protection of the city depends on an opinion that can never be more than an opinion. Socrates signals the difference between the supervisor of the regime and the ruler of the city by restricting the latter to the elders: perfect musicianship is not a matter of age. Potential rulers have to love the city in order to care for it; and they are most likely to love it if they should believe that whatever is to the advantage of the city is to their own as well, and, were it to fare well, should they believe their own welfare goes together with it (412c12–d8). They are therefore to be tested as to whether they would do with zeal whatever they believe is to the city's advantage and would refuse to do what they believe is not. Socrates cannot conceive of testing them for their knowledge of what is in the city's interest. Either there is no such knowledge available, or if it were it would follow automatically that the city's ruler would know that the city's interest is not the same as his own, or possibly, as in the argument with Polemarchus, whatever is knowledge is by that very fact neutral. It is clear, in any case, that Socrates has nested so many beliefs around the love of the city in order that the ruler could never believe that either his love of the city is a belief for him—he is not to say, "I believe I love the city"—or the city's welfare or his own is a belief—he is not to say either, "I believe I'm faring well," or, "I believe the city is faring well." He is to have beliefs about the linkage of things that do not affect the things themselves. The meaning of his own happiness is to be opaque to him.

Socrates wants the potential rulers to love the city; and he devises a series of tests by means of which the tenacity they display in holding on to the opinion that they must always do what they believe best for the city measures the depth of their love. The tests make sure that they do not go directly from the belief that the city's good is theirs to the belief that they must do their own good. The city must always stand between them and their own good. The guardians therefore love the city conditionally and not for its own sake; and whatever may be true of justice, the city belongs to Glaucon's third kind of good. Socrates, however, rather surprisingly, inserts between the criteria for loyalty and the tests for loyalty a discussion of true and false opinion, as if it could make any difference whether the fundamental dogma of the city were true or false (412e5–413c7).

Socrates seems to be solicitous for the auxiliaries who do not pass the tests, for if false opinions are lost voluntarily but true opinions involuntarily, no one who flunks can be punished. Failure is not "tragic," since there is no coincidence of responsibility and nonresponsibility in fatefulness (413b4). Since, moreover, no one is to believe that he changed his opinions willingly, he is not to believe that he lost a false opinion. Those who pass emerge with their opinions intact, and those who fail emerge with the same opinions restored; and their shared opinion is to be grounded in the opinion that no false opinion is good and no true opinion bad. The issue, then, is not so much how to ground the guardians' opinion as how to ground Glaucon's opinion that all the falsehoods which the music education has supplied were means to the establishment of a true opinion: There cannot be a sound argument against the opinion that one's own good depends on the city's. This opinion admits of a twofold interpretation, for one's own good may be taken in the weak sense—one cannot be human without the city—or in the strong sense—one can only be happy if the city is happy. The strong sense is the guardians' fundamental dogma, the weak sense is the city's. Socrates proposes to weld the two senses together in a lie in which, for the city as a whole, being and opinion are one and the same. No citizen can answer the question who he is in any sense unless he says what the city says he is. The city can then become a simulacrum of Glaucon's second kind of good—that which is loved for its own sake and its consequences—if what is one's own in the strict sense can be extended to include one's family. Not even Antigone, however, for all her devotion to her incestuous family, could forget the difference. The city without tragedy is more tragic than any tragedy.

The noble lie is in two parts (414d1–e6, 415a1–c6). The first makes the distinction inviolable between fellow countrymen and all strangers; the second allows for the city's principle—one man/one job—to be almost true in fact. The first is about what separates the city from the outside and makes everyone within "family." It incorporates Polemarchus' view. The second divides the single family into classes of rulers and ruled: Thrasymachus now has a place. The first part of the lie naturalizes the law, the second legalizes nature. The first speaks in simile, the second in metaphor. The land is to be defended as if it were their mother and they were all brothers; but everyone is born gold, silver, bronze, or iron. In the first they are molded by and within the earth, in the second "the god" molded them. The first declares that reality is a dream and they were made perfect; the second declares that all were imperfect but some better than others: there is generation and one does not always breed true. The deviancy of nature makes for community and binds the regime to the country (415a7–b3). The first splits between education in the beautiful and love of one's own and unites them in a patriotic courage founded on right. It is directed primarily to the auxiliaries but in narrative form. The second addresses all the citizens, justifies in language the commercial class can understand why the right to rule and be educated is limited, and enjoins the rulers in the name of the god to show no pity to their own base offspring. Its aim is primarily moderation; it alone speaks of souls (415b6).

The soil makes the city one, the metals structure it. The oneness of the city is then reproduced institutionally through communism. Communism of women, children, and property is the real equivalent to the first part of the noble lie; but the second part denies that communism can be extended throughout the city, since only the best natures and the most rigorous education could make anyone public-spirited enough to give up everything that is his own (416b5–c4). The noble lie gives some assurance to the citizens of baser metals that the guardians and auxiliaries will not gobble them up; but their institutional arrangements cut them off again and make them as remote as the founders. Fraternity and inequality are weakly linked. Some are gold and silver in rank but their weapons are of iron or bronze; others are iron and bronze in rank but they use gold or silver in exchange. The rulers and the ruled live in two time frames at once, and it is only a matter of time before everyone wakes up.

15

HAPPINESS

(419a1–422a3)

The first to wake up is Adimantus. He echoes the objection which Glaucon had made before about the true city; and though he too frames it in terms of enjoyment, what he really means, it seems, is that the armed camp is idle and has nothing to do. They are either no better than mercenaries—*epikouroi* does, after all, mean that no less than it does auxiliaries—or as bad as whores sitting around in brothels (420a1). Socrates on another occasion admits the justice of this, for he wants to see the city at war (*Timaeus* 19c2–8). Adimantus' most important insight, however, is that whatever kind of city it is, the soldiers determine it: it is "in truth" theirs (419a4) and there is something strange if the essence of something is so abstracted and separated from any material manifestation. It is as if in truth the city were theirs but in appearance not. They are ghosts in their own city. It is a peculiarity of the city of arts that as far as function goes, every member of the city could be elsewhere, and the soldiers be hired from abroad if they were nothing but the practitioners of their craft. But unless the soldiers were loyal, they would destroy the city; and their loyalty is mythical and their competence is not. So they had to become attached to the land and yet go unrewarded. They are perfectly just and perfectly miserable. Glaucon was right. Socrates' defense reveals for the first time that the purpose of the discussion was to make the city happy as a whole so that justice might be found in it. Socrates' strategy then was this. Since the issue was that justice and happiness do not go together—happiness consisted of goods the core of which was not justice—Socrates turned to the city of fevered heat in order to reform it enough to admit happiness; and if Glaucon and Adimantus could accept the city as happy, and if he in turn could go on to prove that the animating principle of the city was justice, then, on the analogy of big and small letters, the individual would be just and happy likewise.

Socrates' procedure involves the difficult point that happiness be applicable to a structure. In his comparison, the city is a statue of a human being (*andrias*) and they are its painters; the parts of the body in the image match up with the parts of the city, and we can say that the eyes correspond to the guardians or auxiliaries. Adimantus' objection now reads as saying that the eyes, the most beautiful part of the animal, should be painted with the most beautiful dye, "so as for them not even to appear as eyes." Socrates, then, finds the beauty of the image as a whole to be analogous to the happiness of the city as a whole, and the beauty of each part of one analogous to the happiness of each member of the other. Socrates admits that it is not very important whether a cobbler is poor at his job or not; but it does not obviously follow that the statue painter can dye a toenail purple and not ruin the beauty of the whole. And if, on the other hand, it is the eyes which are dyed purple, it is not obvious why purple cannot symbolize the greater happiness of which the guardians are capable no less than gold can symbolize their excellence. The eyes are to be colored black; there is nothing beautiful about black; but black eyes are beautiful. "Black eyes" must stand at once for the happiness of the guardians and the perfect functioning of the guardians. What, then, is that of which "black" is the image? Socrates seems to identify it with the manifestness of the guardians as guardians. They are never to be mistaken for anything else. The analogy then points to the necessity for the guardians to appear as what they are, but it does not point to their happiness, unless happiness is always seeming happiness. Socrates could have avoided this consequence had he not mentioned the beauty of the eyes but assigned beauty only to the whole and made every part of the whole strictly neutral; but he could not have done so without denying to every part any happiness at all except insofar as each part were capable of looking at the whole to which it belonged. The eyes alone can do this. The guardians then must be able to contemplate the city if they are to achieve happiness; but it is not the guardians but the members of the dialogic city who are in that position. Socrates thus convinces Adimantus of the happiness of the city by having him step back from it. It is then beautiful and he is happy.

Socrates treats the issue of wealth and poverty as the equivalent among the artisans to the issue of happiness among the guardians and auxiliaries (421c8–422a3). Just as they cannot do their job without virtue, so the artisans cannot do theirs if either poverty deprives them of their tools or wealth corrupts them. Socrates understands that Adimantus' question is for Adimantus only a practical question; it does not go to the heart of the matter—to what extent the individual and the city can be understood as parallel and where there cannot be any matchup—for Adimantus did not ask the question in his own name. The guardians' happiness is adventitious; and all they have to do is compel and persuade everyone to be the best they can according to their function (421c1). As long as the guardians do not object, Adimantus will not object on their behalf. Just as the founders will not let either poverty or wealth slip in, they will not let the question of happiness slip in.

16

WAR AND REVOLUTION
(422a4–427c5)

Adimantus' second question opens up a difference between the city and the individual, for the city's need to become as powerful as possible seems to be different in kind from the individual's. Not everyone thinks like Callicles. Socrates' answer is based on probabilities and gimmicks. Their city must make sure, without ever exercising imperial rule, that its neighboring cities, if not themselves as good as it, are corrupt and stay corrupt; and though it may seem unjust to weaken them, the city is doing them good, for they would be worse off if they were corrupt and powerful. Socrates impersonates the embassy of their city and in this way lets us see that the city he is trying to bribe might not believe him, for only the good, he had said, are open to the possibility that others are good. Their city in any case ends up being the unpaid army of every other city in succession. Socrates meets Adimantus' objection, that the city they bribed might become even more dangerous, by denying that any other city is truly a city or any other city truly great (423a7). In the teeth of the evidence, Socrates claims that the rich and the poor are more attached to their own classes than to their common country (Herodotus 4.11). The ignoble lies of others breed presumably less devotion than their noble lie. Socrates, in short, imposes on reality the truth of Thrasymachean precision. Practice demands that the city be error free.

The effect that their idealizing excursion into foreign affairs has on the discussion is extraordinary and sudden. All institutional arrangements, including the communism of women and children which is mentioned here for the first time (423e4–424a2), are of no importance; but music and gymnastic education are held to be the keystone of the city's survival. A pun on *nomos*, which can mean either tune or law, establishes the principle that any departure in music heralds political transgression (424c3–d4). Adimantus is so certain of this that he supplies the evidence: This form of musical transgression, he says, "once it gets lodged flows gently and imperceptibly towards habits and practices; and from there it goes out all the greater into mutual contracts, and then from contracts it comes against the laws and regimes with overwhelming license" (424d8–e2). Adimantus, then, believes that Socrates' city once existed and was Athens, for otherwise he could not possibly believe he knew that musical change leads to political corruption. Socrates himself had carefully distinguished between musical and political rule; and in his own account in Book VIII the causes of change in regimes are quite different. Adimantus, however, seems to have adopted a Thrasymachean distinction against Thrasymachus: to speak precisely of law is to speak of its musical sense; to speak loosely of law is to speak of it politically, and this difference has a temporal parallel in the history of Athens' decline. It is not enough for Adimantus that education distinguishes the city from the gang of thieves; it is necessary that it be the essence of the city and that perfect education once have been real. His indignation at present-day politicians who believe they are "in truth" statesmen has its source in his version of Platonism (426d4–6). He is certain that there once were or now are true statesmen. He is certainly not thinking of Socrates (*Gorgias* 521d7).

17

J U S T I C E

(427c6–434c6)

Socrates finishes off the founding of the city by assigning "the greatest, most beautiful, and principal points of legislation" to Apollo at Delphi (427b3). He declares as plainly as possible that the sacred is of the highest importance to the city and of no concern to them. The city is perfectly good if it is wise, brave, moderate, and just (427e10–11); it is not sacred or it is perfectly good regardless of whether it is sacred. Glaucon interprets a remark of Socrates as implying that he will not look for justice himself but hand over the task to everyone else in the dialogic city; so he reminds Socrates that he had said it was his sacred duty to come to the aid of justice (427e1). Socrates believes perhaps that justice, now that it is armed and protected by the city, no longer needs his help. Glaucon in any case identifies the search for justice with the help of justice, and Socrates implies perhaps that they are not strictly compatible, and however the principle of his own action is to be understood, it cannot be found in the city he has made. He implies therefore that the nonsacred city cannot come to the rescue of justice. The city is incapable of defending itself against the charge that it is nothing but collective selfishness. Adimantus was mistaken to bind education and legislation so closely together.

It is astonishing that justice could have entered the city so surreptitiously that they now need a light from somewhere other than the city to find it. Justice could have been generated out of elements they did ticket as they entered, or it could have split off from something they have already acknowledged; but in no case does justice go by the name of justice in the city. The city is perfectly good (427e7). "Perfectly good," however, does not mean that it is perfectly wise, brave, moderate, and just. It is perfectly good as a city but not perfectly good. The introduction of philosophy cannot make it a better city. Socrates never calls it the philosophic city. The city is good, but it is not healthy, for only the true city was healthy. Glaucon, then, in accepting the city as good, accepts justice as good insofar as it is laborious, and the city is working at becoming healthy. The perfectly good city is imperfect; and its imperfection is the invisibility of justice in it. Should justice therefore ever come to light in the city, the city would believe it was perfect and hence cease to be perfectly good. Justice, however, turns out to be the one excellence the true city and the good city share; but if "just" must be the same as "healthy" when applied to the true city, the good city, which is neither true nor healthy, cannot be just. Justice, then, must admit of a precise and an ordinary sense, and the good city be just in the latter and non-Thrasymachean way. Socrates, then, would have rescued the city from Thrasymachus' attack at the expense of justice as the lawful. Every city, then, becomes a crude version of the good city, for every city is more or less wise, brave, and moderate without any of them being just. Socrates thus gives a preliminary analysis of political life that is not regime-dependent. It is accordingly not law-dependent and not subject to Thrasymachus' criticism of the city's lack of justice.

Whatever other terms apply to any city, none of them affects its being good unless it can be shown that it is strictly incompatible with the four that make it good. "Imperialist," for example, must not be applicable, but holy/unholy, Greek/barbarian, beautiful/ugly, wealthy/poor, urban/rural are all possible. The four terms the good city must admit of need not be applicable to it in the same way. Let us say that the predicate is a saturating predicate if and only if no segment of the subject does not have the predicate, and it is nonsaturating if it is true of the subject but not true of all of the subject. Saturating predicates imply that the subject is in this respect homogeneous, but the subject is heterogeneous if the predicate is nonsaturating. The city then consists of homogeneous and heterogeneous elements. It consists of citizens all of whom are citizens and of citizens all of whom are functionally distinct from one another. The two parts of the noble lie expressed this difference; but since the first part, in making everyone equally a brother, carried the moral that as citizens everyone must fight for the city, "brave" ought to be a saturating predicate. The citizen is the warrior, and Adimantus was right to say that in truth the city belonged to the warriors. The citizen is he who dies for the city. Socrates lists the graves of the dead and all the funeral rites as the final item for which they must consult Delphi (427b7–8). Socrates thus denies that the core of the city is within his competence. In the *Timaeus*, he admits he cannot describe the city at war, and in the *Republic* he denies that "brave" is a saturating predicate and has anything to do with dying for one's country.

The city was originally built to be a paradigm for the individual; it is now presented in its goodness as elementary, and as elementary it will become paradigmatic for the soul. The elementary analysis was originally the letter-analysis for justice, which did not require that the city be a complete paradigm for man. The city could have been ABCJSTD and the individual either as simple as JST or more complex than the city; but now w[WISE], b[BRAVE] m[MODERATE], and j[JUST] are going to show up in city and soul without any overlap or any bond between them; and this is all the stranger since both city and soul are to consist of three parts but admit of four virtues. "Virtues," however, occurs only twice in the entire *Republic*, once of the "so-called virtues of soul," and once in the myth of Er where it may well be a distributive plural (518d9, 618b1). If, then, there is only virtue, the predicates, wise, brave, moderate, and just cannot be additive but must constitute a whole despite the fact that at least two of them are nonsaturating predicates of the city. However this may be, Socrates proposes that, if they do not hit upon justice at once, they can discover it by a process of elimination. We do not really need the example of Socrates' own counting at the beginning of the *Timaeus*, where the absence of the fourth host makes him known to Socrates, to make us aware that justice too can become known by not showing up at all in the good city (428a2–6).

Socrates says that it is plain to him that wisdom is in the city but there appears something strange or placeless (*atopon*) in regard to it (428a11–b1). Wisdom means good counsel (*euboulia*), and it is a kind of science (*epistēmē*), and on account of all the arts in the city, it is reasonable to call it the scientific or technical city. Whether it is as reasonable to call it "carpenter city," as Glaucon does, or "farmer city," as Socrates does, is not so obvious (428c1, 9), for it might then be possible to call the city musical if Socrates' most musical man lived there; but only if he supervised the entire education in the city would the designation truly fit the city. Only those arts, then, authorized by the city and practiced on behalf of the city are predicable of the city. If that wisdom concerned with the city as a whole rules in the city, the city can as a whole be addressed as wise. Socrates does not say that this wisdom figures out how to make the city happy as a whole, and he cannot say that it is concerned with how the city is to be just to its neighbors; he does not even say that this wisdom is a permanent part of the city they have founded. Wisdom is assigned to the guardians but has not been instilled in them, for law may be simply incapable of arranging for the ruling element to have it (428e9). Glaucon, in referring to those they named the perfect guardians, forgets that they did not have science but opinion (414b2), and the science of guarding had been proved in Book I to be the science of theft (334a–b). Wisdom seems to consist of two things: knowledge of the survival of the city and knowledge of what makes a whole a whole. This latter knowledge would be knowledge of how and why the fourfold virtue of the city made it perfectly good; but this knowledge is derivative from the equivalent knowledge in the case of soul—what makes the soul a whole—which Socrates says their very way of proceeding stands in the way of their ever achieving (435c9–d5).

Unlike wisdom, courage is as easy to locate in the city as it is to determine what allows the city to be called brave. This is one country where one cannot speak of a brave people. A city of cowards defended by the brave seems to be the recipe for disaster: there is no second line of defense, and the brave hold most of the city in contempt. Perhaps it is not bad, however unjust it may be, to be trained against one's nature. The warriors, however, are not brave because they fight for the city but because they preserve the opinion of the law with regard to pleasure and pain. The function of the army is twofold: to embody the law and to fight for the city. It does not fight to preserve the lawful opinions of the city. The army, then, must believe that there cannot be these lawful opinions without the city, and it fights for the city as a form of self-preservation. Socrates does not say that it fights for the city as a whole (429b1–3). In his earlier account of their opinions, Socrates had spoken of pain, pleasure, fear, time, and speech as the possible involuntary agents of alteration in their opinions (412e5–413c4); but now he speaks of pain, pleasure, desire, and fear. Then he spoke of tests to guarantee that loss of an opinion would never be held to be loss of a false opinion; now he speaks of such deep-dyed opinions that they could never be scrubbed out. The auxiliaries are the embodiment of the unwritten law. While they are resisting change they are changing. Rulers are indispensable for correcting the inflexibility as well as the drift of unwritten law, for in ignorance of kinds the warriors would tend to treat each new song as a new kind of song (424b7–c4). If Socrates' image for the degree of their indoctrination is to bear any weight, the preparation of white wool would correspond to the perfection of nature by way of music and gymnastic education, for the purple dye corresponds to the laws (430a2–3). The auxiliaries have political courage; they have no knowledge of the terrible (430c3).

With two down and two to go, Socrates does not want to be bothered about moderation (430d4), but justice demands that he gratify Glaucon who now shows not as much concern about justice as he once did: even if he knew how to find justice before moderation, he would not want it to be the first to come to light. Socrates' moderation, which just had him dismiss a possible inquiry into true courage (430c4–6), inclines him not to deal with moderation either. A single-minded devotion to the task at hand is moderate but not just. Moderation is the only good of the city that does not concern itself with other cities; its meaning for the city cannot even be ascertained without Socrates' having recourse to the soul (431a4). Socrates' perfect self-control would forbid him to make any concessions to Glaucon. Whatever may be true of the other two, moderation and justice are not in perfect harmony with one another; and since moderation resembles more a harmony than either courage or wisdom does, it would seem that moderation must cease to be so self-controlled as to be immoderate. Originally, a harmony of courage and moderation was the preserve of the guardians, but now moderation is distributed between two classes, and their harmony is only in a sense the same. The new harmony is between the soldiers, who embody the city's opinion about what is terrible, and the artisans, each of whom knows something. Moderation is the virtue of knowers who acknowledge the right of those who have only opinion to rule them. Socrates indeed made the *Republic* itself possible by indulging Glaucon in his opinion (328b2–3).

Socrates begins with an ordinary expression—"better/stronger than oneself"—which, if taken literally, contradicts itself. He does not give it a sense by saying that when soul rules body, one is better than oneself; instead, though he speaks of pleasures and desires, he proposes that where in the case of soul the naturally better prevails over the worse, there is moderation. The silence about body seems to be dictated by the political meaning, for if ruler and ruled correspond to parts of soul, what of the city corresponds to the body? Perhaps the self-contradiction in "better than oneself" really applies to the city and cannot be reinterpreted to have a satisfactory sense. Politically, in any case, moderation has two meanings. On the one hand, simple and measured desires guide by calculation (with the help of mind and right opinion) those few who are born best and best educated (431c5–7); and in them apparently there is no need for the desires to submit to control; rather, the desires and prudence in them prevail over the desires and pleasures in the many. Socrates implies that the taste of the rulers prevails in the city; he does not say whether the pains of the ruled are also under their control (431c1). According to the second meaning of moderation, on the other hand, the rulers and the ruled have the same opinion as to who should rule. In the good individual, the naturally better rules and there is no need for consent, for it is not natural that the better and the worse have the same opinion. In the auxiliaries, Socrates had extended courage to cover moderation as well (429d1); courage maintained their lawful opinions despite pleasures and desires, but Socrates did not suggest that the maintenance of these opinions involved consent. The necessity for consent seems to weaken the degree of control that reason can exercise in the city. Beating may be more in order where reason is stronger.

Of the three meanings of moderation—the better rules the worse; mind-informed desires of the few control the desires among the many; the same opinion as to who should rule prevails among rulers and ruled—only the last makes of "moderate" a saturating predicate. Everyone utters the same speech and believes it. What binds the city together is an opinion, and inasmuch as everyone has this opinion, what is said of the city can be said of each individual. What would, it seems, be the condition to be satisfied if the city is to be called 'happy' has been applied to "moderate." The three ways, moreover, in which the city can be moderate duplicate respectively the first three ways in which the city is good.

The third sense of moderation applies most strictly to the third class: rulers rarely need to be told that they should rule. Moderation, then, really is a harmony, for through the range of its meanings it is self-binding (431e10–432b1). The city thus seems to be complete without any room for justice; but the principle of its founding turns out to be justice. It is a principle known only to members of the dialogic city (433a4), though everyone in the city in speech acts in accordance with the principle without knowing it, for to know the principle is to know one's own nature and the nature of everyone else. The fourth meaning of moderation is self-knowledge. The justice they find is at their feet (432d7).

A minor deviation from strict grammar indicates that the justice they find and the justice they are looking for may not be the same. The principle in terms of which each one entered the city—whatever his nature was most suitable for had to be his practice in the city—is justice "or some species of this (*ētoi toutou ti eidos*)" is justice. The particle *ētoi* goes normally first ("either") with an express alternative (*ē*);[1] but here the same principle is put forward as the comprehensive definition of justice and as a part of it. Socrates at any rate goes directly from the principle of their founding to a proverbial expression, *ta hautou prattein*, which means no more than "to mind one's own business," and which originally characterized the jack-of-all-trades who did not make anything for anyone else (370a4). The opposite of minding one's own business is meddling, which in Greek is *polupragmonein*, or "to do many (things)." From the "many" in *polupragmonein* Socrates finds its opposite in the "one" of their own principle, one man one job (*hena hen epitedēuein*). Socrates, in short, takes literally the "many" in *polupragmonein* and colloquially the "one" in *hena hen epitedēuein*, so that it no longer entails the perfect adaptation of one nature to one art. Thrasymachus' distinction between precise and ordinary speech thus proves to be indispensable for solving the problem of justice. By applying Thrasyma-

---

1. Cf. J.D. Denniston, *Greek Particles*[2] (Oxford 1954), 553.

chean precision to the proverbial and imprecision to their own principle, Socrates brings about a unity between the individual and the
class-structure of the city. Justice splits between class-membership as
a principle that generates the class-characteristic and class-characteristic as a principle that establishes class-membership. The first principle is positive and enrolls everyone into the city as a knower; but
the second principle is negative and maintains everyone in the city,
once he has been enrolled, and does not let him overstep his job
(433b9–10). Not everyone in the city minds his own business by art,
but everyone in the city minds his own business. Knowledge is the
ticket of admission for each artisan, but knowledge does not keep him
in his place. Once he becomes part of the city, he ceases to be an artisan
and becomes a member of the class of moneymakers. In the course
of Socrates' account, the craftsman yields to the "craftsman or some
other moneymaker by nature," and finally disappears into the chrematistic genus (433d3, 434a9, c7). The structure of the city requires
that one class of the city not do its job in the strict sense. Regardless
of whether individually the job is done in accordance with the highest
standards of knowledge, the artisans must be guided as a class by the
monetary advantage of their primary task. This class, which originally
had been the entire city or the true city, has become what the city of
fevered heat transformed it into, a class that solely looks to its own advantage, and which Thrasymachus had put forward as the ruling class.

The class structure of the city, if it is represented in terms of rank,
looks like that depicted in figure 6. If, however, it is represented in

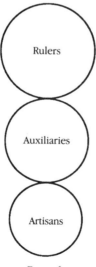

FIGURE 6

terms of numbers, it is its exact inverse, as depicted in figure 7. Now

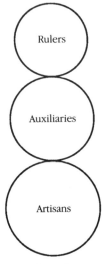

FIGURE 7

if one represents for each class the soul-structure of each individual, the element in terms of its importance for the class varies, as seen in figure 8. The rulers seem to duplicate the class-structure of the city;

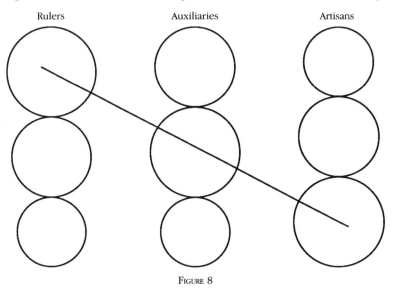

FIGURE 8

but the diagonal represents each class practicing its proper virtue without regard to the bonding of the class. Justice is that principle which adjusts the rulers' soul-structure to that of the other two classes. It is therefore a mistake to regard the ruler's soul-structure as a duplicate of the city's class structure; rather, the city represents a compromise between the ruler, in whom there is no justice that is not identical with his wisdom, and the auxiliaries and the artisans, each of whom, if allowed to be as perfect as the virtue they represent, would resist any bonding with the city as a whole. The artisans are more readily adjustable to the structure of the city the more the principle of minding one's own business is operating and the less the opinion that those who are ruling should rule. The principle is a class-principle and does not require any virtue; but the opinion of moderation must be individual and can only become manifest if there has already been some violation of it.

18

L E O N T I U S

(434c7–441c8)

The *Republic* culminates first in Socrates' analysis of soul. The soul must display the same three species (*eidē*) in it as the city's three genera (*genē*) of natures if moderate, brave, and wise are to be predicable of the individual, and he can be called just because each *eidos* in his soul is minding its own business (435b4–c3). Not only does Socrates conflate once more in the case of soul the comprehensive and the precise meanings of justice, but he declines to keep the structures of city and soul strictly parallel. *Eidos*, it seems, cannot have the same meaning as *genos* (Socrates does not say there are three kinds of natures in soul), but *eidos* must have the rare meaning of part (*meros*) (*Statesman* 263b7 8), though even this is uncertain since *meros* does not occur until after body has been reintroduced (442b11). The soul, in any case, has to be the matchup for the class-structure of the city for two different reasons: the individual is already just by doing his own thing in the city, and the individual, if he really did mind his own business, would not be part of the city. If the individual, then, must be split between soul and body so that he can have his own order and still be a citizen, the body must belong to the city and the soul be the locus of his own justice. In the true city, mind was strictly instrumental and in the form of the arts supplied the needs of the body. It ceased to operate perfectly as soon as music education was brought in to handle soul through opinion and not knowledge. The city thus became less than mind and more than body. Soul, then, cannot be examined with precision without dismantling the city that made it necessary to examine soul in the first place. So that the ratio of true city to good city be put in some relation with soul, a ratio between a precise understanding of soul and the imprecise understanding Socrates offers would have to be established. A precise understanding of soul, if it follows Socrates' own procedure, would have to begin with the making of the individual. Timaeus certainly seems to try to supply such an artifact; but it is remarkable how equally imprecise is his account of soul. Perhaps there are obstacles to a precise understanding of soul that are not entirely due to the present course. The present course, however, does not stand in the way of the introduction of wisdom: from 503b5 to 520a7, the peak of the *Republic*, the words, "philosophy," "philosopher," and "philosophize" do not occur. An inadequate account of soul prepares the way for the perfection of soul. The possibility for soul must be exaggerated, it seems, if there is no precise understanding of soul.

The imprecision of their present course shows up at once: the *eidē* of soul are now coupled with *ēthē*, "character-traits," and both are not in soul but in each of us (435e2). Socrates finds evidence for their presence in us in the national character which Scythians, Greeks, Phoenicians, and Egyptians are alleged to exhibit severally. Not every individual of each tribe has to have the same makeup as his tribe's most distinguished feature, which itself may be no more than what the tribe admires and looks up to in individuals and tries to inculcate through custom and law. The seven wise men of Greece might suffice to attach to all Greeks the label "lovers of learning." Even if, moreover, most members of the tribe were to live up to the national character, could there be an empire of Greeks, Scythians, and Phoenicians? The enslavement of Scythians and Phoenicians would seem to be unjust, however natural it might be that the wise be the rulers, for the Greeks would rule without the wisdom of the Greeks ruling. And should only wise Greeks rule, what unity would there be in such an empire? How could the Scythians retain their fierce love of liberty if they were subjects? The limit to the expansion of these tribes, whether it is due to geography or political defects (Thucydides 2.97.6), seems to satisfy already the demands of justice upon which no rational arrangement could improve. Accordingly, if learning, anger, and desire were three different faculties in us, we would be automatically just, since it would be impossible for any one faculty to usurp the function of any other. Each of them functions as the eye does and not as the pruning hook. There would be justice, then, but without order; and if there were order, a single function of the whole would have to determine that order. The function of the auxiliaries, then, to say nothing of the artisans, is at the expense of the function of the soul as a whole, and every effort would have to be made to ensure that no one impairs his political function by striving to fulfill the function that the order of the soul demands. An auxiliary who passed every test but the last and hence was justly denied admission to the guardians would necessarily be unhappy. Indeed, he might be useless even as an auxiliary and end up making money. In the *Phaedrus*, there are nine kinds of natures and eleven types of erotic soul; in the *Republic*, there are several kinds of natures but so far no types of soul. The suppression of *erōs* has suppressed the very possibility of any manifold of wholes. The parallelism with the city will allow for only one soul-type to be a whole, for only it will be perfectly just.

Socrates does not restrict the class of things which we learn or get angry at, but he does restrict desire to nourishment and pleasure (436a11). Desire, however, is not a class of the city; in the city, it is designated indifferently as the moneyloving or the moneymaking class. The city knows how to translate desires into the calculated means for their lawful gratification (580e2–581a1). The city thus puts a price tag on every desire and regulates its fulfillment. The poor are as moderate as Cephalus: poverty too promotes good behavior and makes the desires impotent. Not only, then, does each artisan alter politically as he shifts from class-membership to class-characteristic, but the virtue possessed by the class shifts on its return to the individual. When applied to the class, moderation meant the acknowledgment that those who rule should rule; when applied individually, moderation cannot mean either the rule of reason or the control of the desires and pleasures, except insofar as both are reflected in the facsimile of grubbing calculation. Even if, moreover, moneymaking could, by channeling all other desires into its own support, induce a kind of moderation, this moderation would not bear to the class of desires the same relation as wisdom does to the rational and courage to the thumoeidetic. Each of them is plausibly to be understood as the perfection, respectively, of its natural ground; but moderation cannot possibly be the perfection of desire unless desire is *erōs* and moderation philosophy. Then we have the paradox of the *Phaedrus*, of an *insaniens sapientia* that does not take its bearings by opinion and adheres to the lawless nature of *erōs* (252a4). In the *Republic* the tyrant is the representative of *erōs* (574e2–575a7); in the *Phaedrus* his is the ninth allotment which, if the tyrant lives justly, obtains for him a better fate (248e3–5). The repugnance with which the tyrant must be held politically nowhere lets up in the *Republic*, for the implication of the Hesiodic ages, that after iron the golden age might return, seems to be too much of a gamble to inspire in Glaucon any wish for tyranny (*Laws* 709e6–710a2).

Socrates formulates a version of the principle of noncontradiction in order to establish the difference between the rational and the desiderative in soul. If he is successful, no one can ever use either 'I' or 'soul' unequivocally in any sentence about his thinking or desiring. 'I' becomes a place like the city in which there are various activities but none that allows for a saturating predicate, and the body becomes essentially the self to which a regime-like structure is attached that threatens at any moment to disintegrate the self. Only impurities in the structure would keep body and soul together. It is, in any case, extraordinary that the highest of all principles should be involved in an imprecise account of soul. If and only if the principle of noncontradiction is violated, does it follow that a difference of agent or agency is involved. But no such principle is invoked to separate the rational from the thumoeidetic or the desiderative from the thumoeidetic. To prove the difference between the rational and the desiderative, which seems to be too obvious to need a proof, summons all of Socrates' effort, for he must disprove himself—he who seems to insist everywhere else that all men desire the goods (438a3–4). Socrates against Socrates is a conflict that only the highest of principles could resolve.

Everything Socrates has done since he abandoned the true city has led to this conflict. Although he admits that the thumoeidetic is the natural base for the sense of right (440c1–d6), he has given a class-analysis of justice that is wholly independent of nature. The natural base of right has been perfected in the double form of moderation and courage, and no argument is given or can be given that they are the equivalent of justice, for they were established in order to find justice. The making of the just city consisted simultaneously in the displacement of the natural locus of justice and the establishment of the natural locus of justice as the core of the city. Justice came to light by denaturalizing the sense of justice. The ignorance of nature is the beginning of right; and the fruit of that ignorance is now before us in the principle of noncontradiction, which deployed against the soul turns it into an 'idea', or a perfectly self-identical being (436e9–437a2). Socrates' spinning top is a mathematical solid whose axis is an imaginary line that only in speech can be said to be at rest and in the top (436e2–3). The principle of noncontradiction helps meet the objections of the captious and evade the difficulties of understanding the nature of things. Socrates is well aware of the evasion. He knows that once the 'ideas' come in the soul will cease to be one of their kind. He calls the principle of noncontradiction a hypothesis (437a4–9).

Socrates begins with a set of contraries. "To nod for assent" (*epineuein*) is the contrary of "to throw the head back for denial" (*ananeuein*), as the desire to take something is the contrary of "to deny" or "to refuse" (*aparneisthai*) and "to bring over to one's side" (*prosagesthai*) of "to push away" or "to reject" (*apōtheisthai*). Socrates sets up two classes of verbs. Most of them designate corporeal actions that are signs of acceptance or rejection of speeches. In one of them he puts "to thirst" and "to hunger." He thus assimilates desire to a *logos*, as if it were an assent to a proposition, or, more exactly, as if it were answering a question (437c5). Socrates does not analyze the question, let alone its physiology, in which what is unknown comes to light as unknown only because it is embedded in a structure of things known. Desire too would be a desire for a something disclosed within desire by its suggested presence, and desire would not necessarily know what would supply what it desired. Desire would then allow for its override by another desire; indeed, desire could be expressed in the form, "I want the pain removed," with nothing but experience to inform one that its removal requires drink or whatever. Socrates speaks of the soul of the desirer as not only assenting as if to a question but also as desiring the genesis of what the desirer wants (437c1–6); but he leaves it open whether the soul desires what it desires for itself. His attempt to get at desire through speech gives it a structure not unlike the spinning top and the city in speech. When Socrates turns to the second class of verbs, he cites a verb that is apparently of his own devising and violates the rather strict rule for the formation of verbs with the alpha-privative, *aboulō* ("to not-want"), that they not be compounded directly with deverbatives.[1] "To not-want" entails the notion of rejection; but if "not to want" were treated as the absence of assent, there would be doubt, and doubt cannot be admitted without allowing for simultaneous states of assent and rejection. The affirmative character of desire brings in its train logical negation as its contrary. Logical negation looks as if it proves that the source of rejection cannot be in whatever the verb of assent represents. That something other than desire puts a check on desire emerges through a syntactic feature of speech, as if the awkwardness of "I want no-cake" instead of "I don't want any cake" showed anything about the nature of desire.

Once Socrates has replaced nature with syntax, he proposes the notion of 'thirst itself for drink itself' (437d8–e8). Any qualification of thirst must qualify that of which the qualified thirst is. 'Muchness' operates on both thirst and drink and yields 'much thirst for much drink.' It now becomes possible for 'thirst itself for drink itself' never to be experienced by anyone (439a2). A grammar of the soul is postulated in order to account for experiences. Socrates does not explain why 'muchness' comes out as 'much thirst for much drink,' but 'hotness' yields the desire for cold drink. The desire for a hot drink would seem to be due to the presence of cold in the body and not in the thirst. Perhaps there never is thirst for a hot drink, and all thirst is for cold drink. In any case, any satisfaction of thirst itself is now impossible, since any drink would never be drink itself and hence would never meet the need of thirst itself. If a sweet cool drink contained within it drink itself, a sip would slake thirst itself while one kept on drinking to satisfy the thirst for a sweet cool drink. 'Thirst itself,' then, cannot be separated from 'drink itself' but must form a syntactical unit which we may call a syntagma, and whose central feature is that it cannot be broken into but must remain whole. For every desire there is a different syntagma, each one of which looks like an 'idea.' An analysis of soul, if done imprecisely, leads to a proliferation of ideas, for it takes its bearings by language. Speech, because it admits of greater precision than fact, produces greater imprecision about facts. Political philosophy too would seem to be caught in this paradox, and its imaginary republics rightly subject to Machiavelli's strictures.

1. Cf. A. C. Moorhouse, *Studies in the Greek Negatives (Cardiff 1959)*, 60–61.

Thirst and hunger now belong to the class of desires (437d2–4), although originally, in the true city, they were needs and not desires and only became desires through the intervention of Glaucon, who wanted the human good. Glaucon's desires, however, did not have the structure of thirst. "I want a couch," if negated, can possibly mean the same as "I don't need a couch"; but "I don't want a drink" is not the same as "I don't need a drink." Glaucon's desires were solely for goods; but Socrates seems to have fused together the analysis of need with the analysis of desire, so the simplicity of a need, which can be at work without any awareness, is mixed with an awareness of need that is fully knowledgeable. Socrates' casual mention of 'love' is enough to show that not all desires have this character (439d6); indeed, Glaucon's desire for a couch was an expression of his real desire that came to light only in his calling the true city the city of pigs. The view counter to Socrates' present argument is that reason and desire are always together, and regardless of whether the good is real or apparent, everyone desires the goods. It therefore would follow that if thirst is always for good drink, and not that only good thirst is for good drink, the abstention from drinking might occur without any external intervention on thirst. Socrates, however, seems to interpret desires as morbid states, like alcoholism and drug addiction in general, or, to use ancient examples, like dropsy and hysteria (*Timaeus* 91b7–d5; Horace c.2.2.13–16). He appears to be adopting the view of those whom Socrates calls in the *Philebus* the dour, who take their bearings by the extremes and whom it is reasonable to identify with the poets (44e4). If, in any case, we accept Socrates' assertion, that anything essentially relative cannot be of something qualified unless it too is so qualified, then if *erōs* is of the beautiful, *erōs* too is beautiful and the god of the poets.

For his argument Socrates gives two kinds of examples; apparently it makes no difference whether thirst is like 'bigger' or like 'knowledge'. It makes no difference whether that which is relative to something exists or does not exist; for whereas if something is bigger, there must be something smaller, there could well be health and disease without there being any science of them. Desires of nonexistent things are thus treated as if their structure were identical with desires for real things; but if desires are always for good things, it would be impossible to be so indifferent. To drink without thirsting, moreover, is common enough, but it requires for its justification an understanding of good. Socrates therefore has to restrict his account to only certain types of desires, for which the model is 'greater/less' rather than 'knowledge of'; but his example of how a qualification of relative terms works transitively makes one doubt whether it is strictly applicable even to thirst. A confusion of two different measures—of relative measure and measure of the mean—seems to have crept into his analysis (*Statesman* 283b1 –289b3). It is certainly true that if something is much greater, something else is much less; but it is not as obvious that much thirst is for much drink. 'Much thirst' may be understood as relative to 'bearable thirst', which would then have a built-in restraint; but in Socrates' interpretation, a measure of appropriate liquidity vanishes into an absolute magnitude unrelated to any mean. 'Thirsty', however, seems to mean by itself 'very thirsty', just as 'hungry' does, for if a host asks, "Are you hungry?" a nod will get him to give much more than he otherwise would. We say on certain occasions, "You were really thirsty," as if we suddenly realized the true meaning of thirst. Socrates treats thirst apart from the being who is thirsty; for if men become thirsty, they must be thirsty for human drink, and human drink means drink good for men, however each man may understand that good. By looking solely at the verb 'to thirst', the possibility of unqualified thirst is realized; but the absurdity of a thirsty soul (439b3), as Socrates expresses it, which cannot drink or slake its thirst makes one see that the ultimate consequence of Socrates' uncoupling of body and soul is the uncoupling of agent and action. Socrates' argument, moreoever, even if sound, leaves loopholes. Let it be granted that the will to drink and the "unwill" to drink cannot occur in the same thing, at the same time, and in the same respect; but nothing prevents the will to drink from coinciding with the will to drink something good. "Just as in the case of the archer," Socrates says, "it's not a fine thing to say that his hands simultaneously push away (*apōthountai*) and drag the bow towards (*proselkontai*), but rather that the hand pushing away is different, and the hand bringing over toward (*prosagomenē*) is another (439b8—11)." Since the contrary actions of the hands are designed to have one result (the release of the arrow), then, if this were the model for thirst, the rational and the desiderative—if they can be imagined to correspond to the two hands—would be joined together from the start, and the target would be the good of which both in some sense were aware.

When Socrates turns from the desiderative to the thumoeidetic, his argument for its distinctness is much less strict. He first tells a story, then appeals to "our" perceptions and to Glaucon's awareness of himself; but apparently he does not hold that the thumoeidetic has a syntactic structure like desire. It no more follows that if there were no longer injustice men would cease to get angry than that if someone is very angry he has experienced a great wrong. Indeed, if the same syntagma held for anger as for desire, the belief that an injustice had been done would require a belief that one was angry, just as the degree of one's anger determines pretty nearly the magnitude of the injury one believes to have suffered. Socrates tells the following story instead:

> "Leontius the son of Aglaion was going up from the Piraeus near the North Wall on the outside; he noticed corpses lying by the place of the public executioner; and simultaneously he desired to see and in turn was disgusted and turned himself away, and for a while he fought and covered his face, but finally overcome by his desire, he dragged open his eyes, ran towards the corpses, and said, "Here they are for you, O miserable wretches, get your fill of the beautiful sight," (439e7–440a3)

The story is part of a proof that the thumoeidetic is not naturally akin with the desiderative (439e4); and the language of the story decides the issue before Socrates can be asked the right question: What is the desire to see the corpses of publicly executed criminals? Since they are called a beautiful sight, are we to infer that it is *erōs*? Since the eyes are addressed, it would seem that anger is speaking, and their satiation results from desire; but since the thumoeidetic does not have a syntax, it could be both the push and the pull, since the respect in which there is a desire to see does not have to be the same as the respect in which there is repulsion. The desire to see could arise from the satisfaction of seeing justice done, and the repulsion from the shamefulness of vicarious revenge. The word translated "miserable wretches" (*kakodaimones*) is a comic word and expresses not pity but contempt.[2] The contempt here is addressed to the eyes, which are made fully responsible for the desire to see; and seeing is identified with eating. The eye is a cannibalistic eye. The eye is a guilty beast. Only anger can create a fully independent living being in order for itself to be satisfied and yet remain innocent. It has given to the eye the syntactic structure of desire. The eye is a belly hungry for a beautiful sight. If, however, the

---

2. *Symposium* 173d1; *Meno* 78a5; cf. R. A. Neil, *Aristophanes Knights* (Cambridge 1901), 8.

thumoeidetic has imposed this structure on the eye, the thumoeidetic must have imposed it on desire in general. The vicariousness of
its own satisfaction (through the animation of a part into a whole)
likewise suggests that the thumoeidetic borrowed the language of
desire to conceal itself. Anger generates syntax; it needs to understand things eidetically, for it knows nothing of nature or the body. It
would thus find no difficulty if the soul were thirsty (cf. 621a3), for
it is hungry for revenge and satiable without its feeding on any other
food than that which it supplies for itself. *Thumoeides*, then, means
not only that anger is always angerlike but that it is the spirit of
eideticization. Its refusal to give in denies the existence of body, for
it identifies itself with the true self, and sometimes treats the desires
as an enemy alien and sometimes forms an alliance with the rational
as if it too were a stranger (440a5–b4). This alliance has already been
exhibited in the analysis of desire in which there was a perfect
cooperation in the eyes of anger between itself and reason.

The alliance between the rational and the thumoeidetic first
showed up in Thrasymachus, whose distinctions suffered from
excessive precision and whose indignation was too good to be true;
and then again in philosopher-dogs, which Socrates could not prove
were a natural possibility in man, and which the entire thrust of the
education showed to be erroneous in principle. Socrates, however,
has been forced by the class-structure of the city to return to a more
sophisticated version of his starting point. Indeed, if that alliance
were as natural as it is now claimed it is, there would have been no
need for the education of the auxiliaries, since any education would
run the risk of corrupting it. It is enough, moreover, to cite the
unrequited or jealous lover to know that sometimes anger sides with
the desires against reason; but that justice and love are wholly
separate and never interfere with one another pervades the *Republic*.
Their separation began with Cephalus' telling the story of Sophocles
and they lurked behind the expulsion of tragic poetry. Oedipus, the
angry man par excellence, confirms and does not confirm Socrates'
position. His devotion to the city, to which he has gained admission
through his knowledge, is total, and his desires can be said either to
have been extinguished or fulfilled through his incest. Either he
lived out his dreams or he never dreamed. His self-blinding too
recalls Leontius. And, finally, his solution to the riddle of the Sphinx
cannot be bettered as an example of eidetic analysis, for though man
is for Oeidpus man living in time, he is without either birth or death.
It is man neither grounded in nature nor sanctified by the gods. The

communism of the best city welcomes Oedipus. Even his self-ignorance, which extends to his being the riddle the riddle of the Sphinx excepts, has its counterpart here: the thumoeidetic, which is the driving force behind eidetic analysis, does not let itself be understood eidetically. Access to it lies through experience and anecdote.

Socrates' claims on behalf of anger exploit the ambiguity of *logos*. The rationality implicit in *to logistikon* (the calculative), with which Socrates designates the ruling element of soul (439d5), does not necessarily carry over into the word *logos*, with which Socrates designates the ruling element of soul immediately after the story of Leontius (the story too he calls a *logos*). He then employs *logos* in an idiom (*logos hairei*) that can mean no less "it's [my] will" than reason requires (440a5, b3, 5, d3; cf. 442c2). The heart has its reasons. Socrates suspects that Glaucon would not assert that he ever noticed in himself or anyone else anger in concert with the desires and against the prohibition of *logos*; and Glaucon swears, "No, by Zeus." His reply, if taken strictly, means: "I, Glaucon, swear that I never noticed it in myself or another." A refusal to admit an occurrence hardly constitutes evidence that there was no such occurrence. The stylized form of Glaucon's oath masks the wish that Zeus punish him if he lies (cf. 444a7). The nobler someone is, Socrates says, the more willing will he be to submit to punishment if he believes himself guilty of injustice. The source of this belief he seems to ascribe to *thumos*, which, in its perfected form as courage, he had made into the repository of the city's opinions. On the arousal of *thumos* at a suspected injustice, it is *logos*, he now says, that calls it back from its fighting alliance with what is in opinion just and soothes it (440c1-d3). That all injustice is willed and that there are no excuses possible have their origin in the belief, generated by the unbeatable nature of *thumos*, that there is no necessity. To will is to be perfectly effective. It would be self-contradictory, in its opinion, to believe a wrong has been done and to refuse to be punished. To accept punishment is to accept the sanction of the law apart from the reason for the sanction. *Thumos* submits defiantly. How then did it come to believe that it committed an injustice in the first place? It must find a scapegoat—desire—and believe that desire is being punished. Desire can be frightened. Leontius gets the satisfaction of seeing justice having been done and of terrifying desire by forcing it to submit to what it will find unpleasant. He can then go away with the conviction that he has brought desire under control while reaping the enjoyment of a double punishment with inpunity. Yet his reluctance to satisfy the gluttony of his eyes seems to go deeper. He calls the sight of executed criminals beautiful. He is shocked into an awareness that the beautiful and the just do not always coincide (443e5; *Laws* 859d2–860c3). His story thus represents the break in the weld between them that Socrates' education was designed to form and expose.

At the beginning of the *Republic*, Polemarchus and his slave detain Socrates and Glaucon. Polemarchus wanted to invite them home; but he asked Socrates whether he saw how many he and his companions were, and then told him: "Well, then, prove to be stronger than they or stay here." Polemarchus, the son of a metic, threatens violence on two citizens. If he carries out the threat, he is liable to criminal charges; but we have no way of knowing whether his companions would have backed him if he had tried. We say, then, he was only bluffing; but why was he bluffing? He wanted to prove that he could rule Socrates; he wanted to exercise his will irrationally. When Socrates suggests that they could be persuaded to let them go, Polemarchus says, "Well, could you in fact persuade if we should not listen?" The will makes itself stubborn willfully. It will not listen to reason or give any reasons. Polemarchus is a bully. His claim that his men are stronger is a claim that his will is stronger. Socrates must yield not because he is compelled to yield or it is to his advantage to yield but because Polemarchus orders him to yield. His wilfulness manifests itself as purposeless and all-powerful. Socrates' account of *thumos* seems to deny that this scene could ever occur; but he could evade that implication in two ways. The first would be that it was only theatrical and Polemarchus was not serious. The word *thumoeides* itself, however, to say nothing of Thrasymachus, implies that it is never genuine but always pretending more or less. Leontius pretended that his eyes were beasts, just as Thrasymachus had launched himself at Socrates "as if he were a beast." The second way of evasion is that which Socrates here adopts: the *thumoeides* is always an auxiliary to the rational by nature unless it is corrupted by a bad nurture (441a2–3). Cephalus must have brought Polemarchus up badly. Socrates' theology had allowed the gods to be good and beautiful but not just; he now declares that the gods could only be just and beautiful through an unnatural alliance between anger and desire. Socrates has used the eideticizing power of the thumoeidetic to get rid of the gods. He has used it against itself. The falsity of the thumoeidetic is its truth.

19

NATURE AND SPECIES

(441c9–445e4)

Socrates has by now presented four structures, two for the city and two for the soul (see fig. 9). The order of finding has inverted the

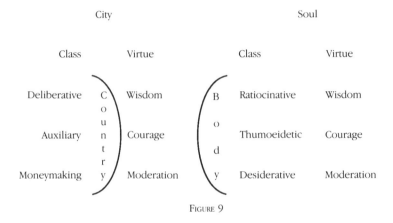

FIGURE 9

order of being. The good city is now an *eidos* (445d8). In conformity with the noble lie it has ceased to be founded and generated out of the true city and become instead derivative from the *eidē* of soul. We are supposed to forget that the guardians were at first broken off from the auxiliaries; now they are as different as the rational and the thumoeidetic. Socrates had begun with natures that had been tied to the divisions of the arts; he then introduced the complex nature of the soldiers whose education was equally complex. Their education, however defective, did not fit them to protect a particular city. The need for particularity, especially in light of the origin of the city in the universality of knowledge, forced Socrates to make the myth, and the myth in turn gave first to the city and then to the soul a class-structure. The original natures became species (*eidē*). This transformation did not work for the artisan-class, nor has there been any proof that the philosophic nature is the same as the calculating species; but this transformation was most successful in the case of the army. They lost their heads and were castrated. They became so defective in themselves that they could only be restored by becoming completely a part of the city. They are the core of the city because they alone fully belong to it as a particular city. Everyone else enters the city because he has a specialized knowledge, through which he satisfies his own needs and everyone else's; but the soldiers enter with a nature and the city makes them its own. It tells them that their bodies are not their own and that the country is their own. The core of the city is alienation.

An individual can easily take on a job not his own, for he has all three species of soul within him; but the classes of the city are incapable of usurpation and are just perforce. The desiderative species of soul, even if it is out of control from the standpoint of the individual, always does its own job. Each species of soul, then, is an imperialistic power that is wholly indifferent to the individual. Desire, by becoming a species, is freed from any limitation of capacity. The ratiocinative too does nothing but calculate, even if it is only calculating how to maximize pleasure. A hierarchical principle therefore has to be added; but such a principle is equivalent to virtue; and if it is part of the nature of desire to be subordinate, it cannot be the case that desire is just desire—a separate *eidos*—but must be by nature a part of a whole. Socrates first mentions part after he reintroduces body. He speaks of the ratiocinative and the thumoeidetic as maintaining a watch on "the so-called pleasures of body" (442a8). They are so-called pleasures of the body because there are only pleasures of the soul (580d7–8). The thumoeidetic analysis of soul attends solely to the labels of things. Socrates then speaks of the ratiocinative and the thumoeidetic standing guard against external enemies "on behalf of the whole soul and the body" (442b6-7); and only then, after the individual has returned, does Socrates speak of parts (442b11). The first part is the thumoeidetic. Its privileged position in the city has given it the right to initiate the making whole again of what it had initially fragmented; but the thumoeidetic puts nothing back in its right place. It is as responsible for "the so-called pleasures of body" as for "the so-called virtues of soul" (518d9). Without this double misunderstanding the city would never cease to practice gangsterism in the name of freedom and self-indulgence in the name of art. The city thus imitates the natural order of the soul by getting everything backwards. It is something for which we must always be grateful. The conformity of the justice Socrates discovered with vulgar justice—no stealing, no lying, no sexual license—turns out to be identical with piety as it is ordinarily understood, for theft includes temple robbery, lying includes perjury, and sexual license includes the neglect of parents and gods (442d10–443a11). A virtue that exists in neither the city nor in anyone who has yet been identified coincides with what is not a virtue. If the justice of the city is, as Socrates says it is, a phantom of true justice (443c4–444a3), then he has violated his own principle—that the images of things cannot be known prior to the things themselves (402b5–7); and there is no connection between either the justice of the soul and the best city or the vices of soul and the inferior regimes. We therefore have to be grateful that Polemarchus and Adimantus interrupt Socrates before he launches into an account of political degeneration and fails to justify the errors of his way.

PART THREE

BOOKS V – VII:
THE GOOD

20

THE WOMAN-DRAMA
(449a1–452e3)

Socrates and Glaucon were prepared to go from the good city to the four kinds of bad regimes; and Socrates tells his auditors that he was going to give an account of how they changed from one to another (449a1–b1). The eidetic analysis of the good city, in which the noble lie presented all becoming (of birth no less than of education) as a dream, was going to be followed by a genetic analysis of degenerate regimes. The making of the good city lent itself to an eidetic analysis; but a deliberate making of the defective regimes seems in principle impossible. Timaeus has to make man both perfect and imperfect; and insofar as he is perfect, he is neuter and the intelligible cosmos is his paradigm; but insofar as the visible universe can be complete only if he degenerates, he must have sexual parts that are useless until he degenerates (*Timaeus* 90e1–92c3). Timaeus' man, then, is ugly when he is good, for not everything he has serves his goodness, and ugly when he is bad, for everything in becoming useful shows him to be unavoidably defective. He is superfluous as artifact, he falls short as becoming. The interest Adimantus and others have in the communism of women and children conceals the demand for a nonmythical account of becoming; but because the demand is concealed, Socrates can thwart them. Instead, he offers them an account of being that confirms the eidetic analysis while replacing the mythical coincidence of education and becoming with the identity of philosopher and king. This too is a noble lie, but it is not a lie of the city.

Polemarchus has learned not to be peremptory and threaten force in the name of others whose consent he has not gained; now he enlists Adimantus, who objects to Socrates' passing over the communism of women and children. Adimantus perhaps is still worried about happiness. Will the army not have any women of its own, or will this too be regulated in light of the city's happiness as a whole? Adimantus' long-smoldering question wins the support of

the dialogic city as a whole, for which Thrasymachus is the spokesman: "Believe, Socrates, that we have all so resolved (450a5)."
Thrasymachus uses the verb *nomizō* for "believe"; it is a denomina-
tive from *nomos* ("law"); so if we overtranslate, Thrasymachus tells
Socrates to regard their common resolution as the law. Thrasymachus has no patience with Socrates' complaint of the extra burden
they have imposed upon him: "What!" he says, "Do you believe we
came here to smelt ore for gold and not to listen to speeches?"
Thrasymachus says they are not unjust; they are minding their own
business and not seeking some Eldorado. He revises the past to fit
the present and gives up money for the sake of his original
understanding of justice. The common good of the dialogic city
crosses their interest in speeches with their interest in women.
Glaucon, whose hunger had to be assuaged by something other than
what the city of pigs could give him, now declares that for sensible
people their entire life is the measure of the kind of speeches they
have been hearing (450b6–7). We expect Phaedrus or Simmias to say
something of the sort; but Glaucon, the meat-lover, has become like
the grasshoppers of Socrates' story, whom the songs of the Muses so
enchanted that they forgot to eat or drink (*Phaedrus* 259b6–c6). The
concern with justice has merged with the concern with *erōs* to
produce an erotic ascetiscism, which again Socrates will have no
difficulty in satisfying (cf. 490a8–b8). After the proof of 'thirst itself
for drink itself' there will be the proof that the lover of anything
loves its entire species (475b4–7). The communism of women, in
which not all women belong to every man but no woman belongs to
any man, prepares the way for love in the abstract.

A whisper initiates the second phase of the *Republic*. It is meant
to be noticed. The revolt which it sparks is as much a sham as
Polemarchus' earlier threat to force Socrates to stay; but now
Polemarchus does not dare to get at Socrates before he has a
conspirator who can express the sense of the House. Just before he
whispered, Polemarchus brought Adimantus over toward himself
(*prosēgageto*). Socrates had previously used this verb to characterize
desire (437b2). Polemarchus, then, desires something; but he does
not conform to the syntax of desire; rather, he stretched forward and
leaned over to Adimantus at the same time. His movements were
contrary to one another with a single aim, for apparently his desire
was coordinate with his shame before Socrates, and together they
were against the *logos*. The whisper represents the gravest threat to
Socrates' proposal on communism—*latentis proditor intimo gratus*

puellae risus ab angulo—, for any private communication between bride and bridegroom would suffice to cancel the publicity which communism is meant to institutionalize. The whisper, moreover, represents not only the risks of sexual conspiracies, but the difference between the publicly stated reason for communism and the rulers' reason. The unity of the city is to be brought about by the ruthless elimination of "mine" and "thine"; but their elimination acts as a cover for the pimping of the rulers, who must have a free hand to keep the class-structure of the city in some alignment with nature. The city in which everything is out in the open by law is the city in which all knowledge of nature is concealed. The essential communicability of knowledge misrepresents the reality of its secretiveness. While the city must divert the soldier away from what is by nature his own, the philosopher's devotion to the truth is in agreement with what is truly his own. The tension between the city and philosophy is ultimately due to the philosopher's selfishness. He does not measure up to the idealism of opinion. He minds his own business.

The issue of women brings in time. Adimantus' question points to the atemporality of eidetic analysis. Socrates, by starting where he did, educated the children before they were born, and hence the sequence of the *Republic* conforms with the provisions of the noble lie (451b9–c1). The education of Glaucon and Adimantus is also atemporal and backwards, for the first things of education can never be the first things simply. Adimantus' and Glaucon's concerns are not the same. Adimantus is more inclined to believe that institutional arrangements are decisive, and the crucial time is that around procreation (449c2–d6). He therefore discounts education and believes the principle "The things of friends are in common" entails universal communism. Glaucon has followed the argument better and sees that communism can pertain only to the guardians, and that the crucial time is between birth and education, which seems most toilsome and to require a division of labor between the sexes (450c1–4). Socrates' two reasons for hesitating to discuss communism formulate the problem as broadly as possible. There is as much distrust in its possibility as in its excellence should it ever occur. He seems to imply that only its possibility would allow for a discussion of its excellence; but though he never proves its possibility, he indulges in talk of its excellence (457e7–458b7). Not even the introduction of time keeps Socrates from talking out of turn. Since women, were it not for communism, would be regarded as private property and a source of private interest, they must in the good city be regarded as equal not only to men but to one another. They seem however, to be unequal to one another in the eyes of men. A distinction, then, has to be drawn between essential equality and inessential difference; but *erōs* seems to dote on the latter. Socrates therefore must show that *erōs* is never particular; it has the same characteristics as mind. If one grants that this holds if at all on the very highest level—Diotima drops all talk of *erōs* when she speaks of the topmost rungs (*Symposium* 210e1–211d1)—, communism must be seen as a device to institutionalize the very highest level as a common practice and belief. The city thus will anticipate the coincidence of *erōs* and mind prior to their true coincidence. The city is destined to misrepresent both *erōs* and mind.

Now that the dialogic city has cast its unanimous vote, Socrates is more worried than ever. Although everything he says is said distrustingly and zetetically, their friendliness and goodwill, of which Glaucon assures him, makes them useless to himself and a danger to themselves (450d8–451b1). The dogmatism of the city in speech has infected the dialogic city. Socrates' piling up of one proposal after another, each more fantastic than the one before, seems designed to disenchant them; but since Glaucon granted that only the irrational is funny (445a5–b5), it would seem that Socrates will be as successful in banishing comedy as he was in banishing tragedy. Wrinkled old women exercising naked in public are as unfunny as philosophers ruling. That nature ensures a shortfall in either case does not warrant the concealment of shame. The city, declares Socrates, has nothing to do with seemings, for it turns out that for the city as the locus of seeming, anything is possible, and given enough time the equality of women will be as acceptable as incest. Since there appears to be no limit once the sacred has been removed to the shape the laws may give the just, the good, and the beautiful, the woman-drama is Socrates' way of determining whether there are any natural limits to the positings of the city. This determination, however, has to be done in the face of Socrates' ignorance of nature; and he accomplishes this seemingly impossible feat by showing that the woman-drama can succeed if and only if there is no human nature. The man-drama began with the guardians as watchdogs of a herd; the woman-drama must suppose that the guardians themselves are a herd (451c8, 459e3; *Statesman* 266a2–5). The man-drama rested on a possible harmony between the artful perfection of weaponry and the most primitive society; the woman-drama rests on the harmony between genetic engineering and communism; but the possibility of genetic engineering dispenses with the need for communism, and the city will solve the human problem when there are no longer any human beings for whom to solve it.

21

E Q U A L I T Y

(452e4–457b6)

Although the discussion of women leads away from the city to philosophy—philosophy is even weaker politically than women, and its practitioners look more like women than men—still the discussion in itself seems to be a cover for Socrates' persisting in his original plan to discuss change of regimes. A city must last. It therefore must have women; but it does not need them for any other purpose than breeding unless it can be shown that their nature can contribute something of its own for the management of the city (455a9–b2). Neither Socrates nor Glaucon can think of anything of the sort; so even if women were special in some way but not of political advantage, they should by excluded. That they are on the whole weaker than men should entail that in a sex-blind test for admission into the city, most would not pass; and those who did would be assigned to the art appropriate to their nature; but the principle one woman/one art has nothing to do with the coupling of male and female. The division of labor and communism cannot consist together. It seems, then, that the introduction of women as more than breeders already represents a compromise with the principle of the city. The guardians are given something of their own that strict justice does not allow, and communism is a way of compensating for its violation. The women may be guardians, but they are still "the women of the guardians" (456b9, 457a6).

The dual function women are to serve gives Socrates the chance to reveal that even in the man-drama the auxiliaries transgressed against the principle one man / one art. Music and gymnastic are now two arts that were assigned to men (452a2–5); previously we might have believed that they were trained in light of these two arts but their own art was that of war. The movement of the argument, however, had led to the need to separate courage and moderation into two species, for otherwise a separation between auxiliaries and guardians could not be made. The women therefore come in at a higher level of the argument; and since Socrates chooses to take "gymnastic" literally as the act of stripping naked, he invites us to take "music" literally as the art of the Muses. Men and women therefore look as if they correspond respectively to the virtues, on the one hand, of courage (or literally "manliness") and moderation, and, on the other, to the arts of gymnastic and music. It would seem, then, that conventionally male and female are believed to have their own nature and virtue, and Socrates was going against the grain of manliness in beginning with music education. Had he begun with the household rather than with the city, he would have proceeded more naturally and arrived more quickly at the highest form of music—philosophy. The closest Plato ever came to this is in the *Statesman*, where the identity of city and household is the starting point and where the course of the dialogue consists in moving the manly young Socrates toward moderation. Though its companion dialogue, the *Sophist,* moves in the opposite direction and takes the moderate Theaetetus toward a form of manliness, the *Sophist* never goes beyond sophistry to philosophy, and however indispensable a movement, it is essentially subordinate to the *Statesman's* (*Sophist* 235b8–c2). Theaetetus seems to be the evidence Plato gives us that it is against the nature of philosophy for the beginning, the way, and the end to be all of the same nature. The sequence of *Sophist-Statesman* is thus fully in agreement with the movement of the *Republic.* Woman, then, comes in too late. The twofold education of the city in speech and of the dialogic city has advanced so far that woman becomes solely an institutional problem. She represents all that the two educations have failed to achieve, but otherwise the *Republic* is closed to her.

The issue of equal education for women begins with its most laughable aspect—nakedness; but Socrates gives no reason why the women must exercise with the men. He certainly does not argue that separate and equal is not equal; rather, everything is to be open to inspection at all times in order to back up institutionally the failure of the education to guarantee in every case devotion to the public good. Nakedness is not part of the natural justice argument; but it is put up front as if the question whether female human nature is capable of being as competent as men's were the same as whether it is capable of doing everything in common with men (453a1–4). War makes it look as if the questions are the same (466c6–d4), for they must train together if the city is not to have two armies, though the greater usefulness of any woman not past childbearing would tend to keep her in the reserves (cf. 460a3–4). The principle that nothing counts except what serves, in terms of which everything concerning women is treated (457b4–5), heralds the idea of the good; but the principle is set against the love of the beautiful that music education was designed to promote. The beautiful came forward in the element of reform, the good is in the element of revolution. Socrates does not say what good the Cretans and Spartans (who first introduced it) found in nakedness; but by speaking of what is repellent to sight rather than of what his audience might find attractive, he subordinates the beautiful to the good and sight to reason (452d3–e2). The unpleasantness to sight of naked old women recalls the story of Leontius, who found so attractive and repulsive the corpses of criminals. The conflict Leontius experienced between the thumoeidetic and the desiderative made him burst out with a comic address to his eyes, "O miserable wretches!" Socrates now reproves the witty for laughing at the uncovering of the mother's nakedness; and he argues that the funny merely depends on any departure from established custom. Yet why we laugh at the ugly and take pleasure in what desire should find as repellent as corpses, seems to deserve as complex an analysis as Socrates gave for Leontius. The laugh might be the noise of shame and due to the sudden recognition that everything beautiful is by law; but it might be no less the triumphant vindication of convention and due to the realization that the old ways are best. Just as Leontius' sense of the nothingness of corpses was overcome by the desire to eke out the satisfaction of punishment, so the laugh at the nothingness of what had been concealed is reinforced by the folly of attempting the impossible. The laugh, Socrates had implied, always signals tragedy.

The general argument Socrates advances for the strict equality of the sexes is this. There is no female nature as such, nor any male nature, but rather nature is any trait with which one is born, for example, baldness. Every so-called nature consists of a string of natures to each one of which there may or may not belong an art that perfects it. Socrates had initially looked at the natural bent of each potential member of the city: if one had a green thumb, one was admitted as a farmer. The structure of the city, however, required that differences of nature, which were coordinated perfectly with the division of the arts, be replaced by the uniform desire for moneymaking. Now, however, it is necessary to reintroduce those differences, so that women too can be considered as human beings with natural talents and aptitudes. This reintroduction of different natures leads back to the original difficulty that no proof can be given that the thumoeidetic nature is the same as the philosophic nature and that either that nature is the same as the warlike nature, or that these three natures cohere in the nature fit for guarding (456a1–9). The argument has led to their separation; and Socrates must argue now on its basis, for only the separateness of these natures makes femaleness look as if it too is just one of many traits that belong to any woman. Socrates' argument sets species (*eidos*) against nature (*phusis*). Species wins by classifying across a natural division. Species-division is in the service of purpose (454b7), and male and female function solely in terms of procreation, while every other species is indifferent to that distinction because each pertains to the soul and knowledge (454d2). Socrates does speak of natures distributed equally across both animals (455d8–9), but this acknowledgment—that man and woman are each a kind of animal and thereby constitute a whole—stands opposed to the speciation of their natures, each species of which is a quality shared in by both but not a part of either. The justice of the city dictates that human nature with its excellence be abandoned and communism replace it. The extreme fragmentation of nature, which the democratic principle of the city imposes, is made up for by a spurious sense of wholeness. Once each man and woman realize that they are nothing but assemblages of bits and pieces, they will be grateful to the city for making them whole again through the community. The city divides in order to unite.

It might seem strange that Socrates should say that men are superior to women in everything, even as weavers and confectioners, and still allow for women to be introduced into the city as anything but breeders (455c4–d1); but the argument is not about superiority but about natural capacity. If men can do everything women are conventionally assigned to do and do it better, then there is no male excellence for which males as males are naturally gifted. There is therefore no reason to believe that a female excellence exists to which equal facilities would give the chance to be developed. The education of men and women is a misnomer, for no saturating predicate of goodness applies to either of them. The women who are educated will be the best of women but they will not be the best women (456e3–4), at least not any more than someone

116

who is the best doctor and happens to be tall will be the best tall doctor. The city's neuterization of human beings thus puts in question any simple teleology and radicalizes the issue of nature. Art combines with political idealism to force a second sailing—the search for truly intelligible species and the whole to which they belong. If the city did not stand in the way of the apparent whole of male and female, and art did not cut across apparently natural divisions, the confidence we have in an immediate access to the nature of things could not be held in check. Without the twin sophistries of art and the city, the descent of philosophy would be as unnecessary as the ascent of philosophy would be impossible. The divergence from the truth converges with the truth only through the city.

22

COMMUNISM

(457b7–466d5)

Aristotle's objections to the communism of women and children are so obvious that it is hardly necessary to prove that Socrates was as aware of them (Aristotle *Politics* 1261a10–1262b35); indeed, the administrative difficulties alone make communism feasible only on paper, and even on paper it is self-contradictory. The structure of the city images the structure of the soul, but the unity of the city images the unity of the body, and the body alone cannot be communized (464b2, d9). Any attempt to model the city on the individual unity of body and soul would be inconsistent with communism, for it would result in the ruler alone being able to speak of the city as his (462c10–d7); but communism is primarily for the auxiliaries (464b6, 466a1). Communism not only takes up the slack in the education, but it also covers the ineffectiveness of the noble lie. It is the regime equivalent of the fatherland, for its marriage arrangements bond the people together in just the way the graves of the fathers do. The regime of the city thus goes back to the illusion of "my country" through the regime itself. The principle, however, that nothing is private except the body cannot establish the goodness of communism, for if "mine" means "my body," there is no natural "ours." To have all things in common is to have nothing to share. Nothing we seem to share through speech, whether it be what elicits or expresses sympathy and starts a resonance in another, can be genuine. The suppression of laughter is particularly telling, for laughter seems to be essentially public; but the imitative yawn, Socrates seems to be saying, holds for every apparent communion (*Charmides* 169c3–6). In the *Republic,* "ours" is used only dialogically. "Our city" and "our regime" refer to what Socrates and the others are founding but to which, however, they do not belong (378b1, 397e1, 462e4; cf. 463a10, b8, 519c8).

Socrates indulges himself in a fancy. He believes he can set aside the natural possibility of communism while he imagines all the arrangements it needs and its advantages. Since he supposes that the understanding of nature would not require a reformulation of the arrangements, his argument amounts to a plea for the goodness of communism in permanent ignorance of what is by nature. Nature, however, can remain unknown only if nature can be discarded. It is not the philosopher or even the wise who should rule but the perfect craftsman who by stamping out every difference could make it impossible for anyone to recognize his parentage; but if he can bring about such uniformity of features, he should be able in time to make all souls the same; and with everyone perfect, he could then abdicate. The true city, which functioned perfectly without any rulers, would thus culminate in the manufacture of citizen robots, and the plural of Athena (Athēnai) would literally come true in this Athens. Body and mind would once more be in harmony. The Eleatic stranger speculated along these lines in his story about a constant alternation between an autonomous universe and divine providence; but he could not decide whether the latter phase was compatible with philosophy (*Statesman* 272b1–d2). It is the paradox of the *Republic* that the philosopher is put in charge of a city that if it existed would not need him. His knowledge of natures, and particularly his knowledge of philosophic natures, is superfluous if there are no natures to be known; and if there were still enough vagary in generation to warrant his interference, so that he could pluck the golden soul from the iron class and demote the sports in the ruling class, he still would not know enough to mate bride and bridegroom. The original split between the city in speech and the dialogic city thus shows up in any city as the split between production and generation. Socrates went from an unachieved city of production to a city of freedom; and now he will go from a city of generation to philosophy. Had not war intervened, Socrates could have completed the city of production in one of two ways, either by eliminating human beings entirely or by introducing philosophy as a nonproductive form of knowledge that shares with the arts the knowledge of cause; but as it is, once the city of production has implicitly taken over again, philosophy comes in as the chief example of the deviancy of generative nature, insofar as nothing can be done to hasten the kingship of the philosopher. The city may ultimately make its citizens, but it will never make the philosopher. Nature in the form of chance frustrates the true city.

It is one thing that the poor auxiliary will be infrequently mated, it is another that the city should lose his or her good genetic material. Many one-night stands are to be the reward for the outstanding, even if the rulers know that the offspring must be exposed; and those who are not allowed to mate will know that no one of the children is theirs. Devices more elaborate than any in a Feydeau farce will possibly manage to avoid these pitfalls; but the number of lies needed seems to mount geometrically, and the women, especially the nurses, must inevitably become the repositories of the city's secrets. A network of lies bridges the gap between the rational and the natural, between, as Glaucon says, geometric and erotic necessities (458d5); but it is only a stopgap until Timaeus' science fiction can become true science and true fiction. In the meantime, however, the language of the city must, it seems, become two languages, one in which the families of the chrematistic class address each other for the most part correctly, and one in the communized classes, where "mother" and "father," "sister" and "brother" are rarely used correctly and then in ignorance; but they are not to be so ignorant as not to know that by nature only one of the fathers can really be theirs. Socrates seems to be proposing a language in which terms of affection and respect are parasitic in their function on what is no longer literally true; and if marriages between brothers and sisters are allowed (461e2–3), since the most beneficial is the sacred (458e4), there can be no rational ground to forbid any kind of incest if the offspring promise to be good. The family is destroyed and its relations kept sacred in order for the city to borrow images whose reality is suppressed. Antigone would feel right at home. Communism is to foster the sharing of pleasures and pains; but education was to make the auxiliaries virtuous. There is apparently no pleasure in virtue, and certainly no pleasure in seeing or hearing of another's

119

virtue, for if there were, communism would be superfluous."Virtue" occurs just once in the fifth book (457a6). Communism, for all its idealism, seems to underline the essential corporeality of the city. The difficulty of its measures gives the impression that if it were successful, it would achieve something grand; but the results of communism seem comparable to the experience of sports fans whom the victory or defeat of "their" teams exhilarates or depresses. Fraternity may enhance this kind of common feeling; but its real aim is to dilute friendships and hinder the formation of conspiracies. One's brothers will always outnumber one's friends (464e5–465b4).

23

W A R

(466d6–471c3)

Whether and how communism is possible among human beings seems as if it cannot be postponed any longer, especially since Glaucon claims that Socrates got the jump on him in posing the question (466d9); but Socrates does postpone it by distracting Glaucon with an account of how the auxiliaries will wage war. The form of Socrates' statement—*peri men gar tōn en toi polemoi*—would have allowed Glaucon not to ask at all (cf. 541b3–5); but as it is, we have a *men solitarium* to which there would have corresponded, impossible though it is, *peri de tōn en tei eirēnei*—"but about the things in peacetime"—that would have been identified with philosophy. Philosophy is not an activity of the city at any time: Socrates philosophizes in wartime Athens as if it were at peace. The discussion of war is a digression in the *Republic,* but everything Socrates has proposed so far looks to nothing but war; and war now serves a dialogic purpose the meaning of which is hard to make out. Glaucon becomes so impatient with Socrates' description of the restrained military practices of the city that he jumps over the issue of the possibility of communism to that of the possibility of the regime (471c4–e5). Socrates had admitted in the case of equality that what is natural and what exists have nothing to do with one another. He implied that as nothing prevents the unnatural from coming to be, so nothing guarantees that the natural will ever come to be (456b12–c2); and he had to prove in the case of communism that it was natural and not that it could ever come to be, for his proposals were clearly blueprints for legislation and as easily promulgated as any other code. The philosopher does not have to become king in order to have communism be established; anyone with the power could translate the speeches of Socrates into laws; but Socrates the philosopher is the only one who can show what his own argument shows he could not: that communism is consistent either with human nature or with his own city. Communism makes a shambles of the good city; and it looks as if war is dragged in to cover that up.

War, however, is no less devastating. There is hardly a principle that Socrates has argued for which the depiction of war does not overturn. If the children of the auxiliaries are to be trained in war at least as well as the children of potters in ceramics, the city must be almost continually at war, and there would be no time for music education even in its ordinary sense, let alone in the sense it obtained in the course of the argument. In order to secure their safety, the children must be spectators of nondangerous battles. It is hard to see how there could be enough such battles for training the children unless the city constantly invented excuses for invading neighbors' lands. These skirmishes must be bloody; it would be miraculous if they all were just. The best young warriors are to have their pick of any male or female they are in love with. Glaucon exacts this concession and at a stroke cancels the control the guardians are to have over marriages. Not only does Glaucon want law to enforce erotic necessities and establish rape as a right, but he has to believe that bravery in war is sexually transmittable and the same as nature at its best. War demands that the noble lie remain a lie and whoever dies bravely in battle be said to be of the golden race. Must Socrates not flatter Alcibiades? Must he insist that the prize of valor be conferred on himself just so that the city will acknowledge on false grounds that he is their rightful king (*Symposium* 220e2–7)? The theology says that there is neither any intermediary being nor any communication between gods and men; but war demands that the golden race be revered when dead as *daimones* and "the god" be consulted as to how to treat them. There is to be no stripping of enemy corpses except of weapons when they win: Glaucon is persuaded it is characteristic of a woman's mind to believe that the body of the dead is hostile. But in the city of perfect equality, what expression of contempt is to be used? Are they to say that this is the way of bitches who get angry at the stones with which they are hit and leave alone the one who cast them (469d6–e6)? The philosopher-dogs are now wholly useless. With the admission that the thumoeidetic and the desiderative commonly, if corruptly, work together on the battlefield, the story of Leontius is shown to have been interpreted incorrectly.

Socrates now proposes to temper somewhat the savagery of their soldiers after he has structured the entire city on the basis of a spurious reading. All the music education will reduce in practice to counteracting the built-in nature of the city. Even though the city is blind to the distinction between Greeks and barbarians, Socrates can find no better way to tame the soldiers than to concede to Glaucon that the city is Greek (499c9), that any war with Greeks is an instance of civil war, and that Greeks are friends and barbarians are enemies by nature (470c1–d2). Glaucon, who is all for a fight with barbarians (471b6–8), has forgotten the noble lie, which had to distinguish between earth (*gē*) and land (*khōra*) in order to keep the city nonimperialistic and ground its right to bar all strangers (414e2–3). Now, however, if Greece is their mother and nurse (470d7–8), there is nothing to stop them from claiming its hegemony, particularly if they come forward with typical hypocrisy as the chastisers of their brothers and punish the rulers of any city which opposes them as war criminals (471a6–b5). Now that Socrates finally promises Glaucon all the meat he craved should he earn it (468c10–e3), Glaucon cannot wait to get started on the realization of the city. He is willing to give up the honor of being a founder if he can get the rewards of a fighting citizen. He knows nothing about the third wave.

At the beginning of the *Timaeus*, Socrates summarizes the structure of the city in speech, but he breaks off his summary just at the point where in the *Republic* he digresses with a description of the city's manner of waging war; and he says in the *Timaeus* that he is not competent to praise adequately the city and its men (19c2–d2). On the basis of the sketch he does give us we would have to agree with him, since his trial attempt to set the city in motion has all but demolished it. Neither the fact that motion and order can never match up perfectly, nor that Glaucon's need for more immediate satisfaction than the austerity of a city in speech can grant him, seems enough to explain Socrates' failure to keep to a minimum the damage war must inflict on any city. Socrates' intent, rather, seems to have been to show how the massive contradictions in the city in speech come to light in practice. The city in speech contains within it incoherencies that prove it to be incapable of uniting justice and happiness; but its incoherencies are not unique to it, rather they characterize the fault planes present in any actual city, which functions not only despite but even because of them. Neither the rational nor the natural limits the real. Glaucon's eagerness to see the city realized, however much of its apparent order has to be sacrificed, expresses his awareness that he can never be happy unless he can become a member of a city somewhat like the *Republic's*. Only in such a city will the duality of his nature, divided apparently equally between the thumoeidetic and the erotic, be comfortable. The apparent reconciliation of this duality in the education of the city erupted on the battlefield, where Glaucon the warrior and Glaucon the lover seem to be equally satisfied. Socrates therefore must now show that the mating of Ares and Aphrodite is a fable of the poets. Glaucon will never anywhere be at home.

24

SPEECH AND DEED

(471c4–474c4)

Glaucon's demand that the good city in speech be realized measures exactly the degree to which he has not understood the *Republic*. That he speaks of the regime's feasibility and not the city's, shows that he has in mind the transformation of an actual city (471c7, e2), one more or less as corrupt as he has made the true city in the second book. His question thus amounts to asking how the purification of the fevered city can be carried out; but since this purification in speech consisted in his own education, he is asking unwittingly how that could be turned into a political process. Once it is seen that Glaucon is asking how the dialogic city can be made real, there can only be one answer. The dialogic city is already real and Socrates already king. Its political reality would require that the conditions for its own dialogic reality be themselves satisfied politically: the overpowering of Polemarchus, the silencing of Thrasymachus, and the expulsion of Cephalus. Not one of them, let alone all three of them, have any chance of success. Even if the first and third could happen—the stronger claim no rights and the sacred disappears—Thrasymachus at his most vociferous and savage is part and parcel of the city. He cannot be banished from that whose essence he is. The realization of the regime, however, depends not only on Plato's being in charge in reality of the dialogic city's conditions; it depends as well on the city's doing knowingly what the members of the dialogic city did unknowingly. The city would have to be educated before it was educated; and if this does not have to hold as literally as it does in the noble lie, it still requires the exile of everyone over ten (540e5). An alliance between Socrates and Pol Pot is inconceivable; but in its absence the argument of the *Republic* would have to cease to be a movement and become instantaneous. The *Republic* can rise only on its own ruins.

The abstention from all food and drink lasts for only one night in the dialogic city; but even if its real counterpart could be kept to a meager diet through the true city's perfect servicing of its needs, there would still be no women for its perpetuation. Plato, however, has done what he could to maintain the survival of the dialogic city. He has translated through a representation the coming into being of the dialogic city into a making; but there is no way for anyone else to do his writing one better. Socrates' narration of the dialogue, which is what Plato records, has hidden his sovereignty even as it has brought to light the community he has brought into being; but it is impossible to imagine that the *Republic* could become simple narration, so that whatever Glaucon introduced—for example, "species" and "nature"—would be indistinguishable from Socrates' own introductions. Had not Socrates impersonated Leontius, the political necessity for the misreading of his story would not have been revealed to us; and yet such a misreading that narration would have achieved is as indispensable for the real city as it is impossible for the understanding of the real city. The dialogic city cannot get more real.

If Glaucon's question is merely practical, it is asking what steps are needed first in order to realize the regime. The answer should be that Glaucon is to persuade the majority in Athens of what he claims to believe, even though they must be persuaded not to be the rulers of what they, along with Glaucon, would be the founders. Glaucon himself may be only possible in Athens, a disaffected offspring of a regime that renders everything feasible unattractive; but it is impossible for his type to be in the majority anywhere (548d8–549a1). Socrates' reliance on the chance coincidence of philosophy and power denies that any political process exists or can exist that will change the odds; and yet paradoxically he couples this denial with the claim that once the coincidence does occur, philosophers could rule, if not forever, then at least for many generations. The philosopher who now exists will suddenly discover on ruling how to produce a class of philosophers to take turns in ruling after his death. Power must surely be miraculous if no inkling of this knowledge is vouchsafed to the nonruling philosopher. Is Ariel the same as political power? O brave new world! The philosopher who is to rule is now available, even though he is so rare that he might vanish for centuries (476b10–c1). Such natures occur and are never the products of any actual regime. They certainly do not come from the auxiliary class (496b6–c3), nor do they need the reformed education of the city in speech in order to become philosophers. They have read their Homer straight.

Glaucon had sworn that he thought they found justice (444a4–10). His question now should have been, since justice is the good order of the soul, whether that order is possible and how it is possible; and inasmuch as the soul's justice emerged from behind the city's ghostly imaging of it, whether the soul's justice could be achieved without the lies Socrates found necessary for the city's justice. Glaucon, however, has given up on the problem of justice as he had originally formulated it, for he now no longer wants the just man to go unrecognized. He wants the justice of the just man to be supported by the opinion of the just city. Fear seems to prompt Glaucon's question. Unless he can surround himself with a like-minded city he will be killed if he follows Socrates. Socrates reminds him of their original quest (472b3–d3). He distinguishes between the discovery of justice, what sort it is in itself, and of the perfectly just man, what sort he would be should he come into being. This distinction was Glaucon's (358b4–6). It had disappeared in Socrates' proposal to see the coming into being of justice in the city (369a5–7); and his argument had been that justice simply is not in the good man and is present only imperfectly in the good city. It is hard for us to recover Glaucon's original perspective, that justice is an "idea" that can show up in the perfectly just man as nothing but will. Glaucon himself had abandoned it, at least to the extent that he conceived a longing for the impossible of another sort. Philosophy is not a means for realizing the impossible; it is a means for ridding Glaucon of the desire to realize the impossible. The charm of the political is so powerful that only philosophy can disenchant Glaucon; and not even philosophy as it truly is can do so. Philosophy too must become impossible and be identified with perfect wisdom before it can exert enough influence on Glaucon for him to remain content with Athens as it is.

Justice may be an 'idea' and never become, but happiness certainly is not an 'idea'. Whether the perfectly just man is happy depends on his coming into being, for only then can one deduce anything about him. The same seems to hold for the good city. It is impossible to speak of its happiness before it has come into being. Socrates likens what they have done so far to a good painter, who on painting as a paradigm what sort the most beautiful human being (*anthrōpos*) would be, cannot show it is also possible for a man (*anēr*) to become of the same sort (472d4–7). Socrates now admits that he did not answer Adimantus' question: happiness does not admit of any analogue in the beauty of a painting. The paradigm, however, whether of human being or city, cannot be nonparadigmatic in the deductions one makes from it. One must be able to read off from the paradigm real consequences even if the paradigm itself is not. Its impossibility cannot affect those consequences. The happiness apparent in the perfectly just man does not vanish in those who fall short of perfect justice. The paradigm cannot function like the pruning hook: some kind of goodness will belong to the surgeon's blade while it is cutting the vine branch. "If you should be granted three wishes . . ." can, it seems, remain hypothetical and still let deductions be drawn. Socrates, after all, had done exactly that with communism; but he could not establish its indispensable precondition—the equality of men and women—without giving up the individual as a natural whole, any more than he could maintain the principle one man/one job and give the city a class-structure. The necessary weakening of principle for the sake of structure, which also haunts Timaeus' science fiction, makes one doubt whether Socrates' suggestion of the relation between paradigm and copy can hold for the city. If Socrates' example is taken strictly, we know that the image of the most beautiful human being can never come to be, for it will then have to be either male or female. Everything in the painting may be recognizably human, even though not every feature can come to be together, or if they all do cohere in reality, other things may accompany their realization that the painter out of ignorance did not depict. Socrates needs to be able to draw a sharp distinction between "centaur" and "human being," if a centaur is not just a horseman and a human being not the coupling of man and woman. The happiness of the happy couple seems to be distributive even if neither of them will be happy apart;[1] but the sexlessness of the painting of the good city, which the comparison with the most beautiful human being entails, does not allow it to be realized in the family. Socrates is stuck with a paradigm to which no approximation as cities are now constituted is possible.

By looking at the perfectly just man, one can decide whether the defectively just man is happy or not; but one cannot look at the paradigm of the good city and decide whether any actual city is capable of supplying happiness. The paradigm condemns all cities (473e4–5); and only if the paradigmatic city itself comes close to being realized can the city be praised. Philosophy must now redeem the city that the twofold education of the city in speech and the dialogic city has already justified. Socrates pulls philosophy out of the dialogic city into the city in speech in order to make it manifest; but it is unlikely to be, as manifest, the same as what it was when it was invisibly at work. Socrates is the king of the dialogic city; he is not the philosopher-king of the city in speech.

Glaucon agrees to the following proposition: Nothing can be executed in action as it is spoken of, for it is naturally the case that action touches on truth less than speaking does (473a1–2). The entire argument of the *Republic* implies that Socrates means that the truth of the impossibility of the city in speech will become more dim once he discusses the way to realize it; but this is certainly not known to Glaucon. What, then, does he make of it? If he thought the good city was an "idea," then its "action" version would necessarily be less true (476a4–7). But it is implausible to have him anticipate the doctrine of ideas; and he lodges no protest later when Socrates lays it up in heaven or in the visible region and not beyond in the intelligible (592b2–3; cf. 509d3). If Socrates means that no action is "true" to the speaking of it, and Antigone cannot bury her brother in such strict conformity with the law that nothing of her own supervenes on her compliance, it is not obvious how Glaucon could suppose that Socrates' speech about the city in deed can differ in this way from his speech about the city in speech. It would seem more relevant for him to recall Thrasymachus' distinction between precise and ordinary speech, and imagine that action must be presented

---

1. Plato's Aristophanes has Hephaestus offer two lovers the chance to become one though they are two while they (in the plural) are alive and to be one instead of two when they (in the dual) are dead (*Symposium* 192d5–e4).

127

in ordinary speech and cannot admit of the error-free doctor. Socrates, however, built that distinction into the very fabric of the city in speech; and no speech about its becoming in deed is going to alter it and make it less true. Homer represented Helen's beauty through a speech of Trojan elders, who said when they saw her that there could be no resentment for the long suffering she had caused, "so terribly like to the deathless goddesses she is" (*Iliad* 3.156–158). The painter of Helen's beauty, even if his intention were the same as Homer's, could not match these lines. If Socrates, then, in speaking of the city's becoming is comparable to the painter, he would be sacrificing something like the elder's experience of Helen's beauty for the sake of showing Glaucon a version of the city that will not engage him so deeply. Glaucon will at any rate realize that he is not destined to be the ruler of such a city.

Socrates answers hypothetically the question whether the good city is feasible—"if philosophers become kings"—, but he seems to contradict himself almost immediately. After he has spoken of the coincidence of political power and philosophy, he implies that if the many natures who now pursue either the one or the other were compulsorily debarred from their singleminded course, the surcease of evils for mankind would be possible (473c11–e5). Why could not a king, then, who was not a genuine philosopher force all the philosophers to assume power? Should the answer be that like knows like and philosophers are undetectable by nonphilosophers, the philosopher must rule as philosopher over a people to whom he looks of necessity like a sophist. Had Socrates meant that the philosopher must worm his way into power, he would not have spoken hypothetically, but he would then be suggesting that there was or could be a private or public rhetoric for promoting the philosopher-king. Glaucon has no political power but only his good will and encouragement with which to defend Socrates against those who are ready to punish him for his proposal; and Socrates, in going on to define whom he means by the philosopher-kings, does not dream of using his arguments in the *Republic* before them, let alone before Athens (473e6–474c3). The *Republic* had almost begun with Socrates' example of the noncoincidence of truth and justice; but he now argues throughout this section on the assumption that not even the total surcease of all human evils would justify the slightest pretense on the part of the philosopher. The philosopher must fall into power; but once he has, he can compel two different natures to fall together. He can be unjust to his own kind while being utterly truthful toward everyone else. If we consider the other possibility, that a legitimate king genuinely philosophizes, we are again baffled as to what effect his philosophizing would have on his rule. He would still be acknowledged the legitimate king and would rule as such. Any actions he took to realize the good city would either lead to his downfall, or, were they found agreeable to his people, not declare him to be the philosopher. If he bequeathed his rule to a philosopher, the philosopher would be forced to become a tyrant, unless perchance he were the king's son. Socrates, then, rightly formulated hypothetically his solution to the problem of human evil. The coincidence of political power and philosophy requires a miracle; but the gods, who are beautiful and good, do not listen to prayers.

25

KNOWLEDGE AND OPINION

(474c5–484d10)

Socrates now develops a complex proof for the necessity of the philosopher-king if what is now badly practiced in cities is to be practiced well (473b5). The proof has seven parts, the last of which is at the beginning of the sixth book: (1) 474c8–475c8: the characteristic of lovers; (2) 475d1–476c1: philosophers and true philosophers; (3) 476c2–477b9: knowledge and opinion; (4) 477b10–478d12: the faculties of knowledge and opinion; (5) 478e1–479d6: the content of opinion; (6) 479d10–480a13: lovers of opinion and philosophers; (7) 484a1–484d10: why philosophers must rule. The gist of the proof is this. There are evils today because no laws are laid down in the cities in accordance with being. The minimum change required is to put in charge of cities those who know the beings and can model the laws in conformity with them. Socrates implies that the philosopher cannot put into the city the order of his soul, for only he can have that order; but the laws of the city, which are essentially in their effect nothing but corporeal habits, can embody closely enough his knowledge. Socrates' proof, then, should not be about the necessary character of opinion but its present character. Opinion can be modeled on knowledge and thus become stabilized. Socrates had worked out in the previous three books another way to stabilize opinion. He assigned to the auxiliaries the task of preserving the city's opinions and called their virtue manliness. Manliness was the dyeing of the pure white wool of music and gymnastic education with the laws of the city. He now seems to abandon that way and proposes instead the direct imposition of knowledge-informed law. Since Socrates' original way was educative, it did not involve any sanctions; but the philosopher cannot legislate without force.

Socrates' proof must pull two ways. Unless opinion and knowledge are wholly separate, the philosopher would not be needed to draw them together, but there would already be some opinions about beautiful, just, and good things that were true; and it would be these opinions the ruler would have to translate into institutions and laws. If this were the case, the philosopher could not be enlisted into the city, for he would have no privileged access to these opinions. Socrates, then, must deny there are any true opinions; indeed, neither true nor false opinion is mentioned anywhere in his proof (cf. 467d9–e2, 477e6). If, however, opinion could never become true opinion, the philosopher's knowledge would be useless for the city. Does the philosopher, then, bring to the city the distinction between true and false opinion? If it is taken literally, the philosopher would have to be at the beginning, since men do distinguish between true and false opinion without any help from the philosopher. Perhaps Socrates means that the philosopher is the first to distinguish between opinion and knowledge, and it is that distinction which, if accepted in the city, would entitle the philosopher to rule. That distinction, however, would itself only be an opinion of the city; and no matter how true an opinion, it would not help to distinguish between genuine philosophers and imposters. The philosophers could never give up ruling as long as there was to be some correspondence between the opinion and the knowledge that opinion and knowledge were distinct. It is not obvious what effect the maintenance of such an opinion in the city would have. Glaucon says that it is obvious what sort the man is who is like the philosopher-ruled city; and Socrates takes him at his word and never describes him (541b2–5).

Socrates begins with a definition of the verb *philein*, "to love" or "to be fond of," in terms of correct speech. He seems to be applying to the verb the Thrasymachean distinction between precise and ordinary speech. To love something means to love everything that belongs to the class that something designates. If a winelover does not like Lesbian wine, he is not a winelover, for he discriminated within the class of wines. Socrates seems to be talking about what we call "——crazy": "He's girl-crazy," or "She's boy-crazy." It is clear enough that the Greek word for patriot, citylover (*philopolis*), cannot be like "winelover," for it is impossible to be a universal patriot. "Citylover" could possibly refer to someone who loathed the country and preferred to be in any town rather than go outside. Socrates himself seems to be a citylover in this sense, but the reason he gives—trees refuse to talk to him—disqualifies him (*Phaedrus* 230d4), for the lover he means has no grounds for his love and knows nothing of the difference between good and bad (475b11–c4). Socrates' first example, *philopais* ("boylover"), seems to resemble patriot rather than winelover, but he appeals to Glaucon as an "erotic man" to confirm the view that

> all those in the bloom of youth, being thought deserving of care and affection, bite and stir up in some way or other the boylover and erotic. Don't you all act so toward the beautiful? One, because he's snub-nosed, will be called charming and praised by you all, and you all say of another who's hooknosed that he's kingly, and whoever's in between the two you say is just right, and swarthy boys you say have manly looks, and fairskinned boys you say are sons of gods; and "honeypales" and the name itself, do you believe it's the fiction (*poiēma*) of anyone else than a lover who is speaking hypocoristically and equably putting up with paleness if it is in season? In a word, you all make up every kind of excuse and omit no manner of expression so as not to lose a single one of those at the height of their youthful bloom. (474d4–475a2)

Socrates' argument seems to be nonsensical, for the fact that someone may love the snubnosed and exophthalmic Theaetetus does not mean that he loves the hooknosed Meletus with long stringy hair (*Euthyphro* 2a9–11; *Theaetetus* 143e7–9). It may be true that every youth is loved by someone; but it does not follow that the class of boylovers and the class of boys are in the relation Socrates suggests. He himself, who claims that he finds almost all boys

131

beautiful, seems not to be in love with any of them, or so at least Alcibiades maintains (*Symposium* 216d1–e5, 222b 3–4). The fanciful vocabulary winetasters employ does not strengthen Socrates' case, for they also speak of undrinkable wines, and Socrates cannot allow for any rejection. Only someone like Richard Porson, who in his love of wine once drank lamp kerosene, seems to be indiscriminate enough, but he did not offer then any excuses and plead that its bouquet made it something special. Socrates' third example, the honorlover, is no better, for the runner who comes in third may have to be content with that, but it does not follow that he loves third-place honors and invents a title to cover up his disgrace. Socrates seems to be trying to give to "boylover" the syntax of "thirst," but with this difference. "Thirst itself for drink itself" now seems to have its counterpart in the philosopher, who has conceived something like "love itself for being itself" (501d1–2), while the opinionlover (*philodoxos*) is the lover of many opinions and corresponds to the variety of thirsts for a variety of drinks. "Boylover," however, which is Socrates' chief example, should, if we correct his conclusion in light of his description, make the opinionlover anyone who loves any opinion and claims that it is beautiful, good, or just. There is no opinion, no matter how irrational and apparently contrary to everything beautiful, just, and good, that does not have its passionate defenders. Lawbred opinion is the comprehensive class of hypocoristics. "If they were not making a procession to Dionysus," Heraclitus says, "and singing a song for the shameful things [i.e., the genitals], it would have been a most shameless performance (fr. 15; cf.fr.5).

Socrates' analysis of boylovers seems to be made needlessly complicated. He does not just collect all boylovers into one class, he personifies that class into "The Boylover" and attributes to the singular personification a love of all boys; but at the same time he denies that the plurality of the beloved boys is likewise unifiable into a singular being which all boylovers are in love with, for, he plausibly argues, "snubnosed" and "hooknosed" could not hold simultaneously for the boy. We know from Glaucon's own confession that his beloved has or had a defective body (402d10–e3); but the inference Socrates draws from it seems wholly unwarranted—that Glaucon loves all boys equally—and it is amazing that, though he does not remember what Socrates is referring to, he accepts Socrates' interpretation of his confession so readily. If all men were in love with Helen, it seems unreasonable to infer that all men are womanlovers, and if all were in love with Charmides, that they are boylovers. But the hypocoristics of excuse, if they are not also the hypocoristics of flattery, seem to express an awareness in each individual case that his attraction to some boy not particularly beautiful does not agree with the lexical meaning of *erōs* as love of the beautiful; and in his unwillingness to give up the opinion everyone has of *erōs*, he devises a term that will negotiate between the boy and the beautiful. The manifold of translations, by means of which every beloved is transferred from the class of youthful bloom to the class of the beautiful, does not let Socrates establish the lover as the lover of the manifold. It is Socrates who is indifferent to those excuses and, in depriving each lover of them, generates the pure boylover. The ticket of admission into the class of boylovers is always particular, but the class-characteristic belongs to no one prior to his admission. Socrates' procedure recalls the Eleatic stranger's, who urged Theaetetus to ignore the pretensions of rank and classify licekilling and generalship together as equally illustrative of hunting (*Sophist* 227a7–b6). Socrates, then, has cut the beautiful away from its would-be lovers and assigned them to be the lovers of a class that they all tried to disguise. The poetry he subtracted from their love, however, not only deprives them of any interest but surreptitiously has crept into his own account. Species (*eidos*) seems to be the philosopher's own hypocoristic by means of which he can love everything he wants to know.

Socrates' misrepresentation of Glaucon to Glaucon makes him the representative of all boylovers (475a3–4). He becomes their collective voice. Glaucon then confirms that the philosopher too is not fastidious in his love of wisdom but loves all of it (475b8–10). The philosopher, then, is not distinguishable from any other lover of anything by his own comprehensiveness, and certainly not by his ability to divide things into their true classes without pretexts. His uniqueness must be sought elsewhere. Socrates makes the philosopher so indiscriminate and insatiate in his learning that Glaucon protests and, in showing himself to be somewhat finicky and snobbish (cf. 522b4–6), finds it strange that lovers of sights and sounds should be classed among the philosophers. He seems to forget a reason Socrates had for his descent into the Piraeus, and how his brother tried to convince him to stay (Xenophon *Memorabilia* 3.11.1). Socrates, at any rate, concedes the point and says lovers of sights and sounds are like philosophers, whom Glaucon in turn now calls true or genuine philosophers (475e3). If such a distinction were applied to boylovers, the sincere or truthful lovers would be those who never employed any hypocoristics but, like Theodorus, would tell Theaetetus to his face that he was as ugly as Socrates.

The philosophers are lovers of the sight of the truth. The interposition of "sight" between "lover" and "truth" renders the philosopher selfless in his devotion to truth. There is no good in it for him, for he is already "true" as he is and stands in no need of the truth to become "true." Appearances never deceive the philosopher. His thought is so powerful that it goes directly to each species that is what it is by itself. Socrates admits that hardly anyone else would agree to this as easily as Glaucon (475e6–7). The agreement consists of three steps: (1) since beautiful is contrary or opposite to ugly, the pair is two; (2) since they are two, each is one; (3) each species of beautiful and of ugly, of just and of unjust, of good and of bad, is one by itself, but by the communion with actions, bodies, and one another each appears as a manifold of apparitions everywhere. Socrates then distinguishes between the philosopher-like lovers of sights and sounds, who cherish beautiful colors, shapes, and sounds, and the true philosophers, who cherish the beautiful itself. This cannot be right. The beautiful itself is the species or the nature of the beautiful itself (476a5, b7); it is not loved any more than is the species or the nature of the ugly itself. Prior to the distinction between those like philosophers and philosophers themselves, all philosophers were in love with every sort of learning; but now that lovers of sights and sounds are lovers of beautiful sights and sounds, the true philosophers follow their lead and become finicky.

There are then two ways open to the philosopher. Either all the species are as beautiful as the beautiful is, and the beautiful is not a separate species, for otherwise the other species are not truly beautiful; or none of the species, not even the species of the beautiful, is beautiful and the philosopher does not love any of them. If he does love them, he must have been insincere and given them each a nickname by means of which he could conceal from himself the ugliness of the unjust and the bad. There is, then, no species whose likeness the philosopher would not incorporate into his laws; and everything ugly, unjust, and bad would show up in the city for which he legislates no less than everything beautiful, just, and good. If the philosopher does not suddenly become partial, the net result of his legislation would be to leave things exactly as they are. Would the philosopher have to be compelled to give up his love of the sight of the truth for the sake of the city?

Socrates has managed to skew the understanding of the philosopher in two ways. The first is that the philosopher does not philosophize.[1] He is not between ignorance and knowledge (*Symposium* 202a5–9, 203e4–204b2); he already knows and loves what he knows. He does not differ from the philosopher-dog. His knowledge and his love are modeled on the sight and the love of the sightlover. There is no reasoning involved for either of them, whether it be about the sight of the knowledge or about the love each has. The second is that the boylover is assimilated falsely to the philosopher, and each is said to be wholly indiscriminate in regard to what they are devoted to; but this nondiscrimination not only impresses on the philosopher a devotion to something he must know as fully as the boylover knows his beloved, but it conceals entirely the truly philosophic activity of collection and division. That Glaucon was the first to employ the word species (*eidos*) blinds him to what Socrates is doing right in front of him. Through the specious assignment of the class-characteristic to every class-member, he takes Socrates' discovery of the class of boylovers as a given. He thus takes each species in each pair of three contraries also as given, and pays no attention to Socrates' first collecting and then dividing the philosophers, with the result that he fails to notice the shift Socrates effects from the neutrality of the larger class to the bias of the two smaller classes. Glaucon's goodwill toward Socrates adheres to the philosophers as well and makes them moral. They become attached to the beautiful, the just, and the good of the city before they become attached to the city.

Socrates now drops the issue of love and devotion for the next section, in which he separates the ranges of knowledge and opinion. He starts with a distinction between the one who practices and believes in the lawfully beautiful things (*kala men pragmata nomizōn*) but not in beauty itself and is incapable, even if one guides (*hēgeitai*) him, to attain a knowledge of it, and, in contrast to him, one who believes (*hēgoumenos*) and is capable of descrying something beautiful by itself, both itself and the things partaking of it, and believing (*hēgoumenos*) neither its participants to be it nor itself to be its participants (476c2–d3). Although Socrates asks Glaucon whether in his view the former is awake or asleep, a postponement of the question leads him to say that the latter lives a waking life.

---

1. The verb *philosophein* occurs three times in the *Republic* (495a2, 473d2, 619d8).

What postpones the question is a question about dreaming, which is possible, Glaucon agrees, whether one is awake or asleep. To dream is to believe (*hēgeitai*) that which is like something is not like but is the very thing it resembles. Opinion, then, must identify likenesses with those things of which they are likenesses, and in making such an identification go on to identify itself with knowledge. In the eyes of opinion, opinion is knowledge, and the things it opines are not likenesses but the things that are of which they are likenesses. The only likenesses so far in their discussion has been of the lovers of sights and sounds to philosophers. Opinion, then, should hold that they are the same. Everything Socrates says of the philosophers must be the opinions of opinion. The philosopher who loves what he knows is the lover of opinion.

If the lover of opinion gets angry when Socrates and Glaucon tell him that he does not know but opines, they will have to soothe him; and Glaucon seems to be more certain that they will have to soothe him than that they will succeed (cf. 480a9–10). In the argument that follows, Glaucon answers on behalf of the lover of opinion (476e7–8), who will acknowledge that what perfectly is, is perfectly knowable, and whatever is not, is altogether unknowable. The lover of opinion, then, claims that he knows perfectly what perfectly is. Socrates suggests that there might be something (*ti*) that lies between what is and what is not. Knowledge, then, covers the range of the coincidence of something and being; and the issue is whether another power or faculty (*dunamis*) covers the range of the noncoincidence of something and being (477a6–b1). Socrates then says that powers are a kind of genus (*genos*) of the things which are, among which are sight and hearing, and Glaucon understands the species (*to eidos*) he means (477c1–5; cf. d8, e1). We are forcibly reminded of the argument with Thrasymachus, in which Socrates distinguished eyes and ears from each other and from the pruning hook. Here, however, knowledge is both like eyes and the pruning hook, since it covers not only an exclusive range but it does so perfectly; and opinion, though its range is as distinct from knowledge as ears from eyes, has no excellence, though we would expect it to be true opinion.

The two criteria which Socrates lays down for distinguishing a power are that it must have an exclusive range and an exclusive product. The substantives "knowledge" and "opinion" designate the ranges, and the verbs "know" and "opine" the products. Glaucon's conclusion, however, that knowledge and opinion are different both in their ranges and their products does not necessarily follow, for a difference in either range or product would make them different even if either the range or product were the same. Glaucon should have paid attention to Socrates' formation of the species or genus of powers which is among the things which are, and asked whether powers are among the perfectly knowable beings, and by what power did Socrates collect them into a class. These difficulties would have brought him before another. To be awake was to distinguish between images and the things of which they are images. If knowledge covered only the latter and opinion the former, the knower would know as little of one as the opiner of the other; but it is essential to knowledge that the inner unity of each being and its participants be grasped, for otherwise there is knowledge without knowledge of cause (516b9–c2). It seems, then, that two different kinds of analysis are going on at once. On the dialogic level it is an eidetic analysis, in which Socrates solicits and Glaucon expresses his assent with the expression, "It has come to light" (478d11, 12, 484a2–6). But on the doctrinal level it is an analysis in terms of being and nonbeing; and while Socrates has given no evidence that anyone knows perfectly that which perfectly is, it is accepted by Glaucon who has been asked at exactly this point to be the spokesman for those who opine (cf. 597a5–7). These two levels correspond to the difference between the dialogic city and the city in speech. In order, then, for the city in speech to be realized, it would have to be shown how the eidetic analysis on the dialogic level could be replaced by the being-analysis. The argument itself amounts to a proof that it cannot be done. Neither the nonidentity of things and their participants nor the constitution of the species of powers admits of a translation into the city's language of being and knowledge.

Once opinion is identified with the range between being and nonbeing, Socrates has to determine what belongs there; and he decides that it is the many lawful opinions of the many about the beautiful, the just, and the good (479d3–5). Lawbred opinion consists in the belief that the beautiful things are many (479a3). Since Socrates had just argued that whoever opines must opine at least some one thing (478b10), and he has asserted more than once that the knower knows the beautiful, the just, and the good to be each one, it is not immediately obvious why a manifold of ones is the distinguishing feature of opinion. The difference between the perspectives of opinion and knowledge must be kept in mind. The many of opinion is from the viewpoint of knowledge, the one of opinion is from the viewpoint of opinion. Socrates has repeated in this case what he had done in forming the class of boylovers. He collects believers of every variety into one class, and though each enters the class with a single identification of something as supremely beautiful, just, or good, the class characteristic is the lawful belief in a manifold of beautiful, just, and good things. Socrates is claiming that there are three or four fundamental hypocoristics that are universally predicated of the lawful customs and practices of every city and tribe. They are the excuses uttered everywhere and always to disguise the love of one's own. They are identical in function to "charming," "kingly," and "honeypale," as boylovers apply them. The philosopher, however, refuses to color any class with any other class. All predication is metaphor in the city. There are no similes. What Socrates has done is to cut each of those predicates away from their law-determined subjects, set them aside each by itself, and asserted their subjects to be the representation of nonbeing. The range of opinion, in which there is many a something (*ti*) and being, is the range of subjects that are not and predicates that are. The subjects are our dreams. "Aphrodite is beautiful," "Zeus is just," "The fatherland is holy" have each submitted to the knife, and what survives in each case is the predicate. Only then is it possible to ask what each of these predicates is.

The discovery of the difference between opinion and knowledge is a discovery of philosophy; but it is only in the perspective of their former identity that their discovery entails that knowledge be attained. Ignorance is unknown to opinion. Every people is the chosen people and inhabits its privileged cave. It is one and there are no others. It is all there is. It is not one of many. The extreme fragmentation of the predicates beautiful, just, and good, into which the exclusivity of each city breaks them, results in a many that makes the range of each seem and be apart from the range that each has for knowledge. Once this many becomes known as a manifold of opinions, however, there is nothing beautiful, just, or good by law that will not come to light as ugly, unjust, and bad by law (538b6–e4). Socrates adds to these the manifold of doubles and other magnitudes. Why morality and mathematics should be juxtaposed is mysterious. In the absence of any claim for absolute magnitude that one finds elsewhere in Plato, Glaucon must surely take Socrates to mean that a magnitude can always be found that inverts the relation of any given relative magnitude. His own contribution of the children's riddle—the eunuch, bat, and pumice—does not further

Socrates' meaning, for in each case—a man not a man, a bird not a bird, a stone not a stone—the contrariety of the predicates does not affect the subject. The true perplexity is whether, once the philosopher has detached unreal subjects from real predicates, he can reattach real subjects to them. The Cave denies such a possibility and claims itself to be the permanent condition of the city.

26

THE PHILOSOPHIC NATURE

(485a1–487a6)

Socrates asserts that the philosophers are uniquely qualified to translate the beings into the laws of the city. He thereby denies that he has done so in his own educational reforms. They were lies and based on lies and not deductions from eternal and unchanging being (*ousia*), a word that first occurs in this sense at the end of the fifth book (479c7). Yet it seems too harsh to denounce what we have read as unphilosophic; rather, two different modes of philosophy have met here, a Socratic way of ascent to the beings and a non-Socratic way of descent from the beings;[1] and of these only the latter, Socrates implies, could allow for the philosopher-king. The philosopher-king bears an uncanny resemblance to the Homeric gods, for whatever they are in themselves and whatever paradigm they have in their soul, the lawful equivalents they devise would have the same apparitional variety Socrates' theology prohibited (380d1–6, 476a4–7). Socrates, at any rate, appears not to know of a single law deducible from the highest beings, for the mathematical sciences he proposes for the city, even if they were derivative from them, fail to provide lawful versions of the beautiful, just, and good. Socrates' own suggestion about the lawful and the just seems to be this. All men living in societies are aware that not everything is permitted to

1. *Phaedrus* 265c8–266c1; Aristotle *EN* 1095a30–b3; cf. R. Kennington, *Review of Metaphysics* XXXV 1981, 71–80.

man. There is some line whose transgression is fatal to the humanity of man. Such a negative formulation expresses everyone's everyone's sense of what is just; and Socrates had made it the principle of the city in speech in the form *ta hautou prattein*, to mind one's own business. The elasticity of the phrase is deliberate, for though there are better and worse determinations of what is one's own, no precise delimitation of it is possible in the city. The bestial and the divine are the two boundaries within which what is man's own is situated; but neither boundary is fixed anywhere except by law, and it is incapable of being fixed otherwise for the city. In the city, the principle of justice may show up as the sacred—"It is not allowed to leave corpses unburied," or, "It is not allowed to bury corpses"—, or in regard to some rule of propriety or property; but the difficulties and even impossibilities that attended the city in speech, once the need for going beyond the true city was recognized, were meant to prove the necessary arbitrariness of political right and consequently the necessity of evil in human life. Now, however, Socrates is confronted not by the city but by a rival account of philosophy through which a return to the golden age would be imaginable. The sixth and seventh books bear to Socratic philosophizing the same relation the city in speech bore to the dialogic city. They represent this rival account of philosophy and at the same time contain Socrates' refutation of it.

Socrates admits that the difference between philosophers and nonphilosophers would have come to light in a better way if that were their only topic. Many things remain for discussion if he is to find the difference between the just and unjust life (484a1–b1). He implies that the life of philosophy and the life of justice are not the same, and that the other way or ways to find philosophy could have been more difficult and longer. He reminds us that he had issued a similar caveat before he discussed the structure of the soul. The soul's structure was seen in light of the city's requirements, and now philosophy too seems to have undergone a similar distortion. A revision of the soul's account could possibly have improved the account of philosophy. The true philosopher in any case seems to have no knowledge of soul, for it is unintelligible as a being not subject to change (*Sophist* 249a9–10). The minimum supplement needed by the true philosophers is an account of the relation between intellect (*nous*) and soul (cf. 490b3), and a proof that any being with soul is capable of those operations of mind they must posit. "Soul" disappeared long before the third wave (458a7), and throughout his account Socrates did not once speak of mind or intellection (cf. 476a10); indeed, Glaucon is the first to use the uncompounded verb *noeō*, and then to remark on the impossibility of a fixed conception of eunuch, bat, and pumice (479c4). No one, however, doubts that there are now in Greece and possibly in Athens those who exemplify perfectly the true philosophers. Glaucon and Adimantus know who they are. Socrates therefore is never called upon to prove their possibility, though they seem to have vanished from the known world since then.

Perfect knowledge of perfect being does not suffice for rule. Experience and proficiency in every other part of virtue are also needed (484d5–485a3). It is this combination that Socrates has to show is possible. In terms of his former image, this is equivalent to putting those awake in charge of dreamers; in terms of his present image, he wants to replace blind guardians who "in truth (*toi onti*) are deprived of the knowledge of what severally is" with those who are not so deprived. "Blind guardians" is a term of abuse, for their replacements are only keen sighted (484c3–4). To have dim-sighted guardians of those incapable of telling the difference between image and reality seems eminently practicable; and Socrates never gives a single example of an image painted by the philosopher-king, unless of course it is the *Republic* itself.

Socrates gives a ninefold description of the philosophic nature. What music education was supposed to achieve in the auxiliaries through harmonizing the two species of courage and moderation is now presented in a revised version as a single nature in which nine qualities cohere. Socrates must now argue for their coherence; but first the two tables:

Music Education	Philosophic Nature
No fear of Hades	Love of learning of every eternal being
No fear of names	Love of truth
No grief	Moderate: no love of money
No laughter	Freedom: human life is small
Truthful	Death is not terrible
Obedient	Just and gentle
Temperature in food and drink	Good at learning (cf. 375a5–8)
Chaste	Good at remembering
No love of money	Witty (*eucharis*)

Music education tries apparently to imitate in the thumoeidetic nature the philosophic nature; and were it not that human nature is not the same as the eternal beings, we might be inclined to say that Socrates already has done what he says the true philosophers must be able to do. If, however, we disregard the dialectical character of that education, which turned it into an education of the philosophic nature from the start, we could say that the indifference of the philosophic nature to everything that is of concern to most men has a fair facsimile in morality, which, however, must take all those concerns in deadly earnest. "I can't be bothered" is the philosopher's version of morality. It expresses his way of minding his own business.

From the disposition and the ability of the philosopher's nature, one should be able to infer everything else about him (486e1–3). The love of truth seems to cause Glaucon some trouble. He might be wondering whether the philosopher could lie as ruler, and be as insincere as Thrasymachus in representing moral indignation. He might also wonder whatever happened to the lie in the soul which all men were supposed to hate. Do all men show a common hatred of falsehood but not a common love of truth (*Sophist* 228c7–8)? Socrates says that strict necessity binds the love of truth to the love of wisdom, for "whoever is naturally in love with something cherishes everything akin and belonging to the beloved." Truth, then, is not loved for its own sake and might in itself be like snubnosed; but the love of truth would prevent the philosopher from making it attractive and coloring it with some hypocoristic. He could have no rhetoric to win wisdom over. The lover of lies, on the other hand, must be like the boylovers and the same as the lovers of opinion. That Socrates is speaking from within the good city is implied by his remark that genuine lovers of learning must from earliest youth desire truth in its entirety; in that case, it is among the auxiliaries who fail to keep the opinions of the city that the future philosophers must be found. But regardless of whether he is speaking of the present or the future, Socrates cannot couple the love of truth with the love of learning if the philosophic nature must show itself when young and still exhibit a love of every learning that makes clear the being that is always (485b1–3). The philosophic young must be the lovers of sights and sounds, for Socrates certainly now suggests that that which is always does not show itself. The original way of defining the philosopher does not quite fit with the way of nature; and in his summary of the philosophic nature, Socrates simply drops the love of being (487a3–5).

Both moderation and courage are now trivial consequences of the philosophic nature. His moderation, which is due to the diversion of his desire and pleasure to a single end, does not differ from the moderation of the passionate chess player or any other hobbyist, whose lack of interest in anything else controls appetite as effectively as calculation. The future ruler has a nature that neither the soul-structure nor the class-structure of the city copies. His detection therefore cannot be left to anyone upon whom either structure has been impressed; and if the philosopher does not rule, his existence would be even more precarious in the good city than it is now. The philosopher is compelled to rule, whether he wants to or not, in order to save his own. He does not rule in order to direct poets to tell stories that will diminish the fear of death, for the natures of interest to him do not need any stories to be without fear of death (386a6–b3). Socrates does not make it clear whether they know that Hades is not, believe that it is not, or do not take it seriously. Perhaps the philosopher-king is supposed to get to them before either the stories of the city corrupt them or they corrupt the city. They are surely not expected, in their love of truth, to be wise enough to keep silent. The superficial convergence of moral education and philosophic nature conceals a divergence that restores in a different way the separation of opinion and knowledge that the philosopher-king was to overcome. The city obtains a ruler to whom rule is wholly unknown. Without any experience of beating he will know nothing of force. Polemarchus' gang never threatens him.

27

THE PHILOSOPHER-KING

(487a7–502c8)

Adimantus cuts in before Glaucon can answer Socrates' question, whether he would entrust the city to mature philosophic natures (487a7–9). Adimantus has become aware that Socrates is talking of not real possibility but natural possibility; he must have noticed that Socrates has put Glaucon in charge of selecting the right natures among the young (486a1, 4, b11, c1). The best of the philosophers with whom Adimantus is acquainted are useless for cities. Would not the rulers of nonphilosophers have to be somewhat cruder? Socrates' argument, which has been of the filament kind, is irrefutable, but it runs so contrary to the facts that it cannot be right. The argument itself shows the uselessness of philosophers, since it is incapable of overcoming experience. Adimantus' own experience has been twofold. Philosophy seems not to be justice, since it is not obviously connected, if Socrates exemplifies it, with the promotion of another's good. Socrates can always beat them at argument, but he is not benefiting them. The constant feeling of being outsmarted cannot be the basis of just rule: Socrates would have made a good general. If, on the other hand, philosophy is justice, justice is not necessary for happiness, since the philosopher as ruler will have to make men happy without their being strictly just. Adimantus is vaguely aware that justice is the dyad of philosophy and city, and that conjunction can never become an equation. Even if, then, Socrates manages to remove Adimantus' unease at entrapment and then instill in him what the philosopher would have to duplicate in his city, Socrates must give up the refutation of Glaucon or else admit that the city cannot be happy or just.

Adimantus speaks of "the truth" and "seeing" in the cities as if neither were weighted with an interpretation (487c3, 6). The way things are for opinion is the way things are. Socrates says this is a true opinion. It is the first opinion labeled as true since the distinction between opinion and knowledge was drawn. Socrates is going to save the opinion and still argue that philosophers should rule. He implies that the opinion would cease to be true once cities see the results of the philosophers' rule (498d6–499a10). For this reason a coincidence of political power and philosophy must be awaited, since prior to the coincidence only a false opinion, spread by opinion-guided friends of philosophy, could prevail over this true opinion. Socrates' argument is in the form of an image. He defends his use of an image on the grounds that the experience of philosophers in relation to cities is unique and cannot be pictured in light of any single thing that exists. All the elements of his image are real except the owner of the ship, who is a composite of all the members of the people. Socrates warns Adimantus that no conclusion can be

144

drawn until this composite People has been reconstituted as individuals. Poets resort to fictional monsters whenever a 'natural' likeness is unavailable and the being that they wish to show has no congeners. In the *Phaedrus*, Socrates had implied that the soul was this kind, and only the monster of undetachable horses, chariot, and charioteer with each of the three parts winged could represent it properly. In the *Republic*, Socrates had made a composite figure out of boylovers, but he did not admit that it was a fiction, and the result was that the philosopher was not unique but comparable to any lover of anything. Socrates' People is the invention of Aristophanes (in his *Knights*),[1] the Boylover is his own. The Boylover cut out the partiality of each lover, the People cut out the varied and possibly conflicting interests of its members. The People always own the city but never run it. They are somewhat deaf and blind and will remain so. No eyeglasses and hearing aids for them. They are now and forever uneducable. Socrates thus breaks the alliance between the educated classes and philosophy. Philosophers are to be given directly to the people, who do not care one way or the other. The owner acquired the ship justly, and since it is at sea there is no danger of war (Thucydides 1.143.5; 2.62.2). There is no need of soldiers to defend its sacred soil and to whose interest some consideration must be given. Socrates, in short, in replying to Adimantus, takes away everything his brother added to the true city. The philosopher could indeed rule a city in which there was nothing but the arts and their satisfaction of the body; but it would still be the city of pigs.

There are, at first, three elements in Socrates' image. The ship is the city, the sailors the politicians, and the owner the people. The city is not the people, and since the art of rule has nothing to do with the rule of human beings, the philosopher can rule the city without ruling them. Socrates takes back more than Glaucon's city; he takes back his argument with Thrasymachus, in which the pilot ruled the sailors and had the art of piloting as well (341c9–d4). The sailors now agree that there is no art of piloting but piloting and seamanship consist in controlling the owner by force or persuasion. The true pilot, in contrast to the sailors' understanding of him, thus comes forward with knowledge of the year, the seasons, the sky, the stars, and the winds; but he does not know anything of the sea, for, since he does not have to be on board (489b6), he has made all his observations on land. He knows nothing of the three waves. An

---

1. Cf. L. Strauss, *Socrates and Aristophanes* (New York, 1966), 103–5.

expert pilot who is a landlubber is strange enough; but since he has never been at sea, he knows nothing of ships. He can steer a ship that might sink under him. He certainly has never made a ship. The pilot is not the designer of the city in speech, let alone the ruler of the dialogic city. Who then is he? He is called a chatterbox and investigator of highfalutin things (488e4, 489c6; *Apology of Socrates* 18b7–c1; *Sophist* 225d7–11; *Statesman* 299b2–c6). He is the Socrates of Aristophanes (*Clouds* 360). Socrates convinces Adimantus that the pre-Socratic Socrates should rule. He convinces him that pre-Socratic philosophy is competent to do what it never dreamed of doing. The Anaxagorean rule of mind over body was as far as it had gone. Socrates has never been wittier.

The surcease of human evils began as an hypothesis—if philosophers rule; it has become a contrafactual—if pre-Socratic philosophers were to rule. Socrates then combines this contrafactual with another bit of fancy: if "People" were first to realize that he needed the philosopher and then among the many competitors came across the so-called useless but genuine philosopher (489b3–c3). It is unnatural, Socrates says, for the pilot to beg sailors to rule them, and we are told the true philosopher is not a boaster (490a2); but still Socrates insists that such a meeting can happen. It can happen, we can grant, if "People" is uncorrupt and has not yet heard from any competitors to philosophy; but in that case he would not know that he was needy, and the philosopher would refine a city that was getting along without him. If, however, the ship of state has experienced a crisis of such magnitude that it is evident to everyone that philosophy is the one thing needful, there must already be rival claimants in the city, and "People" believes he has not inconsiderable knowledge of his own (*Statesman* 290c3–e8). That knowledge consists of the productive arts and their mathematical support (522c1–7; *Philebus* 55e1–56c10). Philosophy, then, would have to pass the test of any other recognized art and the philosopher show he possesses Thrasymachean accuracy (503b5). Socrates at least cannot pass such a test. In his account of the city, neither does the equality of the arts square with the differentiation between rulers and ruled, nor does the city's recognition of the heterogeneity of body and soul allow it to avoid a skewed understanding of both. The city separates what is together and combines what is apart. The pleasures it knows of it attributes to the body, and the virtues it promotes it believes are of the soul. Justice and injustice are necessarily co-present in the city. Any attempt to root out injustice will take justice with it. For Glaucon and Adimantus, who have not followed this argument, the doctrine of the "ideas" is an easy way to inculcate the same lesson. It is an instrument of political moderation and not only of political moderation.

After Socrates has used an image to place the relation between philosophy and the city in its true light, he turns to the imitation of philosophy. The thrust of his argument is obscure. He seems to be saying that cities as they are now constituted destroy most philosophic natures, but there could be a city in which the danger of corruption could be kept to a minimum. That the city is wasteful of talent may be true, but how does that show that the city would cease to regard uncorrupted philosophers as useless? "People" is far from being an easygoing idiot, he is in fact the sophist-corrupter of philosophic natures (492a5–492e1). The insignificant men who now lay claim to deserted philosophy maintain the truth that wisdom is the one thing needful; but the powerful sophists, who are the citizens themselves, indoctrinate and fashion everyone in the city to their ways, and they do not believe that wisdom is the one thing needful. Within a period of fifty years, at least three philosophic natures were born in Athens. Is Socrates asserting that had a philosopher ruled Athens after Salamis there would have been more? Plato certainly does not let us see more than one philosophic nature, and that is Socrates when young (*Parmenides* 130e1–4). According to Socrates' present argument, if a philosophic nature gets corrupted, the evils it would commit would be very great; but since great crimes are not prevalent any more than is undiluted wickedness (*Statesman* 303a4–7), there can never have been many philosophic natures in Athens. The grudging hand of nature is beneficent; a gang of corrupt Platos would no doubt have committed inconceivably grand crimes. If, however, such natures are rare, the evils, whose surcease the rule of philosophy would accomplish, cannot now be intolerable or big enough to merit so drastic a measure. For the philosopher, a marginal diminution of evils and a possible saving of one philosophic nature would follow his rule; everyone else would gain nothing and lose much. There would be new masters, with unintelligible goals and a contempt for human life (486a8–10). The man in the street would have gods on earth and his every other thought would be of suicide. A city whose motto was "A life not passed in examination is not worth living" could not be happy.

Socrates gives an account of the philosophic nature and its corruption in cities prior to his account of the degeneration of regimes. The best regime does not form the philosophic nature. The philosophic nature is natural in a way in which the best regime is not. It comes to be and is not made; indeed, it is always becoming and is distinguished from other natures by its constant motion (490a8–b7). Whether the essence of its nature, which is *erōs*, can vanish in the generation of truth that has been its guide, is of importance only if Socrates has to hold out the hope that the best regime can be realized; it is of no importance for the philosophic nature itself, which does not have to know anything about politics. Even if we do not treat Socrates' claim of a remote possibility for an impossibility, it is not the kind of hope that can guide the future lives of Glaucon and Adimantus. That somewhere there is, and at some time there was or will be the perfect city can only be sobering at any time and at any place. Not one single move can be made to bring it nearer. The first move toward it must be from the top, when and only when—but not even then necessarily—a philosopher has completed his quest. A lover of truth, Socrates says, cannot be a boaster (490a1–7); but how someone who attained the truth would not seem to be a boaster is not explained. He surely would not advertise. Would he be ironical and let Socrates be taken for him? He would, Socrates says, be "beautiful and good" (489e4). If "beautiful and good" has its ordinary meaning, he would be a gentleman and as conspicuous as any other. If "beautiful and good" means that in him there shines through the beautiful and the good, he might not be much to look at and hard to find even if one looked. If he wrote, he certainly could not be as gaudy as Plato.

In his account of philosophy, Socrates shifts constantly between it and wisdom, for he is under the strain of combining it with the political, and before he shows that the dogmatism of the city is of the essence of the city, he shows that the city would yield only to an equally dogmatic wisdom. At the same time, however, he engages Adimantus and Glaucon in a new interest, a concern for preventing the city from corrupting philosophic natures. Whenever they remain uncorrupt now, Socrates says, it is by divine chance (492a5, 492e5–493a2). The issue, then, is whether the chances for philosophy can be improved; and the answer seems to be paradoxically, "No, unless by divine chance." An apparently nonprovidential order allows for the supervention of an apparently nonprovidential order (cf. 498d1–6). It is hard to argue against that. Among the accidental causes Socrates lists, which bring good natures safely to philosophy, he mentions his own: "Our own is not worth speaking of, the *daimonion* sign, for no

doubt it has happened to someone else or no one in the past"
(496c3–5; *Apology of Socrates* 31c7–d6; *Phaedrus* 242b8–c3; *Euthy-
demus* 272e3–4). The *daimonion* differs from the other causes in
the time of its onset—from Socrates' earliest youth—and in its not
being an occasion for reflection on some knowledge. It is wholly
natural. Socrates, then, seems to be saying that either he could have
been a king's son or a fluke of the same kind could have landed a
philosopher in a position in which he would have been compelled
to take power; but since in fact the *daimonion* kept Socrates out of
politics, the *daimonion* could not be what it was for Socrates and
bring about the coincidence of philosophy and power. The *Republic*
itself, one might say, is in its effect on Glaucon and Adimantus the
same as Socrates' *daimonion.*

Socrates could make a case, it seems, against his own *daimonion*
if the city were of the same order of nature as the *daimonion*. The
city, however, cannot be of the same order unless philosopher-dogs
is the truth of the relation between the *thumoeidetic* and *erōs*, unless,
that is, the imprecise understanding of soul is the precise understanding of soul. There are, then, at least two orders of nature, one
to which the city and another to which philosophy belongs. The
political order always requires a completion by law, which at its most
interesting is most arbitrary; and this order either has a deleterious
effect on the second order, so that philosophic natures are far fewer
than they otherwise would be, or, though philosophic natures can
never be but rare, it obstructs any natural way for philosophy. The
Republic represents these two possibilities in Socrates' voluntary
descent into the Piraeus and his thwarted ascent. The thwarted ascent
made the *Republic* itself possible; but those who made Socrates stay
on a whim cannot help wondering whether he could not come and
go as he pleased, and the deviant route through the city could be
replaced, so that once the philosopher reached his goal he could
come back for them. Pre-Socratic philosophy, had it thought itself
through, would apparently have accepted this possibility. If, however,
the thwarted ascent is a necessity for philosophy, and it ceases to be
philosophy unless it is forced to descend, there is a congruence in
the discord of the two orders of nature for which an account would
have to be given on a yet still higher order. The good, or the idea of
the good, is the label on Socrates' incomplete account of that third
order. It is of necessity beyond being.

The unity of the philosophic nature, in which its highest
principle—the love of being or the love of truth—orders everything

else perfectly and by necessity, is not very strong, for it is more susceptible to corruption than inferior natures, and it is particularly subject to the city's assault. Socrates says that each one of the elements of its nature destroys the soul that has it and draws it away from philosophy. He cites courage and moderation, but his remark applies no less to the love of being and the love of truth. Perhaps the highest principle has the force only of logic, and it cannot become a ruling principle unless it is strengthened by the city, which is hostile to it but does wield effective force (492d5–7). Its weakness might also be due to a failure on Socrates' part to articulate *erōs* properly, for, in tracing all big evils to the corruption of a single nature, he abandoned the way of eidetic analysis. The opposition between the many weak natures, to which the city cannot be harmful, and the one philosophic nature denies the existence of kinds that are not derivative from one type. In the *Republic* itself, however, Socrates' account of philosophic *erōs* moves from the language of sight to the language of contact (475e4, 476a10, 484b5, 490b3—5); and his complete separation of these two elements of *erōs*, the distance of sight and the union of touch, shows by itself that even they cannot be harmoniously together in a single nature. That Socrates' turn to nature is marked by so signal a failure is a powerful proof that the way of speciation, which the city had imposed on him, cannot be given up. The errors that likewise attended it might be an unavoidable evil. The resistance to evil that, Socrates admits, the not-good displays, suggests that evil is the toughening element of the good, and the innocence of the good nature is the same as its ignorance of good and evil—and *a fortiori* of its own nature and its limits. The city that stands in its way might thus be the only way it has to come to understand itself, for its selflessness seems to reflect the morality to which the city pretends and cannot fulfill.

Socrates distinguishes between two kinds of sophists, the city itself, which is now understood to be the people, and those the people of the city call sophists. The city lays down opinions about the beautiful, just, and good, to which everyone in the city must conform, while the so-called sophists manipulate the passions of the city through speeches which echo the opinions of the city (493a6—e1). In the sophist's ignorance of the truth about opinion and desire, he calls what the city rejoices in "good" and what distresses it "bad," but calls (*kaloi*) the necessary things "beautiful (*kala*) and just" (*Cratylus* 416b6–d11). The sophist is the spokesman of the city. He identifies good and bad with pleasure and pain, as Glaucon and

150

Adimantus had, and calls the necessary morality (the just and the beautiful). Morality is the hypocoristic of necessity. The sophist thus denies the existence of necessity (Aristotle *EN* 1181a12–15) and in the belief that morality is not pleasure, separates morality from good. Morality, accordingly, is made to look as if it belongs to the realm of freedom; but there are no elements in morality as the city understands it that are not simply necessary, as Socrates had argued from the first book on. Only when the necessary and the moral are understood together can the real difference between the nature of the necessary and the good be established. However friendly Thrasymachus may have become to Socrates, he cannot make the city gentle enough for the philosopher-king (498c9–d1). It would be folly to expect any help from that quarter. The alliance, then, between the philosopher and the shipowner against the sailors is impossible, for with the sailors gone, the shipowner is in fact a wild beast, and the philosopher is wholly incapable of persuading it that the distinction between opinion and knowledge is true; but that distinction, Socrates implies, is indispensable if the people are ever to praise philosophy.

The consequence of this new analysis of the city is that Socrates imagines the wedding between philosophy—deserted by truly philosophic natures the city has corrupted, but still attractive enough in the eyes of highly clever artisans—and a short and bald blacksmith recently loosed from chains and sluiced in the bathhouse, who, wearing new finery, finds his impoverished master ready to marry his daughter to him (495b8–496a10). By appealing to the aristocratic snobbishness of Adimantus (495e2), Socrates disguises from him in the form of parody the way of the *Republic* itself (cf. 496b5, 522b4–6). He thus has him repudiate the true city just as Glaucon had; but whereas Glaucon had wanted the city to supply a basis for human dignity, Adimantus wants the city to have at its top the gentleman wiseman. He finds it easy to believe that the many, when confronted with the absence of contentiousness and vulgarity in his picture of the philosopher (499e3; *Theaetetus* 175d7–176a6), would give up their objections. Socrates therefore warns him again that no amount of persuasion can put the philosopher in charge He must be compelled to translate the order of the beings into demotic virtue (500d4–8); and only then when the people see the result will they cease to be angry at philosophers and believe Socrates. Socrates' proposal requires more than just the translation, it requires that the people know that it is a translation (501d1–3); but since they cannot know that directly, they must infer it from the philosopher looking like the most refined gentleman, whose superiority to the artisan is so obvious to Adimantus.

It is now harder than ever to imagine what necessity could ever befall the philosopher outside the pages of the *Republic*. Socrates compares that necessity to the accidental jingle *genomenon* (what has come into being) and *legomenon* (what is being said) in his own speech, which he then contrasts with the deliberately contrived jingles of an Isocrates or a Gorgias (498d8–e3; *Gorgias* 467b11). Isocrates calls his jingles to our attention; but Plato asks us to take Socrates at his word that he did not aim at the jingle, it just happened that he could make use of it in his argument. Either Plato defies us to prove that the universe is not as artfully designed as his own writings, or he invites us to consider how he has arranged for the necessity of Socrates' descent to appear accidental. To look past Plato the poet is to overlook the philosopher. Indeed, from the moment Socrates begins to describe the way in which the philosopher would rule, there is a confusion between the philosopher's painting a picture of his city and his ruling a city. The philosopher-painters use the divine paradigm for making an outline (500e3); they take the city and the ways of men as a canvas and clean it (501a2–3); they either write or paint laws (501a6); they look at the naturally just, beautiful, and moderate and mix either a flesh-color paint or a manlike copy (501b5); and they either make or represent human ways as dear to the gods (501c2). The confusion of metaphor and reality is so total that Adimantus says finally that the painting (or the writing) would be most beautiful (501c3). He no longer needs its reality.

Socrates' way of speaking of the philosopher-king suggests the following. Philosophy seems to be a rare possibility, even though it alone can make a human being truly happy; but however rare philosophy is, Socratic philosophy is even rarer, even though it alone can know why a human being can be happy only in philosophy. Socratic philosophy is the accidental essence of philosophy. It is both a necessity for philosophy to become Socratic and an accident that it ever become so; just as it is a necessity for human happiness to be found only in philosophy and an accident that there ever be philosophy. The coincidence of philosophy and political power thus seems to represent the coincidence of philosophy and political philosophy in Socrates' thinking. Insofar as Adimantus takes pre-Socratic and Socratic philosophers to be the same, there is a concealment of the difference between them. Socrates knows that no philosopher can know and those who claim to know do not know, for they do not know the city and he knows he does not know because he knows the city. His knowledge of the city is final knowledge, but it can only be final if it is not directly part of the intelligible whole; otherwise his knowledge would not be final or he would know the whole. Socrates knows two things about the city: it is necessary for all men and cannot make any man happy. It is the place where the true difference between the necessary and the good can be discerned, and where the question of man's good and the question of the whole coincide.

28

THE GOOD

(502c9–506d1)

Socrates used two different arguments to justify the necessity for the philosopher-king. The first appealed to nature, the second to the "ideas." Although it could be expected that each class of the city would for the most part breed true, its class-structure would foster injustice unless the philosopher were allowed a free hand to reassign every nature to its proper class—and especially the philosophic natures, which could not possibly be known to anyone but the philosopher. The private interest of the philosopher was then coupled with his public role. He was to legislate for the city on the basis of his knowledge of the beings. Socrates, however, now reveals that that is not enough: knowledge of what is beyond being is needed for the ruling of the city. With this distinction Socrates separates the beautiful and the just from the good. Up to this point Socrates had treated all three of them equally as the hypocoristic predicates of political opinion, but of which the philosopher alone has knowledge and in light of which he was to paint their stable images for the city A theme greater than justice thus comes in after the city in speech has been shown to be marginally realizable (504d4–5). Regardless of whether it can ever come to be, the just city can be portrayed; but only if the just city is within the realm of the real can one ask whether it is good. Morality is idealistic, happiness is not. The appearance of morality, Glaucon and Adimantus had argued, was enough for the acquisition of real goods; and they wanted Socrates to show them that the reality of morality could guarantee happiness.

Socrates now returns to this issue in a form which Adimantus either fails to recognize, or, if we adopt Socrates' opinion, pretends not to recognize (504e7–505a5). Adimantus had accepted the distinction between the lie in the soul and its phantom imitation in speech (382a4–c1); but apparently he did not understand that the lie in the soul that all men hate is the seeming good. No set of opinions, no matter how closely they are modelled on the truth of things, can ever extirpate the bafflement everyone senses about the real good: "It is what every soul pursues and does everything for, divining it to be something, but it stays perplexed and cannot grasp adequately what it is, any more than it can enjoy about the good the sort of stable trust it has about everything else" (505d11–e3). The issue of the goodness of the beings that alone satisfy the demand that the good be real involves in a more comprehensive form the same issue as to whether justice and happiness coincide. Socrates now declares, by the second argument he used to justify the philosopher-king, that neither the city as a whole nor citizen as citizen can ever be happy, for the translation of being into its best possible likeness, which only the philosopher could do, deprives that likeness of the being of the good. The law cannot preserve the beautiful, the just, and the good as each of them is; but whereas the beautiful and the just can still be good if they are not what they are, only the good as it is, is any good. The counterfeit good is no good. Everything in the cave is the shadow of an artifact, but its opening into the light is not just the way out to the beings, it is the way in of the good. The cave cannot but be open to the good and closed to the beings.

The philosophic nature was characterized by its love of being or truth; and since such a nature was merely instrumental for the realization of the city, it was of no interest whether happiness coincided with philosophy. Indeed, the selflessness of the philosopher's devotion made him look like a version of Glaucon's just man, whose incorporation of pure justice was of no use to him. It seemed therefore possible for the philosopher to be as miserable as Glaucon thought the perfectly just man would be. Socrates now says that the *idea* of the good is the most important object of knowledge, for it is by its employment that just things as well as everything else prove to be useful and beneficial (505a2–4). The good, then, must determine the goodness of the beings and the goodness of the knowledge of the beings. Socrates denies that we have adequate knowledge of the good (505a5); but since no possession and no knowledge are any good unless we do know it, we know that it is indisputably good to know the good. This too is final knowledge and anchors one end of the range of Socrates' ignorance, at whose other end is his knowledge of the city. The relation, then, between Socrates' knowledge and Socrates' ignorance, the Socratic name for whose unity is self-knowledge, binds together the three images of Sun, Line, and Cave. A knowledge of what is below being—the city and the things of the city—and an awareness of what is beyond being determine between them the character of Socratic philosophy. That the Cave, however, follows in Socrates' account Sun and Line and does not precede them, even though it describes the permanent situation of man in the city, indicates the difference between the essential order of things and the temporal order of things. The true philosophers are always before Socrates and the second sailing necessarily second.

The good in the first place is the measure of other things with regard to their usefulness for someone or something. It is the limitation on everything else as just itself. The good contaminates all species insofar as they are what they are by themselves (476a6). The good, then, expresses the fitting of the beings to the natures, of which the most important example would be the fit between the philosophic nature and the knowledge of the beings which such a nature desires. What is good for human beings does not ultimately stand in the way of the way to the truth of things. What is right before us in its utmost urgency, though it diverts us from what is most distant from us in its intrinsic importance still keeps us bound to it. Socrates first speaks of our having scientific knowledge (*epistasthai*) of everything else without the *idea* of the good, and then immediately afterwards he speaks of our thinking prudently (*phronein*) about everything else without the good (505a6–b3), as if he wanted to designate the good, through the apparent equivalence of these two expressions, as the single principle in which theoretical knowledge and the thoughtfulness of practice both share (cf. 517c5). We know the image of their joint participation in the Platonic dialogue, and nowhere more conspicuously than in the *Republic*, whose second book began with Glaucon's request to hear from Socrates an account and a praise of justice. The mutual interference of the argument and the action in the course of the dialogue shows that, whatever may hold for the ultimate single source of account and praise, it cannot be as direct and as unproblematic as Glaucon made it seem when he treated his two requests as one. Socrates had first to articulate the question of what justice is apart from the question of whether it is good, and he did so not by suppressing the good but by making justice attractive to Glaucon apart from its goodness in itself. The founding of the city drew Glaucon to justice and limited justice in itself. The action of the dialogue thus exhibited what Socrates now says is the fundamental character of the good; but the good could only have this effect through its not being a part of the argument. Now, however, that the good has become a theme, it is inevitable that only a partial account of it can be given (506e1–3, 509c9–10). The good would cease to be in accord with its function if the good were revealed apart from the limitation that it sets on things.

The two most common errors men make about the good are to identify it with either pleasure or thought (*phronēsis*). In the former case, since there are bad pleasures, pleasure is both good and bad; in the latter, the good is, circularly, the thought of the good. No discrimination in either case is possible, for any restriction on pleasure or thought would have to be based on the good. The good, then, in restricting everything else, cannot itself be subject to any restrictions. It must be the whole that makes the beings parts of the whole. The beings are not as such parts; if they were, it would not be possible to know anything about one without knowing everything about all the others, and the *Republic* could not be devoted to justice to the partial exclusion of everything else. No being, therefore, can come to light before us as something to be known unless it is detachable from the whole to which it belongs. The good, as our interest, makes for this detachability and hence for partial knowability. This is obvious enough. Socrates, however, claims that the cause of the detachment of the beings from the whole is the cause of the attachment of the beings as parts to the whole. The good makes possible both the apartness of the beings from and the participation of the beings in the whole. What Nietzsche calls the optimism of Platonism may not unreasonably be connected with this double claim for the good. The optimism, however, is limited, for the nonbeing of the beings when they are apart from the whole and knowable apart from what they are as parts, precludes the knowability of the beings as parts (506a6–7). Socrates therefore hardly exaggerates when he says that his opinion of the good is ugly, blind, and skew (506c11); but all of its defectiveness would be unknown to him unless something made the satisfying not satisfying (504b1–c4; cf. 354a13–c3). That something is the divination of the good: the soul, which is somehow all things, is not all things.

29

S U N ,   L I N E ,   C A V E
(506d2–516c3)

Of the three images Socrates deploys in succession, none is more puzzling than the sun. Whether the sun is nothing more than an image of the good, or whether the region of becoming and visibility over which the sun rules can be ascribed causally to the good is not clarified. If the former were true, the good and the sun would each cover separately a section of the divided line with no overarching principle (509d1–4), as seen in figure 10. If the

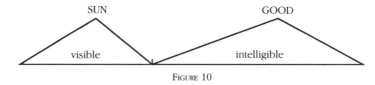

FIGURE 10

latter were to hold, the good would exercise a dual kingship, as seen in figure 11. The good, then, is either a teleological principle

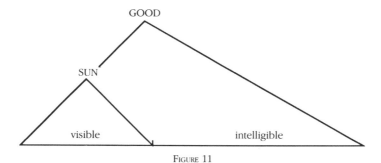

FIGURE 11

of all things, regardless of whether they always are or are ever undergoing generation and corruption, or its causal range is restricted to the things that truly are and Socrates proposes an ontology apart from a natural cosmology. Socrates seems to emphasize the absence of any explicit cosmology when he proposes that a science of solids in motion replace astronomy, and he nowhere suggests that such a science could be the basis of a mathematical physics. Socrates, however, does say that the good generated the sun as its own analogue (508b12–13; cf. 506e3, 517c3); and though Socrates says the sun is the offspring (*tokos*) of the good (506e3), he also speaks of his own account of it as interest (*tokos*) on the principal and possibly counterfeit at that (507a1–5). Indeed, if the good is not a counterfeit cause of becoming, the distinction between being and becoming collapses, and both are equally intelligible. The circumstances of the *Republic* do not allow Socrates to pay his debt in full; and the image of the sun functions initially as a way of satisfying Glaucon without Socrates ever giving him his actual opinion about the good (506e1–3).

The region of the sun, moreover, insofar as it images the good, represents the region of opinion and not of sight; but insofar as the sun is the cause of becoming it images the good as the cause of being, and if becoming and visibility are as closely bound causally as being and intelligibility are, then the sun cannot be the cause of opinion. The sun, then, functions in Socrates' account both as itself and as image. As itself it is a dual cause; and as an image it represents a dual cause. In neither case does it supply a causal account of opinion; rather, it represents opinion within the perspective of opinion, for which the seeing of something as blue is indistinguishable from the opining of something as beautiful, just, or good (507b9–10). The seeing of things is the evaluation of things (508a1–3). The sun, therefore, though it points to the cave, does not acknowledge the cave. It represents a situation to which man has no immediate access. We always come into its light with opinions and surrounded by what we have made; but the sun shines on no artifacts and casts no shadows. It circumscribes a natural horizon that is invisible to man.

In reminding Glaucon of the distinction between the manifold of beautiful and good things and their unitary *ideai*, Socrates designates both as postulates; he says the former are seen and not intellected, while the latter are intellected and not seen (507b5–11). The coupling of sight with a manifold and of intellect with unity is prior to the introduction of the sun as the cause of sight. Light is established as the indispensable bond between color and sight without any indication of its source. Socrates' argument applies no less to the fire in the cave than to the sun (514b2); but the cave's fire cannot be literally understood. Although fire seems analogous to the sun—it supplies the heat by means of which the city makes its artifacts—the cave does not allow for this meaning; in the cave, the fire is analogous to the good—it supplies the fundamental perspective in light of which the prisoners understand all the shadows they see. The cave is closed to the distinction between nature and convention: Socrates calls the sun a god (508a4, 9). It seems, then, that the cave is the invisible envelope of the sun, which by itself corresponds to no human experience.

Socrates' pun on heaven (*ouranos*) and visible (*horatos*) is essential for the sun; but if "heaven" stands for cosmos, as it often does in Plato (*Timaeus* 28b2–4; *Statesman* 269d7–8), and includes earth, then the unity of heaven and earth is no longer visible and represents an insight that denies the very basis of sun and line. The sun thus introduces a distortion into Socrates' account that does not admit of any easy correction. Had Socrates not anticipated his use of the sun, he could have said that the manifold of beautiful and good things is opined and not intellected; but he then would not have been able to argue for something like light as the bond between things. It is not easy in any case to say what that bond might be, for if opinion is to things as hearing is to sounds, Socrates would have to deny that any third item is needed as a medium between them (507c10–d3). The difficulty in pinpointing the analogue to light for opinion reveals the pervasiveness of opinion whenever we express an opinion. The opinions we have about things are embedded in opinion. Socrates had remarked that we might choose the seemingly (*dokounta*) beautiful and just things if there were some good in those seemings for us; but we would never choose them if they did not not-seem to those from whom we expected some good. Others must see them as they seem without their ever saying, "It seems." The fusion of seeing and seeming that is characteristic of opinion has thus affected Socrates' account of the sun. Not only are there no shadows in the region over which the sun presides, but there are no appearances. It is always high noon and everything is right before us. It is timeless and does not admit of ascent.

Socrates deepens our perplexity about the sun when he comes to assign the elements of the visible region to their counterparts in the intelligible (508c4–d10):

Sun: The good or the *idea* of the good
Light: Truth and what is (*to on*)
Sight: Mind
Sight in daylight: Pure Mind
Sight in night lights: Dim Mind
Eye: Soul
Colors: *Ideai* ?
Visible Things: ?

The question marks for the last two items signify the obscurity in which Socrates leaves his account, for though he speaks fleetingly of colors as the colors of things (508c4–6), he does not make such a distinction in the case of the intelligible: "Whenever [soul] focuses on that which truth and being [what is] shed light, [soul] intellects and knows it and appears to have mind" (508d4–6). If "that which (*hou*)" were strictly parallel to colors, the *ideai* would be the *ideai* of the beings and not the beings themselves, and far from being separated entities they would be the classes to which things belong and in light of which they could be understood. Indeed, the word *idea* is used just prior to this passage interchangeably with *genos* to designate the class of light (507e6). Socrates, moreover, assigns to mind as to sight two states, for neither one of which is either mind or sight responsible. One can turn the soul to face being; but if the mind is then pure it is due to the presence of Truth, and to its absence if it is then dim; but in neither case does the mind have any control over its own state. It is always the same mind with the same capacity for being enlightened (508d2). Mind does not think or reason its way to a state of being enlightened.

As the sun is the source of daylight, so the good is the source of truth; but though Socrates speaks of night lights, he does not say what their source is. If the plural is distributive, he is referring to the stars and planets; if the plural is the collective of concreteness, he is pointing primarily to the moon (516a9–b2). In the latter case, he would imply that the sun is the indirect cause of whatever we see when our sight is dim; and since daylight is restricted arbitrarily to the seeing of colors, shapes would be what was visible in the moonlight. When, however, Socrates turns to soul, he says that soul opines whenever it turns to that which has been mixed with darkness, but he is silent about that which supplies the light in that darkness. Is there for the soul in the state of opinion something that reflects the Truth of the good? Such a reflective body can only be the fire in the cave: if the fire were not a reflective body but supplied its

160

own light from a source that was not even remotely connected with the good, then the cave would not be open to the light and the soul would not have the nature to divine that the good is something (cf. 516c1–2). The soul would then be perfectly satisfiable within the cave, and the opinions we have would not be the opinions of the beautiful, just, and good but of *x*, *y*, and *z* to which wholly equivocal names were attached. Whatever may be true of beautiful and just things and everything else we postulate, the soul's divination of the good is not hypothetical: It is incapable of being suspended and put in doubt. The good, then, must overarch both being and becoming, at least in the sense that the fully real intrudes into becoming through the soul's divination of the good. It supplies "the indispensable being of becoming" (*Statesman* 283d8–9).

If daylight and nightlight bear to one another the relation of sun to moon, then the good must supply the light of both Truth and opinion; and when it supplies the light of opinion, it must be below the human horizon and its light reach us by reflection. The variety and changeableness of opinion, or the manyness of opinion, shows that the truth of things becomes fragmented in its reflection, and nothing in opinion allows for its one-to-one-correspondence with anything in Truth. That virtue is one but seems to be four is an ever-recurring example in Plato of the general question whether the fragmentation of truth breaks up only into arbitrary bits and pieces, or whether there are not only shards which cannot be fitted into the whole of truth but natural breaks in opinion as well that allow for a rational articulation. The *Republic* is obviously a representation of the city as containing both kinds of elements. It therefore forces us to ask whether Truth is responsible for what we may call the natural conventions of the city, and if it is responsible how it is. The difficulty we have in answering this question is due directly to the absence of the *Republic* from the account Socrates now gives. The ascent from the cave is made without any use of the ascent of the *Republic*. Although the ascent of the *Republic* has alone made it possible for there to be a representation of its ascent, sun, line, and cave are blind to what made themselves possible. At the center of the *Republic* stands an account that is alien from its own setting. It pretends to be prior and is posterior to the discovery of political philosophy. It is the second sailing in the guise of a first sailing.

The exposition of the good by way of the sun gives to Truth a prominence it otherwise might not have had. As light binds sight to colors, Truth binds mind to being. Light, however, does not keep-sight and color apart; rather their separation comes from the distance between the sun and us. This distance, in turn, brings about a separation of heat and light, so that the sun no less brings things into being without burning them up than displays them in the light without blinding us. Since the good likewise makes the beings both be and be known, the good must be at a certain distance from them in order that, on the one hand, the beings be in themselves and not simply be swallowed up in the good as final cause, and, on the other, the beings be displayed before the mind and not overwhelm the mind in the brilliance of Truth. If the good, moreover, causes the beings to be while it itself is beyond being, a distance between mind and the beings is necessary if the beings too are not to cease to be in an Aristotelian contact of being and mind. (Aristotle *Metaphysics* 1051b17–30). Such a conclusion, which merely follows from drawing the consequences of the analogy, leads to two questions. What is the distance between mind and being that Truth unites? And what causes the distance between mind and being? The analogy with sunlight certainly allows for Truth to be the bond and not the separator; but if that which separates them were not Truth, then mind would know being in a perspective that would be inaccessible to it. Only if Truth both separates and binds can mind know being as being.

Being as being, however, has two meanings. It stands for both being and the truth of being. Being as being is being by itself; being as the truth of being is being as part of the intelligible whole. The condition, then, for the distance between mind and being must be the difference between the beings as they are in themselves and as they are as parts of the whole. Since Socrates later says that the sun must be figured out to be the cause of the things that come to be and come to light (516b9–c2), the good too must be figured out to be the cause of the being of the beings and of their being known; but since the beings cannot be known before the good is known (506a6–7), Truth does not light up the beings as they are in the light of Truth. Truth must distance the beings from their being parts of the whole. It must part the beings from the whole and keep them apart from each other and the whole; and only insofar as it keeps them apart does it bind them to mind. Truth, then, is the fragmenting light of opinion, and any ascent from opinion must be on the basis of what opinion discloses. It is the contradiction in the manifold of opinion from which one begins the ascent to the unity of the *idea*. The moonlight of Truth is all that can ever be available to us.

Since the phrase "light of the sun" is perfectly clear and its supposed parallel "Truth of the good" is not, Socrates seems to invite us to make good the parallel by taking Truth (*alētheia*) literally as a compound of the alpha-privative and *lēthē*, and *lēthē*, in turn, not in the sense of forgetfulness but as cognate with *lanthanein*, to escape the sight of or be latent. "Truth," then, would mean disclosure or discovery, and "Truth of the good" the disclosure of the good. The disclosure of the good would mean not only that Truth discloses the good (just as sunlight lights the sun) but also that the good discloses the beings, just as the sun lights up colors. The beings do not disclose themselves, but the good discloses them for mind in the element of Truth. The truth in whose light the beings are laid out does not direct the attention of the mind either to the cause of itself or to any one of the beings. Truth is totally transparent to mind and totally indifferent to the beings. Its indifference to what it discloses seems the price to be paid for its transparency. The good, then, is not manifest in the beings that the good discloses. It is the undisclosed ground of all that it discloses for thinking. Whether the beings are good is not disclosed with the disclosure of the beings. The disclosure of the beings hides something. It hides not only what causes the disclosure but the fact that the cause of the disclosure is the cause of the being of the beings (509b6–8). That which discloses and that which is disclosed are bound together in an undisclosed way. They are manifestly separate and secretly together. The disclosure of the beings, then, must be also the concealment of the beings, for the mind does not know through the disclosure of Truth that it is thinking the beings. Mind, therefore, is not thinking the beings when it is thinking the beings, and this is only possible, we have argued, if the beings are disclosed apart from what they are in the whole. So an even more literal translation of *alētheia* would seem to be necessary. Truth is not disclosure but disclosing, the being-in-the light of the latent. This manifesting of the immanifest is the Socratic question, What is (*tí esti*)?

Three things are sunlike (*hēlioeides*): light, sight, and eye, and of these the eye is the most sunlike (508b3). Three things are goodlike (*agathoeides*): truth, knowledge, and soul, and of these the soul is most goodlike. Inasmuch as Socrates is so insistent that no member of either triad is respectively the sun or the good, opinion—which Socrates had previously characterized as a dream state in which likeness and identity are equivalent—would be inclined to identify any one of either triad with respectively either the sun or the good. The soul, then, is not the good; it is not the cause of either the being of what is or the knowability of what is, anymore than the eye is the cause of color and the visibility of color. In the absence of any natural cosmology, we do not know whether the soul is either an alternative or a supplementary cause of becoming; and though the soul would then be the bond between being and becoming (as the receptor of one and the supplier of the other), the single link between coming into being and coming into the light would be broken.

However this may be, the soul in the present account is not causal. It most resembles existentially the good as the cause of the being of the beings in its awareness that the good must be real; but it is not as obvious how soul most resembles cognitively the good as the cause of the knowability of the beings. Since it seems impossible for the soul ever to obtain full knowledge of the beings, the resemblance cannot consist in any direct mapping of the beings onto soul. But since it also seems that the virtue of soul which makes for happiness does not depend on the attainment of full knowledge, there is in the soul a divergence between its virtue and its knowledge that does not hold for the coincidence of Truth and being in the intelligible. This divergence shows up in a Platonic dialogue as the finiteness of its action and the apparently endless perplexities to which it gives rise. The *Euthyphro* is complete not because the question, What is the holy?, is answered, but because Socrates persuades Euthyphro to give up the prosecution of his father. The wholeness of the dialogue is due to the achievement of that good; and the dialogue is beautiful insofar as its parts have been measured by that good to fit together in a whole. Now if we imagine the question of the dialogue to be no longer under the constraint of its action, the true perplexity would emerge as a perplexity for soul itself whose action would consist in the working out of that perplexity in light of all other true perplexities that the set of all dialogic actions would engender. The soul, then, would be most goodlike if the *ideai* in their totality had their image in a finite structure of finite perplexities in soul. Soul would thus be the eidetic structure of ignorance whose activity would be both endless and bounded.

So general a picture, however, of the cognitive and existential likeness of soul to the good tends to blur the essential difference between the universality of argument and the particularity of action. Since no science can direct the acquisition of science, not even the science of the good, it is never the case that any perplexity is ever wholly free from the perspective in which it first comes to light as a perplexity and makes it a matter of concern. It therefore seems to follow that the soul of any philosopher, no matter how varied his experiences of perplexity might be, would be related asymptotically to the eidetic structure of ignorance which is soul, and without a natural cosmology it is impossible to say how such an asymptotic relation is to be understood. The soul is not a construction as the city in speech is, for it is more certain that it is than that the city in speech can ever come to be; but it still could be the case that the bearing of the city in speech to any actual city is not unlike that between soul, as it emerges in the sun-image, to, for example, the soul of Socrates. Under the inspiration of the Muses, Socrates will later propose that every city is a degenerate version of the good city; but since there cannot be an "idea" of soul as that which is always itself in never being itself,[1] it is not obvious how the variety of defective souls is related to soul. That the structure of the city and the structure of the soul are parallel to one another may be taken in any case as expressing this problem without solving it.

Line links sun and cave. Insofar as the line itself is a mathematical construction, and Socrates discusses at the greatest length the procedures and hypotheses of mathematicians, the link between the natural horizon of the beings in themselves and the human horizon of educational experience seems to be mathematics. That link is unknown to the line, for not only does it precede the cave, but there is no suggestion that the mathematicians are aware of the cave, or, if they are aware of it, that it would affect their mathematics. An illusion is built into the sequence of sun, line, and cave that one has to dispel if the misleading position of the line is to be discounted. The division between Books VI and VII, which separates sun and line from cave, is a fortunate reminder of the fact that Socrates offers the line from the start as a continuation of his account of the good, but the cave gets tied in with them only after it has been given by itself. Socrates, indeed, after insisting that mathematics alone drags the soul away from becoming to being, denies that mathematics does more than dream about being (533b6–c3); but to dream, according to Socrates, is to mistake likeness for identity, and such a mistake is characteristic of opinion. The line is surely more sober than the sun, which led to

---

1. This is the minimal meaning for the definition of soul as self-motion.

Glaucon's funny outburst (509c1–2), but its precision may be a more insidious form of obscurity. The order of number may not match exactly the order of things.

The translation of sun into line requires that three dimensions be represented in one dimension. The linearity of the fourfold experience (*pathē*) of soul does not allow for either the sun or the good to show up on the line. The soul of the line is without depth: It is the soul without the divination of the good. The hypotheses and constructions of mathematics suspend the good. On the line the soul is present only in the section of trust, which includes "the animals around us (*ta peri hēmas zoia*)", every kind of plant, and the entire class of artifacts (510a5–6); but the soul vanishes everywhere else. In neither section of the higher part of the line does soul think soul. The line precludes self-knowledge. It is not just the soul, however, that the line devalues, so that it no longer most resembles the good, but Truth too undergoes a comparable devaluation. Clarity (*saphēneia*) takes over from Truth (509d9, 510a9, 511a7, 511e2–4). Clarity makes us surreptitiously the standard; it is the subjective side of Truth. Mathematicians believe it is not worthwhile to give an account of the things they postulate, "on the grounds that they are evident (*phanera*) to everyone" (510d1). The human informs the line, but the human is not accessible through the line. The sun did not illuminate everything within the human horizon, for as the cause of becoming, nurture, and growth, the artifices of man were not subject to its light. On the line, however, the drawing (*graphein*) and molding (*plattein*) of mathematicians are indispensable (510e1–2, 527a6–b1). Their constructions determine what it means for something to lack clarity. Lack of clarity is assigned to the section Socrates calls imaging (*eikasia*). It is not the same as the region over which in the sun-image the night lights cast their dim glow. The difference between day and night is lost on the line; it is replaced by a difference that, if Socrates' list is complete, allows the sun to show up not as itself but only in its reflections in water and mirrors. Things and their shadows and images belong together under the sun; but the line separates them as if it were an accident that things are always somewhere, but they could be as placeless as triangles and squares. The line gives a spurious version of the possible truth that not everything that is is in place (*Timaeus* 52b3–5). The sharp distinction between the visible and the intelligible, with which Socrates began, left unclarified the relation of heaven and earth, whether they do or do not constitute a cosmos; and this unclarity has affected in turn the line, so that its

standard of clarity must be without any natural orientation and indistinguishable from the precision of mathematics.

Socrates identifies the sections of the line most peculiarly. He
does not start with trust but with imaging. Shadows and reflections
are distinguished before the naming of what reflects and casts
shadows. The domain of trust (*pistis*) is first that which the domain
of imaging images (510a5, 10). The ratios of the cuts in the line grant
to trust the same degree of clarity to imaging (*eikasia*) proportion-
ally as intellection (*noēsis*) has to thought (*dianoia*) (510a8–9); but
trust is so trustworthy that it is immune to thought. That the things in
its domain are, is so certain that the questions of what they are and
how they are cannot presumably arise; but since in fact they do arise,
and for no one more than Socrates, it must be solely in the
perspective of the line that the human horizon is as certain
cognitively as it is existentially. The reasoning possible within trust
has been arbitrarily denied through the false assimilation of opinion
to sight (509d3, 510a9). Such an assimilation, which the cave as an
image represents, is possible only within the cave. The line therefore
precedes the distinction between nature and convention; it precedes
philosophy, the absence of which term from sun, line, and cave has
already been noted. The trust assigned to the human horizon seems
to entail that imaging means no more than distrust and doubt. "I can't
quite make it out" and "It looks like a tree" seem to be the kinds of
utterances Socrates is thinking of (*Philebus* 38c5–10). For us, of
course, who have read the *Sophist*, it is all too easy to assume that the
problem of being lurks in this cut of the doxastic. But it only lurks
there, and that is its significance: the line jumps over the perplexities
within the doxastic in order to make it plausible that thought can stay
entirely within the intelligible. Once it is granted that thought must
begin in the lower part of the line, the possibility that thought in its
ascent could ever cut itself off from it vanishes. The only evidence for
this, however, within the construction of the line, consists in the
well-known fact that Socrates' demand that the upper and lower
sections be cut in the same ratio as the line as a whole was cut leads
to the equality of the two central sections, trust and thought. Socrates'
silence about this equality is of the same order as his silence about
the problem of being that the nonbeing of image raises.

Socrates proceeds to cut the intelligible in a way which conforms with the primacy he had assigned to imaging over trust in
cutting the doxastic. Glaucon does not understand. Socrates says the
cut is made at the point "where soul, in using as images the things

then imitated, is compelled to investigate one section of the intelligible by proceeding not to a beginning but from hypotheses to an end or conclusion" (510b4–6; cf. 511a7–8). Thought, then, looks at the section of trust only as a source of images and, without any knowledge that the things of trust are images, proceeds to treat them as if they are images. Poets, of course, do this all the time, either when they liken one thing to another within trust—"My heart is like an anvil unto sorrow"—or when they liken something within trust to something outside the experience of the senses—"That beats upon it like the Cyclops' hammer." Marlowe's lines well illustrate how opinion collapses opinion and sight; but it is surprising that the same practice should be ascribed to mathematicians. Since nothing initially seems to suggest that Socrates is thinking of solid geometry, it is not obvious why thought should start with the things of trust and not with the already available two-dimensional shadows and reflections of imaging. Thought seems to duplicate the natural power of light to image insofar as it represents to itself what has come to be, whether by nature or by art, as having come to be through what it thinks. Socrates later says, however, that among the shadows and images in water are the artifacts drawn and molded by the mathematicians, and it is these they use as images (510e1–3). So Socrates is thinking of solid as well as plane geometrical models; but then his first description of the dianoetic section is misleading, for the phrase "the things then imitated" (510b4) would not refer to the entire range of trust but only to those things the mathematicians themselves have made and not to men, animals, and plants. Such a restriction would be in accordance with the ordinary meaning of the word imitation (*mimeisthai*); but it would be tantamount to denying to thought any access to the truth about things not of its own making. Is it possible, then, that everything within the range of trust is to be understood as an artifact? Socrates did speak of the craftsman (*dēmiourgos*) of the senses, and how lavish he had been in his making of the power of seeing and being seen (507c6–8). We also know that only if an art could replicate human beings would the structural defects of Socrates' city in speech be eliminable, and that in Book X a god makes the unique paradigm of couch and table. Thought, then, either uses as images only the visible models it itself makes or, since everything that either becomes or is has been made, thought can confidently use anything visible as an image. Nothing, however, in the passage requires the latter view, and it is certainly safer to accept the narrower interpretation. The other possibility seems to be due simply to Socrates' presenting thought in light of the doxastic before he explains to Glaucon that the things it treats as images in the domain of trust are what it itself has put there.

Socrates divides his first account of thought into an account of hypothesis and an account of construction. The postulates of calculation and geometry include odd and even, figures, and the three species (*eidē*) of angles; and the constructions are the seen species (*eidē*) thought itself makes. Since the seen has already been identified with the opined, the square the mathematicians draw is something opined to be a square; and though they may speak about it, they do not think (*dianoeisthai*) about it but about that which the square images, for they make their speeches for the sake of the square itself (510d5–8). Thought speaks of the square it has drawn on the basis of its own postulation of squareness. Thought is the imagination of intention. It separates what it is talking about from what it is thinking about. It separates speaking from thinking without giving any thought to the separation. It thinks of the visible as imaging the thought as if the way in which water reflects a tree is the way in which a drawn figure reflects a thought figure. The mathematicians fail to notice that the resemblance is itself a postulate, for a drawn square resembles an infinite-sided polygon as much as it resembles the square itself: "square" is merely its label. Socrates brings this out in two ways. He uses the verb "to be" in his description of thought only once, when he says of its constructions that their shadows and images *are* (510e3); and he says of the mathematicians that they seek to *see* those very things which one could not *see* by any other means than by thought (511a1).

There seems to be a kind of willfulness in thought that recalls Thrasymachus' rejection of ordinary speech in favor of a precision that left reality behind. The implicit modelmaking in Thrasymachus' notion of regimes, each one of which was in strict conformity with its ruling element, seems to have its counterpart in mathematical hypothesization, which desubstantializes the domain of trust in order to treat it as an imaging of its own unquestioned hypotheses (511a6–8). Socrates' own city in speech was built on the basis of Thrasymachean and non-Thrasymachean elements. Insofar as the city was nothing but the city of arts, with its guardians too being the precision craftsmen of freedom, the city received a perfection comparable to that of a painting of the most beautiful human being whose possible existence was irrelevant. But insofar as the city in speech was shadowed by the dialogic city, there was a continual

169

correction of the hypothetical precision of the city in speech, and this most clearly showed up in the differences between the education of Glaucon and Adimantus and the education proposed for the city in speech. That difference recurs on the line in an idealized form as that which distinguishes thought from intellection (*noēsis*). Although the city in speech exemplifies perfectly an object of the intentional imagination, the dialogic city falls far short of the dialectic power of intellect. There is a break in the line that the line represents as a continuum between thought and intellect. The cave is the representation of that considerable break in the line. The cave brings the line closer to the way of the *Republic* itself.

There is both a shorter and a longer account of intellection; but the longer account is far shorter than the longer account of thought (511b3–c2). In neither account does Socrates say that the species of intellection are, but Glaucon, in interpreting what Socrates says, speaks in terms of being (511c4, 5, d2). Glaucon sees that the task of dialectic is immense, but he does not doubt that it is possible, for he never reflects on the relation between the dialogic city and dialectic. The word "dialectic" is from the verb to converse (*dialegesthai*); it seems to designate the conjunction of the speechmaking (*logous poieisthai*) and the thinking (*dianoeisthai*) that thought itself had separated. Dialectic does not start from the beginning, which can only be hypothetical, but starts from where we are. It starts from what are in reality or literally (*toi onti*) suppositions or hypotheses (511b5). These suppositions can only be the things of trust from which the constructions or images of trust have either been subtracted or regarded as nothing more than opinions (510b7–8). The suppositions of thought are the manifold of opinion treated as opinion and not its hypothesized replacements. That mathematical postulates are self-evident and consistent is their attraction; but that opinions are obscure and self-contradictory makes them the true starting-point for philosophy. The species of courage and moderation and their relation to virtue, and the species of man and woman and their relation to human being, are obviously possible topics of the dialectic Socrates sketches here; but the inconclusive way in which the *Republic* has dealt with them in the course of seeking after the single species of justice makes one realize the extent of the difference between the first steps of dialectic and the completeness Socrates envisages, in which each part of the whole would not alter in light of our interest. The *Republic* has certainly advanced up to the principle of the whole, but not without images; and it will soon descend from it and come back to justice, but its descent too will involve images and leave much in the dark. We have a measure of the difference between the *Republic* and the movement of *logos* itself when we consider that Socrates will prove to Glaucon that the just man is happy without ever showing him even his opinion of the good (533a1–7). Glaucon will be satisfied before it is reasonable for him to be convinced that the rulers of the city he helped to found can know what Socrates says is indispensable if they are to rule. The good for Glaucon is as fragmentary as his understanding, but all the same it is complete. It is this notion of the good as good for something that is missing from Socrates' description of intellection. It is *logos* without soul that moves so easily from start to finish.

Each of the three images of sun, line, and cave differs as an image. The structure of the sun is likened to the structure of the good; but it is not claimed to be a natural likeness, so that whatever shows up in the sunlight has its intelligible counterpart in the Truth. The unresolved ambiguity of "heaven" precludes it. As for the structure of the line, though it is said to match the fourfold experience of soul (511d7), it assumes the competence of geometrical proportion to represent what it itself admits is beyond its competence to represent. Thought postulates the unpostulated and extrapolates the highest section of the line. It simply assumes that as imaging is to trust, so it itself must be to something else; but dialectic might well consider thought to be an interpolation between itself and trust. The cave, however, is a 'normal' image, however strange Glaucon might find it (515a4). Socrates first makes up a picture that Glaucon is to look at and then tells him the prisoners are "like us." The situation in which we are from childhood is re-presented to us. Its strangeness consists in the fact that no shadow on the wall does not have its source in us. Our waking life is a dream, and everything is inside our heads. There are no gods behind the parapet but only the human beings who carry implements of every kind and shape, statues of men (*andriantes*), stone and wooden animals, and all sorts of artifacts (514b8–515a1). The cave thus represents the city as if the noble lie had succeeded completely, and nothing was even dreamt that was not a shadow of an artful contrivance; but it differs from the noble lie in its not being noble but a representation of the implicit intention of every system of convention to block out everything that it itself has not stamped and admitted into the city. If the dog is there, it is domesticated; if the bird is there, it is a bird of omen; if the tree is there, it is holy; and if man himself is there, he is unknown.

171

Socrates goes out of his way to have the prisoners cast stationary shadows of themselves on the wall while they watch moving shadows of images of themselves (515a5–8). In the wholly human world man is the self-ignorant measure of all things: only he and his shadow always remain unchanged. The cave is thus the representation of the intentional imagination of thought, which represents what it itself has postulated. Socrates' true city now returns in a modified form. It is enveloped by the mathematical sciences that support the productive arts with the addition of imitative arts as the conveyors of the city's authoritative opinions. Law and art have been united to keep out nature. The figures of the mathematicians, as they show up on the wall, are of the same order as the shadows of any other artifact. They are both twice removed from reality.

A distant fire burns high up and behind the prisoners (514b2–3). Since the artifacts behind the parapet are nearer the fire, their shadows are always larger than the shadows of the prisoners themselves. Their greater size suggests that the human beings who carry them are the ancestors: "They were giants in those days." The ancestors would be as human as the prisoners; and the non-existence of divine legislation would conform with Socrates' theology. The depth of the cave would thus be a temporal dimension; but the ascent from the cave seems to be entirely spatial. There is no suggestion that an archaeology of the city would be necessary in order to leave the cave. The ascent from the cave is not through the cave. The released prisoner does not stop to question the puppeteers who are on the far side of the wall. The wall of the cave does not stand in the way of his ascent, but magically vanishes along with the puppeteers. The ascent from the cave bypasses the *Republic*. It thus represents a pre-Socratic version of philosophy, for which it is still possible to look directly at the beings without any recourse to speeches. Socrates represents the experience of ascent but he does not represent the way of ascent and therefore not even the experience of ascent. Though Socrates imagines that someone is outside the cave who questions the ex-prisoner and drags him out and up to the sunlight, the image does not allow for their conversation to be an element in the ascent itself. When the caveman emerges, he sees phantoms of men in the water, but he does not talk to their originals (516a7).

The sole mention of conversations occurs among the prisoners of the cave (515b4). In these conversations, whatever they see they hold (*nomizein*) as the beings (515b4–5). The identification of shadows of artifacts with reality is sandwiched in between two remarks that apparently do not bear on it. The first remark is that some of those who carry the artifacts are speaking and some are silent (515a2–3), and the second that the wall of the cave echoes the utterances of those who are speaking, and the prisoners believe each passing shadow is the speaker (515b7–9). There seems to be no necessary correlation between the series of echoes and silences and the series of shadows and lit areas. Nothing compels us to believe that the carriers are addressing their remarks to the prisoners rather than to one another, for if they were and were thus to be interpreted as the founders and legislators by design of the city, the silence of some would be inexplicable. We must imagine, then, that on occasion the carrier of an image of a tree or of a dove is talking, and the prisoners believe they hear oracular noises from the shadows of these objects, which some among them claim to be able to interpret (cf. 515b10). In general, then, the speeches of the carriers do not necessarily have anything to do with the artifacts they carry. The sequence of shadows and the sequence of sounds could be out of phase, and whatever opinions the prisoners form would thus arise from the haphazard identification of shadows with sounds. Unreal subjects would be tied in with real predicates: "Aphrodite is beautiful" and "Zeus is just."

The second sailing of Socrates starts precisely from the arbitrariness of speeches in the cave, and the realization that it is possible to examine the predicates without the subjects.[2] The predicates are forms of the good, and the good is not hypothetical. The pre-Socratic philosopher, however, rushes past the speeches of the city and claims to know directly the true originals from which the artifacts have been copied. He believes it is easy to discriminate between Zeus and man, for man is not himself a question. The pre-Socratic is like Oedipus: he knows that the solution to the riddle is man but not that the solution is enigmatic. Both the pre-Socratic philosopher and the Socratic philosopher begin in the same way. There is no disagreement between them about the need to distinguish between nature and convention and that this involves a general denial of any reality to the highest beings of the city. To make a cut between these subjects and their predicates is common to both the pre-Socratic and Socratic philosopher; but the former dismisses the predicates as so much babble—their inappropriateness to their subjects is self-

2. Maimonides' *Guide* begins with a procedure very similar to this.

evident—and believes he can replace the subjects with their true originals. Not Oceanus and Tethys are the origin of all things but water; not Ares and Aphrodite are the efficient causes of everything but strife and love. The city has mislabeled the beings, it has not misidentified them (515c9–d1). When the ex-prisoner returns to the cave, he needs some time to adjust to the indistinctness and irregular succession of the things he saw above in all their vividness and uniformity, but they are fundamentally the same things.

On Socrates' last day in prison, after the officials had removed his chains, he bent his leg and rubbed it with his hand, and as he rubbed it, he said:

> How strange, men, does this seem to be which men call pleasant. How wondrously is it naturally related to that which is in opinion its contrary, the painful, the fact that though the pair of them is unwilling to be present together in the human being, still, if one pursues one and gets it, he is pretty nearly compelled on every occasion to take the other too, just as if the pair of them has been attached from one head. And it's my opinion, if Aesop had realized this, he would have composed a story [*muthos*] how the god, wanting to reconcile them in their warfare, after he failed to be able to do so, joined their heads together into the same, and it's on account of this that to whomever one of them is present the other follows afterwards. (*Phaedo* 60b3–c5)

Socrates gives two accounts of his own experience. The first is descriptive and registers a perplexity; the second is mythical and assigns a cause. The first brings together nature and opinion; the second is necessarily hypothetical—it appeals to the highest principle—and yet assumes what holds for opinion to be true. Pleasure and pain are for the second account originally two separate heads that have been subsequently brought together; in the first account they are always together and there is only one head. The causal account, which is ultimately mechanical, presupposes a teleology that failed: whatever is, is a falling away from a perfect model. The first account proposes to replace the opinion of pleasure and pain with the species, and in the species to discover the cause. The first account begins with the echoes of the cave. It is through and through Socratic; but as the *Republic* shows, the first account needs the second way as well. The dialogic city cannot come to be unless its participants make the city in speech; and the ascent from the cave must begin with the attempt to recover the beings that are in truth before the descent can become possible. The turnaround to face the cave must follow the turnaround away from the cave. This double turn Socrates calls on occasion *muthologein* or the speaking of myth (376d9; *Phaedo* 61e2). It is his name for the unavoidable impurity of dialectic (*Theaetetus* 196d7–197a4).

Socrates does not speak of the pleasure that would accompany the release of the prisoner from his chains, but only of the pain he would suffer in standing up, turning his neck around, and walking up to see the light (515c7–8). His release is under compulsion. The painfulness of the ascent points to the recovery of the body. On one's ascent the artifacts in themselves are shown, and one is puzzled to say, when forced to answer, what they severally are (515d4–5). Socrates does not say that it is the discovery of their solidity that is the decisive experience for determining the greater truth of what lies outside the cave. The line dropped two dimensions from the sun, and though the standing, turning, and ascending are all corporeal, the image of the sun, under whose dominance both line and cave are, does not allow Socrates to give enough weight to the decorporealization of everything within the cave. The city, which has its origin in the cooperative satisfaction of the needs of the body, turns out to be nothing but shadows. Through Glaucon's rejection of the city of pigs, the soul by itself took over from the individual unity of body and soul which initially the city was intended to image (369a1–3). The ex-prisoner understands at last that the city is Hades, where there are only ghostlike bodies called souls (516d5–6, 521c2–3). That to be means to be body is the necessary first step out of the cave. This is the truth in the false claim that the healthy city is true; but the etiolation of the body is the false response of the city to the divination of soul. The city passes off an image of body as soul (518d9–10). Philosophy in its first ascent detects the fraudulence of that simulacrum; but it does not detect its truth and denies being to everything it cannot lay its hands on (*Sophist* 247c3–7). Its horror of unreality begs the question of the goodness of the real that the denizens of the cave, Glaucon and Adimantus, are at least aware of. The soul can only be recovered by a descent.

If we on our own were to put together sun, line, and cave in a single picture, it would look like that reflected in figure 12. Yet Socrates tells Glaucon that sun, line, and cave are to be

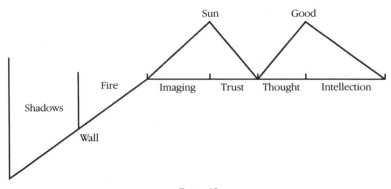

FIGURE 12

superimposed on one another (517a8–b6), as reflected in figure 13. Such a superimposition, however, is difficult to interpret, for in

Sun and Moon

Imaging	Trust	Thought	Intellection

Fire   Good

FIGURE 13

the ascent from cave to sun, there is no place for thought. Once one leaves the cave, one first sees most easily shadows and then phantoms in water, afterwards the sky at night, and only then the sun itself in its own place (516a6–b7). Mathematics and its visible constructions along with its intentional objects have vanished, for the city in which the arts are perfected has vanished too. The difference between the natural and the conventional horizon is ignored, and becoming and making are identified. Socrates, it seems, wanted to indicate that the mathematicians are prisoners too, and their constructions and theorems duplicate the cave and do not transcend it. Although Socrates goes out of his way to insert solid geometry into the series of mathematical sciences, it is the only science for which he does not claim any special power to advance the soul closer to being. There is nothing less solid than the solids of solid geometry.[3]

In order to make sun, line, and cave cohere, a different kind of superimposition would seem to be necessary, in which the two

3. Cf. J. Klein, *Commentary on Plato's Meno* (Chapel Hill 1965), 65.

sections of the cave (in front of and behind the wall), the two sections of the doxastic, and the two sections of the intelligible part of the line are only diagrammatically separable, as seen in figure 14. In fact,

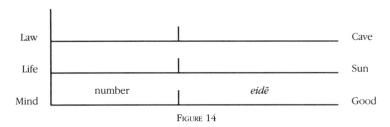

FIGURE 14

however, we live in all three orders at once, and the distinctness that the line has extended from itself onto sun and cave would have to yield to the partial penetration of sun and good into the cave and the partial penetration of good into sun. The genetic and the eidetic would have to be thought together (517c1–4). It would thus be impossible in principle to know prior to reflection in what and in what form the truly intelligible shows up in the cave or in the sun. The radical difference between an automatic recognition of the beings and a reasoned conclusion about cause could no longer be maintained (516b4–c2). Thinking is present throughout the entire range of the line. The order of discovery and the order of being would not necessarily be in an inverse proportion to one another, so that the most remote from us would have to be the closest to what is. The conspicuous might well be the invisible. Oedipus' name designates simultaneously the swollen feet from his infant bonds (*oidai pous*) and the knowledge of orientation (*oide pou* or "know where"). They belong together by nature and are only tragically apart.

30

ASCENT AND DESCENT

(516c4–521b11)

The disorientation that the ex-prisoner experiences on his ascent does not differ from the disorientation he would experience on his descent. In both cases he would not be able to make out what was there to be seen. The indifference experientially of the difference would seem to require a double turnaround, so that one does not confuse blinking in the dark with the blinding of the light (*Sophist* 253e8–254b1). In Socrates' account this is not a difficulty, for he assumes the completion of the ascent before the return. Socrates thereby seems to imply that what the Cavemen say while the ex-prisoner is still bewildered among them—"He lost his sight when he went up and it's not worthwhile to try to go up" (517a3–4)—would be irrefutable unless there was a guarantee of success. A partial ascent from the cave cannot be justified in the cave. Just as Glaucon and Adimantus believed the city in speech was not worthwhile unless it could come into being, philosophy is made to conform to the self-proclaimed success of the city, and, if the philosopher is always ridiculed in his ignorance, he is condemned before the dogmatic wisdom of the city. No philosopher as such, Socrates implies, should ever risk his life in attempting to free and lead the Cavemen up, for, should they ever get their hands on the perfectly wise, they would kill him (517a5–6). The Cavemen are the prisoners of the wise; only if their hands were tied would he venture to return. The coincidence of wisdom and power is the nightmare that lay hidden in Socrates' counterexample to Cephalus; but the coincidence of philosophy and power is ridiculous.

A version of that coincidence is the dialogic city, and for the first and only time Socrates tells Glaucon what he has had to undergo at its hands. Imagine, he says, the ex-prisoner during the time of his readjustment to the cave, "compelled to compete in lawcourts or somewhere else about the shadows of the just or statues of which the shadows are" (517d8–9). The phrase "statues of which the shadows are" can refer only to one of the artifacts behind the parapet, all of which are presumably invisible to the prisoners. This statue of justice can only be Glaucon's perfectly just man, whose statue, Socrates said, Glaucon had polished so vigorously for the comparison-test (361d4–6). It was Glaucon, then, who, in his objection to Socrates' refutation of Thrasymachus, had stopped in his ascent from the cave at the artifacts outside the wall and mistaken them for the real and his own liberation as complete. Glaucon had taken the prevailing opinion about justice and brought it to the highest degree of Thrasymachean precision. He claimed that it was an image of justice itself and asked Socrates to dispute about that intentional image as if it were the real thing. Glaucon had presented the impossible as an image of the truly real, and Socrates was to prove that a lifeless being was happy and the wholly imaginary was good. It has taken this long to bring Glaucon up to see behind him the city. Glaucon admits that he had forgotten it (520a5).

Glaucon's failure to remember the cave after his ascent from it makes that ascent seem to be nothing more than a habituation to another environment and not to differ in kind from political indoctrination. To be enlightened is to be brainwashed. Socrates therefore must distinguish indoctrination from what he calls conversion (*periagōgē*). The cave is a place of constraint because the soul is as naturally "agathotropic" as the eye is heliotropic. It is against the grain for the soul to be treated as if it had any need of habits, or as if there were something like the doing of philosophy without philosophizing. One becomes just by acting justly. There are no conditions in which the soul automatically becomes just. Communism is an illusory version of Truth in whose presence the soul knows. One does not become wise by acting wisely. There is no manner of thinking that induces thinking. To go through the motions does not end up in the initiation of the motion. To philosophize is not to emulate a philosopher. Habituation is gradual and incremental; there is never any bewilderment or blinking on the way to habit; but philosophy is impossible without bewilderment, for it begins in wonder and stays informed by wonder. There is no science of wonder. Socrates speaks of the conversion of the whole soul in order to express the completeness of the break with the familiar (518c8). Philosophy is characterized by "breakthroughs." The way of ascent is abrupt (515e7). It is the practice of dying and being dead.

We now have a paradox. Socrates' education of Glaucon could not be more different from such an ascent. The *Republic* works so smoothly that even what seem at first like breaks are reinterpreted to restore a specious seamlessness. What severally distinguishes sun from line, and both from cave, seems to represent the kind of break that signals the possibility of a philosophic conversion; but Socrates papers over their differences and pretends that the three images fit perfectly together. His harmonization of them culminates in his denial that to force the philosopher to descend would be unjust. His descent presupposes not only that a complete ascent is possible, but that the cave makes possible a complete ascent. Wisdom is an idol of the cave. No sooner does Socrates set up the proportion that as cave is to sunlight so habituation is to conversion than he turns around and asserts that the good city in deed is a privileged cave, in which an institution of its own devising exists that helps the best prisoners to escape from the cave. The institution cannot be private, for then those who believe they are living on the isles of the blest might have an obligation to the institution but certainly not to the city. If the permission or indifference of the city, on account of which the institution exists, were enough to create an obligation to the city, then only the philosopher who was born and lived outside society would be without any obligations. Not even if the philosopher-king picked out someone with a good nature and turned him to philosophy, would an obligation exist. The philosopher-king would have to be acting not only with the willingness and support of the regime, but he would have to be acting as king and not as philosopher. "Philosopher-king" rejects in its very formulation the principle of one man / one job. If Socrates' own definition of justice is to hold, regardless of whether it is in the strict or loose sense of minding one's own business, Socrates cannot but be proposing that they be unjust to the philosopher. The violation of right is the foundation of all political right. The philosopher's descent into the cave is a debt he owes to the city; but it was Cephalus who defined justice in terms of paying one's debts.

The *Republic* exemplifies the ascent of philosophy in the element of political habituation. Socrates gets Glaucon used to philosophy without any conversion to philosophy. He reproduces in him the forced union of philosopher and king. Not only does Socrates have to admit, however, that to comply with justice is to be unhappy (520e4–521a4), but he has to justify the philosopher's compliance in language that betrays the spuriousness of his argument. Socrates says that it is "our task" to compel the best natures to ascend and descend (519c8–d7). And when Glaucon asks in surprise, "Shall we not be doing them an injustice?" (519d8), Socrates launches into a speech in which he tells the philosophers: "We generated you as guardians and kings for yourselves and the rest of the city, having been educated better and more perfectly than the Cavemen and more capable of sharing in both tasks" (520b5–c1). But Socrates has done no such thing. He has suggested that the best natures should be given the best education, but he has certainly not educated anyone even in the dialogic city to the degree of competence necessary to assume the rule of the city. His defense of the city's justice precedes any proposal of his own as to what a city-sponsored philosophical education would consist in. Why, then, does not Socrates let the philosopher go free? By arguing for the justice of the philosopher's descent on grounds that contradict the truth about justice, Socrates startles us into this realization: no one has a nature designed to rule in the city. Some are born to be farmers and others to be blacksmiths, but though some are born to the purple, no one is born to rule. All political rule is derivative from and parasitic on the natural rule of soul over body and of mind over soul; but the nature in which such rule is best realized is a nature geared solely to philosophy, and only if the impossible were not impossible would it be right to divert that nature from what is by nature right. The city in which there was no ruling element Socrates called the true city.

31

MATHEMATICS AND DIALECTICS

(521c1–541b5)

The sequence that Socrates establishes for the mathematical sciences—arithmetic, plane geometry, solid geometry, kinematics, and harmonics—is not a sequence of ascent. Harmonics is not closer to either being or the good than arithmetic. This sequence, moreover, is not the same as their dialogic sequence, in which astronomy first follows plane geometry and then, after solid geometry is inserted, is itself eliminated and replaced by kinematics. The correct sequence is arrived at through two errors: the first is Socrates', who corrects his mistake after he has rebuked Glaucon for his popular defense of astronomy (527d5–528a8); the second is Glaucon's, whom Socrates rebukes again for identifying spatial "down" with becoming and spatial "up" with being (528e6–529c4). These corrections illustrate dialectics and bear to mathematical education the same relation that the dialogic city does to the city in speech. The good shows up not in solid geometry but in Socrates' urging Glaucon to think of himself first when he defends astronomy; and the kinematics that is genuinely dialectical is in Socrates' remark that in his eagerness to go through everything swiftly he slowed himself down (528d7–8). It is, then, in the arguments for mathematics rather than in mathematics itself that the ascent of dialectics is to be found, for the consequence of the established sequence of mathematical sciences is to make all of them possible in the cave. Not only does the future development of solid geometry depend on the city's support, but the replacement of astronomy by kinematics allows for the mathematicians to study the motions of solids while they are prisoners and stay undistracted by the imprecise reality of planets and stars. Thrasymachean precision culminates in mathematics, which like Thrasymachus' own chrematistic art antedates the distinction between nature and convention. That distinction, Socrates admits, has been always experienced as vehemently as would be the discovery of one's own illegitimacy (537e1–539a4); and there is nothing in mathematics as such that would ease the shock.

All the arts of the city make use of number. Agamemnon, the general, is ridiculous when tragedy ascribes to Palamedes the discovery of number and order, and presents Agamemnon as ignorant of the number of his armada as of his own feet. Glaucon goes even farther: one cannot even be a human being unless one can count and calculate (522e3–4). Tragic poetry, it seems, does not locate the human in either the city or rationality. It focuses on what is pre-Promethean and pre-political in man. The ancient quarrel between poetry and philosophy turns on this issue as to where the human is to be located. If mathematics contributes something to the understanding of the beings and the good, it is through the reflection it forces on what it means to be human. Political philosophy must side, at least initially, with mathematics over against poetry: at the heart of Socrates' true city was a perfection of the arts that mathematics alone could make possible. The coupling of the warrior and the philosopher through the knowledge of number represents as dramatically as possible the monstrous character of political philosophy, for which there cannot be any ascent without descent (525c4–6). It is easy enough to kill the enemy if they are ciphers (*arithmos*) and nothing counts but the bodycount.

Socrates' argument for the periagogic power of number begins with a misunderstanding on Glaucon's part. Socrates distinguishes between two elements in perception, those that do not invite intellection to further examination on the grounds that perception has adequately judged them, and those that urgently encourage it to further examination on the grounds that perception is doing nothing sound. Glaucon believes that Socrates' second group includes those things that appear far away and paintings that employ shadows to represent depth (523a10–b6). It is perfectly clear to Glaucon that Socrates refers to them. Since Socrates has something else in mind, his distinction is not perfectly clear and, in failing to take Glaucon's perspective into account, exemplifies what Glaucon thinks he means. Glaucon's distinction cannot hold for the prisoners of the cave, for the distance between themselves and the shadows is fixed and they have no knowledge of the third dimension. Socrates' distinction, on the other hand, can be drawn within the cave; indeed, Glaucon has only to imagine (*dianoou*) three fingers seen up close, while Socrates is speaking, and he does not have to see them at all. "Each of them," Socrates says, "appears surely as a finger, and it makes no difference whether it is seen in the middle or on either end, whether white or black, whether thick or thin, and anything of the sort; for in all these cases the soul of the many is not compelled to ask the intellect what finger is, for sight was at no point indicating to intellect simultaneously the finger to be the contrary of finger (523b11–d6)."

Socrates does not deny that the Socratic question, "What is?," may be no less applicable to the finger than to the beautiful, the just, and the good; but he implies that thought awakens automatically in everyone when it is confronted with a contradiction in what perception reports about any kind of magnitude (523e3–524a10). If Socrates is referring to relative magnitude, it is remarkable that throughout the discussion not one comparative adjective is employed;[1] nor is it any easier to understand why sight can be said to recognize short and long and yet fail to see shorter and longer. Socrates had previously restricted sight to color, but now he supposedly enlarges its power to include the knowledge of absolute size. Perhaps one can imagine sight abbreviating its report to, "The finger is short," but not if it cannot also expand it to, "This finger is short relative to that finger." Thought is not puzzled by the contrariety of the predicates but by the identity of the subject. It is the indifference of sight to the difference between a long and a short finger that provokes thought. For sight, each finger is a finger regardless of its predicate; but thought cannot allow the same thing, namely finger, to be both short and long unless short and long are not two but one. Thought denies coherence to any class that consists

---

1. *Phaedo* 102b3–6, which introduces an apparently similar argument, shows that that argument is different.

of members that admit of contrary predicates. Agamemnon would have to have two left feet to satisfy thought, for how else could a foot be both right and left? That we see the same thing simultaneously as both one and many is too much for thought (525a4–5); and thought resolves the difficulty through separating the one and the many. Such a separation makes number possible, where the many of the number belongs solely to the ones in their togetherness and not to each one in their separateness. Thought thus postulates species that are of a wholly different kind from the species recognized by perception. The latter are the species as trust takes them, in which same and different are together and we do not doubt that they are; but the species postulated by thought, in which same and different are apart, are hypothetical, and we say, "Let them be." How, then, can Socrates ascribe a higher status to the latter and claim that mathematics turns the soul to the contemplation of what is? The short answer is that he does not. The contradiction that thought finds in the contrarieties of perception forces it to raise the question, "What is the one itself?", and it is this question that is periagogic. Socrates makes the philosophic issue turn on the thought-provoking difference between two kinds of class-formation. Arithmetic or number theory does not enter the discussion until after the Socratic question has been formulated (525a9); but it would not have been formulated unless the bodiless, imperceptible, and indivisible ones of arithmetic had not cast into doubt the species of trust. It is the postulation of their being that transforms the beings of trust into questions.

Glaucon finds it easy to agree that geometry is a science of that which always is (527b7–8). Socrates, however, does not now say anything in defense of the view that there is a circle itself or square itself any more than he had in the discussion of the line; rather, he points out that all the speeches of geometry speak of actions and they do so as if for the sake of action (527a6–b1). There is a massive contradiction between the constructions of geometry and the theorems of geometry (527a1–4), and Socrates does nothing to resolve it. What the contradiction does do is to cast doubt on the distinction Socrates had previously made between speech and action, when Glaucon had agreed that action was less in contact with truth than was speech (473a1–4). The construction of a perfect square is as problematic as the construction of a perfect city. What Socrates has done is to insert once more the way of the *Republic* into the higher education of the best city, but only insofar as the students of geometry stand back from what they are learning and ask what they are doing in their practice. As long as the students believe that what they intend is not what they are speaking about, geometry cannot be periagogic. There is no ascent from the cave without self-knowledge.

In order for Socrates to connect the universality of abstraction with the intellection of being, the positing of an indivisible one on a line without width must be taken as more than just a sign of human wilfulness. Socrates does not explain how mathematical objects differ in this respect from the city in speech. Glaucon could therefore infer from his not being able to perceive the city he and Socrates are talking about that it too has the capacity to turn the soul around. That the city in speech does in fact have this capacity does not depend on its standing in for the city as *idea*, but rather on its capacity to reveal the nature of political life and the envelope of unreality in which every city exists and without which none could exist. It is the nonbeing of the city that directs us to being; and the nonbeing of the city is most apparent in the contradictions of the city in speech. If mathematics, then, were comparable to political philosophy, it would be the impossibility of discriminating among the self-identical ones of arithmetic that would force the soul to turn around and realize that the truth about being cannot lie entirely within the competence of mathematics. The ontology of arithmetic is caught in the impossibility of thinking together the two things it needs equally, a Parmenidean unity and an anti-Parmenidean manifold of indiscernible ones. It would therefore be the suppositional character of mathematics rather than the propositions and theorems of mathematics itself that would serve philosophy (533c1–3). Number, then, is no more periagogic in itself than the city is, for philosophy is as indifferent to the refinement of the one as to the vulgarity of the other (522b4–6).

PART FOUR

BOOKS VIII – X: THE JUST

32

THE FALL

(543a1–550c3)

It is not obvious why the last three books of the *Republic* are necessary. Glaucon has long believed that it is better to act justly and be just regardless of circumstances and consequences (445a5–b4); and he has just acknowledged once more that the city it would be worth legislating for is not within his power or his knowledge to found (534d8–e1, 540d1–541b1). The second and third parts of the *Republic*, Books II–IV and Books V–VII, were each generated out of Thrasymachus' theatrical anger, on the one hand, and his distinction between precise and imprecise speech, on the other. Socrates took the first and made anger both central to the city and that in light of which the soul's structure was to be understood. He likewise took the second and brought it to the conclusion that wisdom in the strict sense should rule the city, and that the education preparatory to that wisdom was mathematics, the locus of precision itself. Socrates thus split the connection between spiritedness and reason by treating each separately, and still gave the impression that the alliance between reason and spiritedness was maintained. That alliance was grounded in a twofold idealism: the selflessness of the thumoeidetic and a wisdom that dispenses entirely with the body and sense perception. If the issue of justice has not yet been settled, it must be due to the distortions to which the city has subjected the understanding of the soul and philosophy. In the rehearsal of the qualities to be looked for in philosopher-kings, Socrates replaced the love of truth with the hatred of and indignation at falsehood, and shortly afterward rebuked himself for expressing his indignation and pseudo-anger (*hōsper thumōtheis*) at the Aristophanic ridicule of philosophy (535d9–536c7). As long as wisdom is not possible and philosophic natures are defective, justice itself, he implies, will find fault with philosophy and the city will be justified in rejecting its only possible salvation. Justice, then, can be truly understood only after everything Thrasymachus represented has been discarded. Only in the element of degeneration and the defective can justice come to light. Demo-cratic Athens is the condition for the possibility of Socrates (561d2).

What kind of man will resemble the city whose rulers are philosophers is so obvious to Glaucon that Socrates does not describe him (541b2–5); but once Socrates reminds Glaucon of where they digressed at the end of Book IV, it ceases to be obvious, since, according to Glaucon, Socrates had described there the good city and the man who resembles it, though he could have presented a finer city and a finer man (543c7–544a1). Glaucon implies that there are three kinds of good men: the warrior, whose education was outlined in Books II and III; the philosopher-wiseman of Books V–VII; and the communized man of the same books whose education is not enough to make him king. The good city seems to be the only city in which the ruler does not embody the character of the regime, for it is not the philosophers but the soldiers, as Glaucon observes, who care for the city (543b7–c3). The good man, moreover, whose son becomes the timocratic man, not only has a family but has never ruled and may not philosophize (549c2–6). He resembles Mr. Bennet of *Pride and Prejudice* and seems possible in any but the very worst and the very best of regimes. There are, then, at least four types of good men of whom two are regime dependent and two independent of the city. It is not easy to say who is the happiest. If the issue is happiness and justice, then only political men are relevant (544a5). Neither the philosopher to whom Socrates awards the palm nor Odysseus to whom the myth of Er does for minding his own business has anything to do with rule. Insofar, however, as men do reflect the cities they rule, the kind of justice exemplified in each re-gime will support the same justice in the ruler, and Glaucon's demand that the effect of justice in the individual be considered apart from the consequences cannot be met. What Glaucon has come to see since he posed his question is that happiness is not possible within the cave no matter who rules. The question now is, Is it by being unjust that one can be happy? Does injustice make up for the unhappiness insep-arable from political life? This question requires another defense of the city, in which it is not the rational city of the arts and philosophy that stands against Thrasymachus, but the sacred city that resists the bestialization of man. Socrates' second defense of the city thus leads to another confrontation with tragic poetry. Thyestes, he admits, is the truth about the man who is like the best regime (619b7–d1).

Socrates proposes to combine an eidetic account of the four mistaken regimes with a genetic account. His proposal requires that the best regime had once existed, for otherwise the faults of the second-best regime would not be due to itself but would be inherent in any city regardless of will or knowledge. A nongenetic account would present timocracy as the best regime one could have under the most favorable circumstances, and no one would be to blame for its injustice. Timocracy, however, is that regime in which the thumoeidetic, untouched by any music education, is most in control; and the thumoeidetic is where the sense of injustice lies. It would seem, then, that the thumoeidetic must postulate the prior existence of a regime from which timocracy has degenerated, just as the indignation of the timocratic son is on behalf of his wronged father, whose wife and servants fill the son with stories of all the indignities the husband and master has had to endure (549c2–550a1). The genetic account complies with the necessity for perfect beginnings from which man has wilfully fallen. Socrates, however, is not prepared to satisfy this necessity, for his account of the good and the beings was noncosmological; he has no other choice but to call on the Muses, who in being playful are to speak tragically as if they were in earnest (545d7–e3). If Socrates had not demoted astronomy, he would not be in his present fix; but he had no choice if he was to pretend that an ascent from the cave was possible without the discovery of nature. The promotion of mathematics led to the disappearance of the sun, under whose sway all generation had been put. Socrates, it seems, needs Timaeus in order to show the best city in space and time; but not even Timaeus would have sufficed, for Timaeus put asexual man at the beginning and traced the completion of the cosmos to his fall. Socrates, then, must resort to the Muses who keep man a sexual being and offer the mumbo-jumbo of "the nuptial number."

The Muses deny that the rulers of the best city, though they are wise, are capable of knowing enough at any time to figure out a program of eugenics; but they imply that at the beginning of the city, which coincides pretty nearly with the beginning of the cosmos, the offspring of the rulers shared in the same order of perfection as the cosmos. If the rulers made any mistake in their marriage arrangement, the cosmos more than made up for them; but when the cosmos had degenerated, there was nothing they could do to compensate for its exhaustion. The rulers seem to be ignorant as well of the Muses' first principle—corruption belongs to everything that comes into being (546a2–3)—and to have taken the initial success of the city for their own success. The Muses themselves, in turn, seem not to know why philosophers had to be kings: even if marriages in the golden class failed to produce golden children, the rulers could demote them and discover in the bronze and iron classes golden souls. Socrates' arrangement assumed from the start the deviancy of nature, but he had to renounce the inevitability of the coincidence of philosophy and power. The Muses, on the other hand, can assign a definite time for the best city, but they have to deny that unmixed golden souls survive into the iron age. Socrates had argued for the possibility of the best city at any time and at any place, but only after the full development of the arts and the degeneracy of the city. The Muses say the best city is impossible now and will not recur until the cosmos runs its course and is reborn. They deny as well the possibility at any time of perfect wisdom (546a8–b2); but Socrates had to argue for the possibility of wisdom in order to make the descent of the philosopher less unjust than it otherwise would be. The Muses seem to be true to the present while telling lies about the past (cf. 382c10–d3). Their serious suggestion seems to be that philosophy is always a matter of chance. The rulers' neglect of the Muses consists perhaps in their belief that philosophy could be successfully bred, and that the best soldiers make the best philosophers. Once the regime succeeds in inculcating the noble lie, it is destined to fail. To neglect the Muses is not to know how to tell apart the truth and lies like the truth (546d3–547a4).

The Muses go on to say that faction breaks out between iron and bronze over against gold and silver (547b2–c4). Gold and silver should stand for rulers and soldiers; but iron and bronze cannot represent the artisan and commercial class, since Socrates had laid down the principle that as long as unanimity in the ruling class remains, the regime cannot alter (545c9–d3). Iron and bronze, then, must represent the soldiers, and silver the silverplate of their education. Since iron and bronze aim at the acquisition of land and houses, and the compromise reached allows for their private ownership, it is not immediately clear why the Muses speak as if concessions were made on both sides. Part of the agreement consists in the enslavement of those whom the rulers had formerly treated as free and friends; and this enslavement is not a demand of iron and bronze insofar as they represented the chrematistic class, but of the soldiers, who, no longer gentled by philosophy, have domination of others as their single goal. The breakdown of the regime is not due to the emancipation of desire but of the thumoeidetic, which, just as in the Leontius story, disguises itself behind desire. The will to enslave is inevitable if moneymaking is publicly disallowed; but though it is unjust, it satisfies spiritedness more than money could. Even its injustice, however, preserves something of justice. Now that the soldiers are no longer required to practice music, but their sole concern is war and the guarding of the city, they strictly comply with the principle of one man/one job. As the forced union of philosopher and king made clear, only the dilution of the principle of justice can stem the evils of justice.

Timocracy imitates both aristocracy and oligarchy, neither of which shows up in it in a genuine form. Its common mess does not serve to foster communism but to separate the men from the women; and its desire for money is not for displaying or spending it but as a kind of honor (548a6, b4). The love of honor and victory is the single most conspicuous element in it; and it arises from the thumoeidetic being in control (548c5–7). The desire for recognition had never before been ascribed to *thumos*, though it showed through plainly enough in Thrasymachus' anger, and Adimantus believes that its presence in Glaucon makes him out to be the model of the timocratic man (548d8–9). Socrates, however, implies that Sparta would not suit Glaucon, for he is not as headstrong and unmusical as the timocrat. Like the philosopher-dog, the timocrat is both savage and gentle; he is gentle to the free and savage to the slaves, for he does not have contempt for slaves but remembers the injustice of their original enslavement. The slaves now are strangers within the gates, strangers who ensure the proper degree of harshness in the soldier without the illusion of the noble lie. The enslavement of one's fellow citizens is an ignoble lie, but it is at least as effective as the noble lie: one's slaves are an enemy from whom one benefits. The thumoeidetic man vents his anger at those who were once his equals and displays his deference to those in power whom he wishes to replace. He distinguishes between what is higher and lower than himself without there being any real difference in either case. His own position is essentially unstable. He must be therefore the engine of all political change. In Socrates' true city every citizen was assigned his proper place, for a specialized knowledge completed the nature of each; but the soldier had a nature that only opinion could control and no knowledge could perfect. He is forever on the lookout for something to perfect him, and he is always restless because he senses there is nothing.

The father of the timocrat is a good man who follows the principle of the best regime and minds his own business. He is willing to be diminished so as not to be bothered; but his wife is distressed that her husband is not one of the rulers and sees herself diminished among other women on account of it. Her husband is as indifferent to money as he is to her, and she tells her son that his father is not a real man. The slaves are worse; they speak of justice and revenge, and urge the son when he grows up to punish all his father's wrongdoers. The love of honor is inculcated in the son by those who cannot be honored in their own right, and who wish to feel that they are ruled by those whom others recognize as worthy of rule. Honor is a vicarious compensation for an inequality that cannot be overcome. Socrates thus implies that the characteristic of timocracy is always manifest among those out of office: they are displaced persons. Socrates had hinted at this when he first called timocracy "the honorloving regime" and then switched to names in which the "loving" was suppressed and which were more in accordance with the names of other regimes (545b5–7). If this turns out to hold generally—the principle of the regime is never embodied in the rulers—then Socrates has discovered the most common cause of change, and he would be arguing against Thrasymachus that the interest of the rulers is never the same as that which animates the laws of the regime. This disparity would have one further consequence. A judgment could be passed on the relation between the justice and happiness of the individual in himself apart from the support of the regime whose principle he represents, for it would never be the case that the rulers of any city show to the fullest extent the impress of its ruling element. Even in the best city the philosopher does not philosophize when he rules.

33

O L I G A R C H Y
(550c4–555b2)

Oligarchy is a regime in which the rich alone rule (550c11–d1); it is not a regime in which moneylovers rule, for they might well be the energetic poor. It is not even a regime in which the wealthiest individual rules (though the principle of the regime seems to entail it), any more than in a timocracy either the individual who has accumulated the greatest number of honors or even the one most devoted to obtaining the highest honor rules, for if that were the case, the tyrant would be the perfect timocrat and oligarch combined. As Socrates had remarked earlier, those who inherit wealth are not overly fond of money (330c1–2); so even if the first generation of oligarchs exhibited the principle of the regime, it vanishes in their descendants and yet they go on ruling. There is, moreover, already in Socrates' best city a class of moneylovers; but it is not suggested that they take over from the timocrats, or that oligarchy results from the triumph in a civil war of the bourgeoisie over decayed aristocrats. Oligarchy comes from the top; its love of money does not originate in desire but in the thumoeidetic. Although the expenditure of secretly stored wealth is an individual affair, it is the mutual competition among the families, once they see what others are doing, that makes it a characteristic of all the timocrats (550d9–e3). To make money is a point of honor; it has nothing to do with money as a means for gratification through consumption. Socrates now opposes wealth to virtue, as if virtue and not honor were the spirit of timocracy (550e4–551a6). Virtue in itself is not the principle of any actual regime; it is always a retrospective interpretation of those who came later and who, having fallen further, ascribe it to motives that have ceased to be intelligible to them. The ancestors of the moneylovers were obviously not rich; so obviously they must have acted out of virtue (cf. 556d7). The belief in perfect beginnings seems to belong to political life as such.

The genetic account of the regimes seems to contain two divergent elements. The first consists in the movement toward tyranny that is latent already in timocracy; the second consists in the movement toward less and less mediated satisfaction, or the growth of sensual desire. The second is essentially private, and whatever satisfactions the artisan class has or is allowed to have do not require the usurpation of rule. The hyphen in "philosopher-king" cannot conceal the divergence of these two elements even in the best regime. Political life is always in need of a supplement. The contempt in which the best hold it seems to survive in the various ways the rulers of inferior regimes try to force something alien to rule to be satisfied through rule (346e3–347a6). Money is the most obvious example. It must be more than a means of exchange and acquisition if it is to serve as a title to rule; but it still retains its primary function so that the oligarch can hold on to something more solid, he believes, than the shadows of the cave. It is not for nothing that we call the rich "men of substance." The son of the timocrat follows in his father's footsteps until he sees him stumble against a reef of the city and lose all his property (*ousia*); he then turns to the accumulation of capital as security against the arbitrariness of political honor and disgrace (553a9–c4). He is humiliated by poverty and seems to interpret the restoration of the family's fortunes as a form of revenge. His turn to moneymaking is prompted by the same considerations that drove his father into politics. Socrates, however, claims that the future oligarch overthrows the rational and the thumoeidetic and installs in their place the desiderative and moneymaking part of the soul; but the language of its installation—the desiderative is the great king of Persia whom the timocrat's son decks out with tiaras, necklaces, and sabers (553c4–7)—shows that the thumoeidetic is still at work. Desire wants satisfaction, not admiration and honor, let alone the pleasure in the enslavement of others. Only the thumoeidetic, if it is not exercising the profitless art of war, can turn directly to moneymaking without the intermediary of some craft to which every artisan in the chrematistic class is bound. The apparent unleashing of desire is in reality a version of pride latching onto something more subject to the individual's control than political honor can ever be. There is no political equivalent to the expression "a self-made millionaire."

Not all the faults of oligarchy are peculiar to oligarchy. The first that Socrates lists—the ruler is without knowledge of rule—is true of every regime except the best if such knowledge involves all that he had assigned to the philosopher-king; but if there is something like political wisdom, an oligarch is as likely to have it as anyone else, and since their own wealth is at stake, perhaps oligarchs have a greater incentive than most to defer to the prudent among them. Socrates' scheme does not allow anyone to be sensible and calculate the effects of strict compliance with the principle of the regime; and he is right to discount prudence insofar as no regime can make it an essential requirement for rule. Thrasymachus' error-free ruler is impossible as long as the laws of the regime determine the actions of the ruler. From time to time every city stands in need of rulers whom the city has not succeeded in taking over completely; and in this sense the philosopher represents the liberation from the law upon which the survival of any regime depends. It is behind the back of the Cave-dwellers that the cave is open to the light. They survive crises through something that is equally against their will and their knowledge.

The second fault Socrates finds in oligarchy—that the city splits into two cities of rich and poor—was especially true of the best city, in which the wealthiest class was the lowest and the poorest class the communized warriors and rulers. As Aristotle remarks, wherever there is not perfect equality, the rich and the poor are going to have opposed interests; but the poor that Socrates is speaking of are not those who work for a living but the unsuccessful moneymakers among the former rulers, who without any skill form the enemy within the oligarchy itself. The rich need prodigals in order to become superrich; they can feed their own greed only if others do not practice their version of moderation. They deplore what they must promote. They are forced to create the future leaders of democracy in their attempt to live up to the limitlessness inherent in the desire for money. The criterion for membership into the ruling class can be fixed at any amount ; but the principle of the regime does not admit of any check on acquisition. It is as inevitable that Crassus arise as that Caesar replace him. Oligarchy produces two kinds of drones: beggars and thieves (552c6–d1). That they are both nonproductive recalls the nonproductive soldiers of the best city, who had monopolized all the weapons and kept even the farmers from defending their own land. The thieves must be their descendants, for they retain the waspishness for which they were originally selected. They are ex-soldiers who believe the city owes them a living, and they take what they believe is theirs. But where do the stingless drones or beggars come from? They cannot be former artisans, for oligarchy is no more likely to foster poor businessmen in the chrematistic class than any other regime; and if they had a skill they should always be able to find employment. Beggars too must believe the city owes .them something; but unlike their bolder brothers they remain lawabiding and conceal their resentment in asking for a handout. The divisiveness of oligarchy thus consists in splitting in two the unstable mixture of domination and servility that constitutes the thumoeidetic.

Socrates believes that only if in the soul of the individual oligarch the equivalents of beggar and thief obtain, can he prove that he resembles the regime to which he belongs. He grants that the rulers in an oligarchy look as moderate as any of the former rulers, and by holding money in the highest esteem and satisfying only the necessary desires, they have effectively enslaved all the other desires as pointless and vain (554a2–8); but, he claims, drone desires emerge despite their self-control. To have money is to imagine the spending of it, and to imagine the spending of it is to conceive of the desire to do so. If one can one wants. The oligarch impoverishes something in himself that shows up as either criminal or abject. Even though it serves no purpose, he defrauds orphans because he can get away with it; and he refuses to spend money on anything noble or beautiful. The oligarch gains recognition (*eudokimei*) for his seeming justice (*dokōn dikaios*), but he does not care for recognition (*eudoxia*); he does not mind if he is despised. Oligarchs do not rule in oligarchies. They are indifferent to the regime that supports them and let it be known to everyone that they think small. The drone desires of beggary are political and concern the love of honor and victory (554e7–555a6). The political becomes vestigial in the oligarch, for though he remains enslaved to the conventions of the city, he has seen through its seemings. He prides himself on his realism. The oligarch represents the ultimate taming of the thumoeidetic. He is the best that most cities most of the time are capable of. He is the first who is said to be just, even if it is only for show; for out of fear he does not use his power to the extent that he could. That naked force and fear are now first mentioned as instruments of control both politically and psychically is simply due to the extravagance of the Muses' conceit that the fully rational regime once existed (552e2, 553b8, 554c1; cf. 548b7–8). A decent form of self-imposed violence, Socrates admits, constrains the oligarch (554c12–d1). He has internalized the collective selfishness of the city for which education has ceased to be important. The oligarch is the cringing cur of the philosopher-dog. The bark and the bite linger in the timocrat: he punishes.

34

DEMOCRACY

(555b3–562a3)

Socrates maintains a total silence about the demos in his account of democracy. The word itself never occurs. The demos figures largely in his account of tyranny, but as long as he is discussing the origin of democracy and its character, he never explains how the demos came to be. The demos must have been present from the start; they were in fact the first members of the city, all of whom were equal to one another in the contribution they severally made to the city and the benefits they severally received from the city. The leaders of the demos, however, do not come from the demos. They are former oligarchs on whom their fellow oligarchs have grown fat. They are beggars with stings, filled with hatred of a regime that encouraged in them, out of a stingy avarice, the spirit of extravagance. Oligarchy cannot remain true to itself and stop the growth of these beggars. Over against Thrasymachus, Socrates shows that here is a ruling power that cannot serve infallibly its own interest unless it compromises with what it takes to be its own principal good. These beggars, then, must supply the impulse for a democratic revolution. Their hatred leads for the first time to the killing of fellow citizens (557a3). Killing follows for another reason as well. The recovery of pride demands it; the lean and tough poor realize that it must be owing to their own vice that the wheezing and out-of-shape rich are in power, and they must show there is nothing to them (556c8–e1). The view that money is virtue dies hard.

Democracy rests on two inconsistent principles—equality and freedom. Equality determines the distribution of citizenship and offices (557a4–5), freedom declares one can do whatever one wants (557b4–6). The second principle is nominal, for it ignores the conditions for real possibility (cf. 557b7). Dreaming is a large part of democratic possibility, and when dreaming has become fully realized, it has become tyranny. The difference, however, between equality and freedom can be traced back to the difference between class-characteristic and class-membership that haunted the city from the beginning. The democratic equivalent to the individual credentials of knowledge with which each artisan entered the city is the whim of everyman to become what he wants. The democratic equivalent to the fusion of the class of desire and moneymaking is the poverty of the people. Poverty as a common state of want characterizes the demos as a political entity; poverty as a consciousness of need informs each member of the demos and makes of them together a manifold of equally intense and equally exclusive desires. Democracy begins as a regime in which every sort of human life can be found separately; democracy ends up as a regime in which everyone is every sort of human life together (557c1, 561e3). "Role-playing" is a theory possible only in an advanced form of democracy.

Democracy is a theoretical regime, not only in the modern sense of the term—Herodotus has someone say of it that it has the most beautiful name, *isonomia*, that is, equality before the law (3.80.6)—but also, more literally, as an object of contemplation: its beauty like a richly embroidered cloak of many hues can be appreciated better if one looks at it than if one wears it (557c4–9). The attractiveness of its variety comes to light if one stands off from it and comes to it as a stranger. Socrates now says that their whole enterprise is in a sense the revelation of the true purpose of democracy (557a1–e1). Its good is their own two cities: the selection of the best city in speech from the democratic supermarket of regimes and the exhibition of democracy in action in their establishing the dialogic city by the equality of the vote (450a3). Freedom of choice can be realized fully only in the medium of speech. If Socrates alludes to Aristophanes' *Acharnians* when he remarks that there is no compulsion to go to war when the democratic city is at war (557e4), then comedy comes along with philosophy as the reality behind the fantasizing of democracy. Pericles' funeral speech is the extraordinary tribute Thucydides pays to the democratic imagination; and in the *Republic* Plato conveys the same in Glaucon's thought-experiments. Democracy alone made it possible for Glaucon to imagine that one could be as invisible as Gyges and by the will alone resist the most terrible tortures (558a4–8). Democracy discounts education just as much as Glaucon ignored the effect of habit; and again like Glaucon democracy overestimates the prevalence of outstanding natures (558b1–c1; cf. 562c2). It can encourage, however, individuality while it maintains equality only because it finds two kinds of men inconceivable: the criminals who must be punished and the ambitious who tell it they are well disposed. Evil and power are to it unreal. Democracy, to be sure, is not as easygoing as Socrates makes it out to be, but he exaggerates its mildness in order to connect the conditions for the *Republic* itself—no force, no piety, no anger—with its larger setting. Democracy's failure to enforce its decisions and protect itself parodies philosophy, for which everything is open to revision.

The genesis of the democratic man parallels the genesis of democracy and can apply only to the rich. Poverty would prevent the growth of what Socrates first calls expensive and non-moneymaking pleasures (558d5); but he drops pleasures in his longer account and speaks instead of the differences between necessary and non-necessary desires (558d9). The democratic man has desires which only the sons of oligarchical fathers could satisfy. Socrates expands the notion of necessary so as to include any desire whose fulfillment does us good; he calls non-necessary any desire that either does not do us any good or does us harm, as well as those that one can get rid of if one works at it from youth onwards (558d11–559a6). Necessary desires go far beyond the needs for which the true and healthy city was designed. Glaucon's desire for relish can now be called necessary, since its good was part of his own education. Even Adimantus' and Polemarchus' interest in the communism of women was a necessary desire, for it prompted the digression on philosophy. Indeed, it looks as if necessary desires are elements of what Socrates calls logographic necessity and go to shape every Platonic dialogue. What seems to be precluded is *erōs,* which is never fulfilled and whose goodness is obscure. Socrates, then, reintroduces the good into desire but not the desire for any apparent good (as if this distinction were known to desire). He puts together the desire for life and the desire for the good life and calls both natural desires and fully rational desires necessary. He thus can pun on "chrematistic" and count the oligarch's insatiety among the necessary desires, for his desire is not necessarily deleterious to either body or soul, and it is useful (*khrēsimon*) for keeping every other desire under control (559c3–d2). Socrates forges an alliance between philosophy and oligarchy. It is an acknowledgment that he and his friends need the excess of oligarchy no less than that of democracy.

Although democracy seems to be the least political of regimes, Socrates adopts the language of politics to describe the transformation of the oligarchical soul into the democratic (559e4–561a5). There are military alliances, factions and counterfactions, exile and return, seizure of the acropolis, and the revaluation of words. Desire seems to fight too hard if its only goal is pleasure. It wants to win. The struggle is led by speeches and opinions (560c2). The youth who listens to them is the son of a successful oligarch whose lack of education and knowledge and rejection of everything beautiful make it impossible for him to help his son to stand against the assault of speeches, however amateurish. Those speeches speak not on behalf of pleasure but of truth. They plead for shamelessness as manliness, insolence as good education, anarchy as freedom, and luxury as magnificence. They claim to want the return of the virtues which the education of Books II and III were meant to instill and oligarchy banished The overthrow of boorishness, effeminacy, and foolishness—the names now given to measure, moderation, and shame—is in the name of freedom. Democratic freedom comes forward as the freedom of which the soldiers of the best city were supposed to be the precision artisans. It is through and through thumoeidetic without the illusion of the noble lie. In the Hesiodic scheme of things, democracy corresponds to the age of heroes (546d8–547a1).

The lucky democrat who when he is older becomes more sober recalls Cephalus (561a6–b5). He indulges in everything and sticks to nothing. He has no habits that interfere with taking up any fancy, whether it be philosophy or aerobics, for all desires have become equal through their coming from the outside in the form of speeches. They are advertisements to which nothing in the democratic soul responds but which out of indifference it might as well taste. Such a leveling of desire seems to be possible only if the desire for money has preceded it and discovered a universal means for satisfying anything regardless of whether it is a need or a whim. The democrat has a credit card for a soul that tells him, "Master the possibilities!" The regime itself, however, displayed the greatest variety of distinct types; and it is not at once obvious why "rugged individualism" ends up as the homogenization of mass man. A twofold characterization of justice held in the good city. The principle of its class-structure—each minded its own business—took on a supplement in the case of the soul-structure of the ruler, so that each of its parts minded its own business perfectly. That "perfectly" could not hold for the city, since its two lower classes were informed by opinion and not knowledge. In democracy, however, the principle of justice in the weak sense becomes the principle of each individual and no longer of a class, since everyone now belongs to the people and all class-structure has disappeared. This principle was originally attached to the jack-of-all-trades who was the alternative to the division of labor that founded the city. The jack-of-all-trades satisfied his own needs; the politicized jack-of-all-trades in democracy satisfies all his desires, which the prior accumulation of wealth has made possible. Socrates, then, is arguing for the goodness of the original split in the two forms of justice. As long as there is some class-structure one is not what one belongs to; but the elimination of any class function socializes the individual completely, and he becomes necessarily nothing but the regime and incapable of virtue. He reproduces the whole of which he is part through imitation. He becomes a poet without talent or knowledge. He thus needs poetry more than anyone else to supply in speech the models that he can never become. Everyman now enters the cave willingly and watches the movies.

35

TYRANNY

(562a4–576b6)

When Socrates had first proposed his fourfold scheme of genesis of regime and regime-character and genesis of regime-individual and his character, he deviated slightly in the case of tyranny and the tyrant. He spoke of the tyrannized city and the tyrannical soul (545c3–4). His scheme committed him to distinguishing between the genesis of tyranny and the tyrant, on the one hand, and between the character of tyranny and the tyrannical character, on the other. The widening gap between the ruler of a democracy and the democratic man seems to culminate in the possibility that the tyrannical man never rule and lack the support and the rewards that rule alone would give him. The tyrannical character is a real type and as far from power as the philosopher. The happiness of each can thus be assessed in its correlation with justice apart from the opinion of the city. By his assigning all of seeming to the regime, Socrates can satisfy Glaucon's demand for the real in the judging of the individual. That Socrates can match up the separation of seeming and being with regime and individual through what seems to be a wholly neutral scheme should not surprise us. Even in the true city, where there were no rulers, the city had the latest in technology and the citizens slept on the ground. Glaucon's objection to that divergence seemed plausible; but Socrates' argument had been that it is the failure of the individual to be in phase with the city to which he belongs that keeps him free, and the gravest threat to freedom arises when the individual embodies the regime. The injustice of political justice is all to the good.

Politically, democracy is majority rule; but its spirit is classlessness or the absence of any distinction between ruler and ruled. Its spirit shows up in individuals who are oblivious of the needs of the regime. They are democratic; they are not democrats devoted to the rule of themselves. A delegation of power therefore must take place, in which rulers are chosen to maintain the spirit of democracy without any need for the demos to participate in its own maintenance. The flipover from freedom to tyranny is due to the attempt to actualize freedom through the elimination of all class-differences.

In order to crush the opposition to equality that the rich do in fact put up or are believed to put up, the tyrant is necessary. The tyrant's own interest in getting rid of everyone who stands out in any significant way coincides with the democratic principle of freedom as equality. Only the demos with perfect equality among its members survives the tyrant. The trivialization of all differences so that changes in style and fashion seem to be transformations in essence, establishes the uniformity at which the democratic spirit aims and tyrannical power brings about. Effective control in a democracy always devolves on the drones of the thumoeidetic class; the stingless among them buzz about the speaker's platform and drown out anyone who rises up against their leader (564d4–e2). Their leader becomes a wolf not, as Socrates claims, from a man but from a dog who originally protected the flock of artisans from strangers and had to be educated to refrain from devouring his fellow-citizens (565e3–566a4). That education never succeeded fully. A false analogy between the gentleness of watchdogs and of philosophic natures controlled the education in the city in speech and was corrected only in the dialogic city. The genetic analysis that Socrates, with the help of the Muses, linked at the start with an eidetic analysis of regimes conceals another eidetic analysis. Through this second analysis the truth of the thumoeidetic comes to light slowly by the gradual casting off of the false interpretation of the Leontius story, which denied that *thumos* and desire are ever in alliance against reason. Thrasymachus pretended to be a wolf by art; the real wolf is at the heart of the city. He is the tyrant whom the philosopher-king for all his own spuriousness has made it possible to detect.

Socrates presented the final triumph of democratic elements in the soul of the oligarch's son with all the fanfare and language of the Mysteries (560d8–561a9). He spoke of extreme democracy as drunk on the unmixed draught of freedom (562c8–d2). He thus prepared for a digression on tragedy, the highest form of Dionysiac celebration and the one, Socrates claims, most suitable to democracy and tyranny (568a8–d4). This digression occurs just before Socrates and Adimantus between them make demos and tyrant into father and son. The political is now constituted by the family and the sacred; and their destruction, which the best city was to achieve, now returns in a poetic form. The son robs and beats the father; and Demos, who was never generated, becomes holy. Socrates enhances the dignity of the people and attacks the tragic poets who, he claims, are the wise associates of tyrants; but, as Adimantus makes clear, the tyrants with whom the tragedians live are on the stage. Adimantus quotes from Euripides' *Trojan Women* the phrase "godlike tyranny" (1169). Hecuba speaks it in the course of a speech in which she regrets that Hector's son was killed before he enjoyed "godlike tyranny." The language of tragedy makes the illegitimate legitimate. It operates at the same time democratically and anti-democratically. It assigns to figures of the heroic age a word which, though it cannot but retain all its Athenian meanings, might designate an Oriental king who had not necessarily been an usurper, and yet 'tyrant' would still imply that no one else is free and before whom everyone bows down as if before a god. A democratic audience is persuaded to sorrow for a barbarian's loss of godlike tyranny. They are made to imagine the immoral amorally as the beautiful divorced from justice. In the context, this carries two implications.The outstanding survives the onslaught of democratic equalization through its translation into the imaginary; and Demos listens with regret to the failure of his own son. The tyrant is the embodiment of all democratic wishes—he does whatever he wants—and the object of all democratic desires. He is Eros.

Had not Socrates emulated poetry and personified the demos, he would not now be able to give a separate account of the genesis and character of the tyrannical man. By his grafting the genealogy-model of the individual onto the regime analysis, the tyrant becomes distinct in origin and way from the tyrannical individual. The tyrannical individual sleeps in almost everyone and becomes known in dreams, when one does not hesitate to try to have intercourse with one's mother and any other human being or god, slay anything, and indulge in every kind of food (571c9–d3). Socrates calls these desires the desires that transgress the law; he does not call them unnatural. They are essentially divorced from real possibility, for there are no gods apart from the gods of poetry who are sexually available. It is an unlawful desire to sleep with them but it is not punishable by law. The desire is determined by the law itself, for the law must first establish the beings which are then imagined as being violated. The nonbeings of the law are safe from violation as nonbeings and as lawful beings. The gods are objects of non-necessary desires: they are not necessary for either survival or well-being. The law has established them as objects of desire, for in surrounding them with prohibitions it has planted the desire to transgress those prohibitions and thereby rooted their existence. In dreams, then, the soul realizes the triumph of the city. Translegal desires are desires that violate the fundamental requirements of the city and acknowledge fully the fictions of the city.

Socrates does not prove that translegal desires are desires; it simply follows from his discovering them among non-necessary desires. But the actions he mentions—incest and cannibalism—are perhaps not only brought into existence through the law but also classified by the law. Is cannibalism a form of gluttony, and incest a form of eros? Glaucon was not just hungry when he dismissed the city of pigs and demanded meat, and Thrasymachus not just greedy when he demanded money. Satiety of food or drink is said to be the condition for such criminal dreams (571c5). One may wonder whether hatred of the enemy does not stimulate imaginary cannibalism (*Iliad* 22.346–7; Vergil *A.* 4.601–2), and hatred of the falsehood that one's mother is not a sexual being imaginary incest. The denial of any difference between man and beast or between parents and children seems to be the ultimate consequence of democratic equality (562c7–563d1). When Socrates described how dogs, horses, and donkeys behave in a democracy, as if they were as good as anyone, Adimantus said that he spoke his own dream (563d2–3). Once the extreme tenderness of the democratic soul—which becomes irritated at the slightest constraint, whether expressed in written or unwritten laws (563d4–e1)—unites with the universal hatred of the lie in the soul, the thumoeidetic dreams of a revolt against the city. Knowledge does not inform those dreams, for the thumoeidetic must preserve the city's opinion about the holiness of the mother and the unholiness of human flesh in order to set out to prove that there is nothing there to inspire awe or shame. It seems, however, that the thumoeidetic cannot be involved, for Socrates goes on to argue that *erōs* is the ringleader of all unlawful desires (572d8–573d5). If this Eros were Socrates' and Diotima's, the objection would be sound; but this Eros has been winged by the poets and given the epithet "tyrant." The poets' Eros is not only desire but the object of desire as well, through which the lover makes the beloved an agent of his love and fully responsible for it. Eros is thus wholly full as beloved and wholly empty as lover. He combines the total abjection of the lover with the total domination of the beloved. But slavery and freedom when split apart were the drones, Beggar and Thief, and Eros the tyrant is their poetic reunion (575b6–9, 575e2–576a6). Eros is the thumoeidetic made whole; it is a fiction. In incorporating this fiction, the tyrant is driven to acknowledge that which does not exist, and which has not existed for any ruler or citizen before him—the fatherland (575d3–9). Once democracy has dismantled all class-structure, what remains is the other half of the noble lie, which by claiming that the land was the mother of the citizens made incest inevitable. The incest of Oedipus is the truth of Thebes' autochthony. The tyrant is the true believer in the lie of the city stripped of everything that made it noble and good. The collapse of education and class-structure exposes the bestiality of unalloyed patriotism. "Fatherland" and "People" tend to be the two slogans borrowed from Right and Left of every tyranny; and the tyrant himself must cherish his two fathers as the ultimate barriers against nothingness. If he can punish them, they must exist. The dream of Everyman that the tyrant lives out is still a dream.

36

THE THREE COMPARISONS

(576b7–588a11)

The sixteenfold analysis of the four mistaken regimes has laid bare the city and the soul without order or structure. This is the city and the soul that concern tragedy. Its tyrants violate the fundamental laws of the city that antedate any regime and through their punishment confirm those fundamental laws. Socrates now has to do the tragic poets one better: without recourse to the gods and the sacred he must show the tyrant, stripped of his tragic garb, to be suffering the greatest misery (577b1). The translation of dream into reality through tyrannical power, upon which Socrates' case depends, cannot be done. It involves either the impossible—intercourse with a god—or the improbable—incest and cannibalism. Tacitus' *Annals*, one might say, supplies the hard evidence that Socrates admits he does not have (576e6–577b5). But that evidence might also be considered tainted, since Tacitus, after he has quoted the opening sentence of a letter Tiberius wrote to the Senate, alludes to Plato's *Gorgias* and the ninth book of the *Republic* (6.6). And Nero, who in the murder of his mother comes closest to the tyrant of the *Republic* (14.1–8), comes closest to the tragic tyrant as well: he tried to murder his mother with a theatrical prop, he wrote poetry, and he assumed the roles of tragic figures on the stage (15.65, 16.21; Suetonius *Nero* 21.3). Such a coincidence between theater and politics suggests that the reality of the tyrant consists in his unreality—Tacitus calls Nero *incredibilium cupitor* (15.42)—and he is nothing but the ungrounded opinions of the city (576c3–4). The tyrant Socrates and Glaucon are looking at is the shadows of the cave in the light. The tyrant is Eros. He represents the complete politicization of desire that first showed up in Leontius; but by now the thumoeidetic has pushed its way entirely into the desiderative and fused with it. Anger and love are one. Their separation has been the thrust of the *Republic* ever since Socrates introduced their union in the philosopher-dog. The philosopher-dog was Glaucon, who we are told is no less thumoeidetic than erotic. His speech on behalf of unjustice was, with all its inconsistencies, the expression of his double nature, which he now repudiates. In the last three books of the *Republic*, Glaucon does not find anything funny.

Socrates offers three comparison-tests of the just and the unjust man. He divides the first into two parts, of which the first involves a direct reading-off of the tyrant from the tyrannized city, or so Glaucon believes; but Socrates points out to him that he has been speaking of the private man whose misfortune has not compelled him to become a tyrant (578b4–c3). These tyrannical men are not immediately recognizable, for their regrets and fears, wailings, groans, and lamentations are never displayed in public. If, however, the tyrant succeeds in killing or exiling everyone outstanding in the city, the remnant must be the homogenized demos, each of whom is the tyrannical man: everyone wants to be somebody and regrets the choice of the life he made the moment before. The democratic man is the tyrannical man. His spokesman is the tragic poet who shows him to himself and teaches him how to grieve for his unsatisfiable longings.

The second part of Socrates' first comparison-test consists of a thought-experiment. He asks Glaucon to imagine the situation of a large slaveowner plucked by a god from the city and set down in some isolated spot with his wife and children (578d11–e8). This picture is meant to correspond to the tyrannical man becoming a tyrant. Socrates thus splits the regret of the tyrannical soul away from the fears of the actual tyrant. If they were co-present, the tyrannical experience would be that of remorse and the fear of punishment, or guilt; but as it is, the actual tyrant experiences the cave. He is forced

208

to stay at home in the prison of the city and cannot go abroad to see the sights (579b3–c2). He resents everyone who does get outside and sees anything good. The tyrant seems to be Hobbesian man, with the hand of everyone raised against him, but the fear of violent death results in the shutting of the cave. Socrates has thus succeeded in convincing Glaucon of what seemed impossible: seeing, which Glaucon put in his second class of goods (desired for their own sake and for their consequences), is a good of which the most unjust man through his injustice is deprived. Socrates' strategy accordingly now becomes clear. His second and third comparison-tests are designed to deprive the unjust man of, respectively, thinking and health, the other two goods in Glaucon's second class. The tyrant, then, is the prisoner of the cave who wills its illusions. His impotence is a direct consequence of the impossibility of breaking the connection entirely between the human soul and the reality of the good.

Glaucon is called upon in the second test to judge in point of happiness five types of man. It is unclear whether he realizes that these types are all possible in the early stages of democracy and are not identical with the rulers of the corresponding regimes. Socrates himself refrains from identifying the most royal man with the actual king of the best city. He merely says that he rules himself royally, whereas the most unjust and wretched man must be the tyrant who rules tyrannically both himself and the city (580b8–c5). Socrates therefore can now casually identify the philosopher with the just man without the assumption that either the best city has perfected the philosopher or the philosopher is the wise man simply (583b2). Socrates drops, however, any political correlation for the three types—philosopher, honorlover, moneylover—that match the three parts of the soul. While he has identified the philosopher with the just man, he cannot identify the unjust man with either of the other two types: neither the love of honor nor the love of money is in itself an obstacle to the practice of justice as the city understands justice.

The political neutrality of the second comparison-test is deceptive. The thumoeidetic is still ranked higher than the desiderative (583a8–9), and the desiderative is still given its politicized label "moneyloving." Socrates, however, now assigns their own desires and pleasures to mind and anger respectively, and, though he admits that the desiderative is polyeidetic, he does not conclude that it cannot have a single pleasure (580d10–581a1). Granted that there might be a pleasure in making money, it would belong, according to Socrates, with the pleasure that fathers take in their sons and poets in their poems: it would no longer cover eating, drinking, or sex. Socrates now gives the desiderative a new name, *to philokerdes,* the love of gain or profit. *Kerdos* is not a common word in the *Republic* (Adimantus used it once [366a2]), and *kerdaleos* hardly more so, but Socrates twice denied that he was convinced that injustice was more profitable than justice (345a3, 7). The gainful, then, is the good for oneself, and the desire for one's own good, now that the just man and the philosopher are one, should not be separated from philosophizing. Socrates' second comparison-test, in restricting the love of gain to the lowest part of the soul, makes thinking too pure. Thinking wins on the basis of a false understanding of soul. The philosopher seems to win because he can claim to have greater experience of the other two pleasures than either can of his. He can say whatever he wants and no one can contradict him. It is his opacity to everyone else that seems to make him the winner. Glaucon has a lot to do with his winning. He speaks of the pleasure that comes from learning of the beings, and the enjoyment that is the philosopher's alone of the vision of what is (582b4, c8). Glaucon seems to have postulated an experience beyond the experiences he can have had. On the basis of the renown he won at the battle at Megara (368a3), he assures Socrates that the wise, like the wealthy and brave, are honored by many (582c4–6; cf. 581d7). No one honors the lover as such; success is an indispensable condition. Unless Glaucon the herald lies sincerely on his behalf, the philosopher-king is impossible. It is a good thing Glaucon was not told about the good.

In order to assign justice in the strict sense to the philosopher exclusively, Glaucon believes it is necessary to assign him thinking in the strict sense—pure mind in contact with pure being. But justice in the strict sense applied to the soul as a whole, and thinking in the strict sense, endowed as it now is with its own desires and pleasures, does not involve the whole soul, let alone the whole individual. Mind apart from soul, and soul apart from body seem to be implicit in the proof that without justice thinking is impossible. Socrates, however, offers another argument that does not involve either implication. He argues that the philosopher, in arguing for his own life as the most pleasant, is minding his own business and being just in the loose sense. The philosopher argues; neither of his competitors can argue and still keep to their business, for the ambitious would have to win and the moneymaker have to profit from the argument in order to justify the time spent away from what they do. Their experience allows them to make a claim but not a defense of their claim. They need mouthpieces like the poets and Thrasymachus; but neither the poets nor Thrasymachus can be trusted not to toot their own horn. To spend a life making speeches is the only life that includes as a matter of course making speeches about a life of making speeches. Socrates now calls the philosopher a speechlover (582e8).

Glaucon had classed health as something cherished for its own sake as well as for its consequences; he implicitly challenged Socrates to show that health could not be had unless one was just. Socrates' third comparison-test takes up this challenge in a twofold way. No one, Socrates will argue, regards health as a good unless he is in pain, and health is possible only if one is strictly just, i.e., has a perfectly ordered soul (586d4–587a1). The argument once more is about pleasure, but until it is over, there is no mention of desire (586d5). There are perfect satisfactions of the mind but no desire for them. Socrates never mentions false opinion and the awareness of ignorance. Since he wants to prove that hallucination (*phantasma*) belongs to the experience of almost all pleasures that are not of the mind or directed by the mind, any pleasure that attends on the recovery from an error would be as perspectivally determined as the recovery from any illness. Socrates' model is pleasant smells, whose absence arouses no desire and whose departure no regret. They are pure because they are neither good nor bad. If knowledge were as pure, it would cease to be important to us; like junk food it would not stick to the ribs. The mortal now comes in (585c4),[1] and Glaucon will conclude that it is nothing (608c8). A confrontation with poetry is unavoidable.

Socrates begins with the ordinary understanding of the contra- riety of pleasure and pain, and a quietness of soul (*hēsukhia*) between them. He then proves, by an appeal to a physiology of pleasure and pain as motions, that the middle state, which must now be understood as the absence of motion, cannot in itself afford any pleasure or pain; it appears to do so only through a comparsion with either pain or pleasure. It is admitted that the speeches of the sick about their pain are true, but not that there is nothing more pleasant than health and they had not realized it before they were sick. The sick are not allowed to revise their opinion and resolve in the future to take their pleasure in being healthy. With the intrusion of a

---

1. *Thnēton* ("mortal") occurs six times in the *Republic*, twice in quotations from poets (331a8, 386d1), twice in Book X (611a7, 617d7), once at 416e7, and here.

physiology of pleasure, health ceases to be an Aristotelian mean and becomes instead a mathematical point at which one can only look and judge at a distance but never experience.

The consequence of this argument emerges in the likeness Socrates now applies to pleasure and pain. It starts from the premise that there is in nature an up, down, and middle (584d3–4). Anyone, then, in moving to the middle from down believes that he is moving upwards. If he stands in the middle and looks from where he moved, he believes he is nowhere else than up, "if he has not seen the true up." If he then moved back again, he would believe and believe truly that he was moving downwards. Socrates, however, does not discuss the more interesting case of someone, like Timaeus, who believes there is no true up or down (*Timaeus* 62c3–63e8). When Timaeus got in the middle, he would certainly see that he had moved up, but he would not believe it; he would call his experience of the pleasure, which was comparable to that movement, a hallucination, but he would not conclude that there was a nonhallucinatory pleasure. When, moreover, Timaeus moved back again, it would appear to him that he was moving downwards, but he would not believe it either; and in experiencing the pain comparable to that movement, he would not believe it was true or pure pain (584c2). He would always be buoyed by his belief-grounded hope that he had not yet reached bottom and a return was imminent. Timaeus may of course be mistaken, but his false opinion is clearly different from his hallucinations; and Socrates is truly mistaken to identify false opinion with hallucination. Such an identification makes philosophy impossible, for even if Timaeus were conveyed to the true up, he would not believe it. One cannot arrive at the true up unless one has started from there and knows it. The movement to the truth is forever barred.

Socrates, however, corrects this account with another. Hunger and thirst are now emptinesses of a corporeal condition, just as ignorance and folly are of the soul's (585a–b4). They are all needs and not desires. Socrates returns to the true and healthy city before desires had come in through Glaucon's rejection of the city of pigs. His argument, then, is a reflexive argument: Socrates convinces Glaucon that he is more truly filled with the *Republic* than if he had dined on pork. His needs and not his desires have been satisfied. He should now know that he could never be satisfied with meat, tables, and couches. At the same time, however, Socrates introduces the more and less into being and knowledge. The filling of soul is truer than the filling of body: one is less inclined in the case of knowledge than in that of food and drink to mistake the movement away from emptiness as fulfillment. The healthy city, in which mind and body operated perfectly, appeared more complete than any city that succeeded it; but the philosophic state of being between empty and full does not mistake gray for white. It knows itself as a mixed state. To the philosopher, partial knowledge, then, does not present itself as complete knowledge. Philosophy neither possesses Helen nor fights over her phantoms (586c4). Filling of soul is "truer", *alēthestera* (585b9). It is the greater disclosing of the not-yet disclosed.[2]

37

POETRY

(588b1–608b10)

The statue Glaucon had made of the unjust man had no soul. Socrates now has Glaucon picture such a soul as a monstrous version of the tripartite structure he had devised for soul in light of the class-structure of the city. There are still three looks (*ideai*) to the soul, but each is no longer a simple part: appetite is a complex beast with heads of savage and tame beasts able to be grown from itself; the thumoeidetic is a lion which can be snakelike (590b1); and the ratiocinative is a human being in whose likeness the outer envelope is fashioned. It is as hard to picture the inside and outside together as it is to picture the inside by itself. If the man is put in front, as in Centaurs, the many-headed beast could form a circle around the

---

2. It might be observed that the number 729, which represents the greater degree of pleasure of the philosopher's life over against the tyrant's (587d12–e4), can be assigned to the divided line as follows:

A	B	C	D	E
Tyrant	Democrat	Oligarch	Timocrat	Philosopher

AB is 9, BC and CD are each 81, and DE is 729 (9:81::81:729::90:810). So CDE represents the soul-structure, and ABC its phantom image (unnecessary and illegal desires [587c9]). If 729 represents the number of days and nights in a year (588a3–5), the sun shines only over DE.

equine extension, and the lion could bring up the rear; but if the lion keeps the place the needs of the city assigned to it, the picture defies the imagination. Socrates now admits that the thumoeidetic is never tame, though like a snake it may be charmed, and there are tame elements of desire that do respond to education. The most disturbing element, however, of the soul in speech is the man within. He too must be imagined to have within him the same monster. Man, then, is an ever-receding image of man. Since a perfect matchup between the inner and the outer man is precluded, the human as such does not exist. Socrates is forced to replace the man within by the divine (589d1, e4), and thereby admit another kind of monster as the alternative to the original.

Socrates makes it clear, in his gentle persuasion of the praiser of injustice, that this alternative is not always available. The condition for its possibility is a city with laws that promote the beautiful; and the only city whose aim was to inspire a love of the beautiful was the city in speech. No real city has anything but shameful laws. Despair, then, seems to be inevitable if the soul's natural shape conforms with Socrates' present picture: only the most musical of educations could so articulate the fusion of forms that one could even speak of a tripartite soul. The forced parallel to the class-structure of the city thus becomes justified, for some version of it is a necessity for any city: the city imposes on the soul a crude replica of its own crude structure. That suffices to bring some order to most men most of the time, even though the city requires a restructuring of the true order of soul, so that the leonine and ophidian come between reason and desire and split their natural harmony. That harmony survives in the city only in a corporeal form, in which reason solely serves the satisfaction of need, and approaches more or less the true and healthy city. Anything over and above the true city in the city diverges from its true psychic counterpart in philosophy—the harmony of reason and desire—and infects desire with all the growths Socrates had made evident in the sixteenfold analysis of the four mistaken regimes. The apparently natural shape of the soul is thus its political shape, which, manifest in dreams, reveals the strain to which the city has subjected soul. The political against the political is the stuff of poetry. Poetry represents the monstrousness of the politicized soul without its basis in the eidetic structure of soul. It is interested less in courage as the respository of all lawful opinions than in envy and wilfulness, and less in the socially useful love of money than in the polymorphism of desire. Socrates' rejection of poetry is at the same time the rejection of the tyrant whom poetry serves up to its audience of tyrannical men.

Socrates analyzes poetry in two ways. The first presents poetry in light of being, the second in light of the good.[1] It is not obvious how the two ways fit together, for though the poet is three removes from the truth in both, he is third from a god in the first and third from a human being in the second. Socrates begins with couches and tables in the first, and with bit and reins in the second. Couches and tables belong to the city of fevered heat, and, in Socrates' presentation, the division of labor has advanced so far that the couchmaker and the tablemaker are distinct; but though horses are not said to belong to either city, the artisans who make bit and reins—the shoemaker and the blacksmith—do belong to the true and healthy city. Couches and tables were luxuries; they heralded an expansion of the arts that catered to consumption and among which were all the arts of imitation, including painting and music (373a6, b6). The horse, on the other hand, first occurs as an example of a thumoeidetic animal whose human usefulness depends on rule (375a12). The expansion of desire and the need to be ruled went together, for the first led to war, and war in turn led to the structuring of the city and the soul. The expansion of desire was Socrates' response to Glaucon's concealed demand to be somebody or at least to have the possibility to become somebody. To satisfy the conditions for that possibility involved the city in war and the consequent subordination of the individual to the city's needs. That subordination made it finally possible in turn to be somebody who was good. Politically, the relation between being something and being good controlled the relation between the city and the regime, the spurious unity of which was the noble lie. Individually, education took a corresponding twofold form, in the first of which the love of the beautiful could make a citizen better than the city itself would ever be, and in the second the love of the truth could make him superior to the best possible regime. Poetry, then, is necessarily subject to a twofold attack. It has not understood fully either individuality or goodness.

Socrates admits that he does not understand what imitation (*mimēsis*) means, or, more literally, what it wants to be (cf.590e1). He

---

1. The difference between the two arguments resembles the difference between eikastics and phantastics in the *Sophist* (235c8–236c7). It recalls as well the two principles of Socrates' theology.

proposes to proceed in the usual way: "We are accustomed surely to posit some single species (*eidos*) in regard to the manifold of each thing to which we apply the same name" (596a6–7). His examples are many couches and tables, for each of which "we are also accustomed to say" that there is one *idea* at which the craftsman of either artifact looks when he makes couches or tables; and the couches and tables are those we use, but neither of the craftsmen makes either *idea* itself (596a10–b10). That the posited *eidos* could be the same as the *idea* of the craftsmen seems impossible, for the *eidos* is initially a question—"What is that which makes every couch a couch?"—and the *idea* is an answer to which the couchmaker has complete access. Couchmaker as accomplished Platonist is not easy to accept. The *eidos* and the *idea*, however, are identified after Socrates introduces the maker of everything (and everything includes gods and all the things in Hades below the earth), and tells Glaucon that he too could make everything he mentioned by carrying around a mirror. Glaucon agrees but distinguishes between these appearances (*phainomena*) and the beings in truth (*onta tei alētheiai*). He agrees that the painter makes an apparent couch, and that the *eidos* couch is that which is a couch while the couch a couchmaker makes is not perfectly that which is. It is astonishing that Glaucon's "beings in truth" are deprived of perfect being so easily, and that he does not ask Socrates how he can possibly mirror gods and the things in Hades, or, after he agrees that the god makes the couch in nature, ask who makes the gods the painters paint.

We ourselves are equally baffled as to what Glaucon makes of all this and what Socrates is driving at. The real couch on which one cannot lie seems to express the meaning that Glaucon invested it with when he demanded that Socrates supply him with one. Couch and table are artifacts embedded in law and convention, as Glaucon recognized expressly (372d7); they encoded Glaucon's wish not to be a pig, which any "real" couch and table would satisfy only partially. Glaucon wanted to be more than an Athenian without ceasing to be an Athenian. Socrates' version of that longing is his account of god the couchmaker. The god, "whether because he did not want to or some necessity was upon him not to make more than one," made one couch, "because, should he make only two, one would come to light of which both in turn would have the *eidos*, and that would be that which couch is and not the two." Socrates continues, "The god, I suspect, in knowing this, wanting to be really [*ontōs*] a maker of a couch that really [*ontōs*] is, but not of some couch nor himself to be some couchmaker, made just one to come to be by nature" (597c1–d3). The unique couch is a product of the god's will to be a unique couchmaker and have no competitors. He wants to be somebody who is the only member of his own set. He is not going to reproduce what gives him the title to be who he is, for his reality depends on there not being anything that he himself has not made. His will, therefore, has nothing to do with knowledge, for otherwise whatever he knew would be something he had not made. His human counterpart is also never said to make his couch by art.[2] Any couch one can lie on, no matter how crudely made, is a couch, just as the couch the painter makes with all his skill belongs to the same class as the image Glaucon sees in his mirror. With the replacement of knowledge by will, the first argument about imitation comes to depend on the total breakdown of the class-structure of city and soul, so that the individual on his own can make something of himself. He wills to be unique. "One god/one job" now becomes the principle that governs each human being.

Accordingly, when Socrates discusses painting, he slides from the artifact to the artificer and has the painter make phantoms of makers (597e10–598c4). The issue of knowledge is first raised in the context of imitation. It arises after Glaucon has misunderstood the import of god the couchmaker and assigned to him universal demiurgy. God the couchmaker must have been one of infinitely many gods, each one of whom willed without knowledge to make something unique and who thus answered the democratic criteria of freedom and equality. Socrates was setting up an opposition between this manifold of demiurgic gods and the imitator who can represent anyone and violate the principle of natural justice. The gods of the poets are too few to satisfy the individual will, which, in the absence of any political purpose, can now dream of truly becoming a craftsman of freedom. It is not possible to be oneself—to mind one's own business, or, as we say, to have one's own space—unless one raises some claim to superiority. If someone pushes us aside as we are walking along minding our own business, we are likely to say, "Who do you think you are?" as if to say that if he were somebody he would have the right we believe he usurped. The poets pose a grave

2. The first occupations with the *-ikē* suffix, which designates an art, are painting and imitation (598b1, 6), and they occur after the first argument is complete. Earlier *tekhnē* is concealed twice in the word *kheirotekhnēs* (596c2, 597a6), but it has no effect on the argument.

threat to our claims. No mother, after she has heard Thetis' lament for Achilles, *ōmoi egō deilē, ōmoi dusaristotokeia* ("Woe! I am wretched. Woe! Unhappy mother of the best son"—*Iliad* 18.54), can ever believe that her grief at the loss of her own son is as perfect. She falls short of a perfection to the reality of which the poet himself is supremely indifferent (472d4–8). The poets foster the apolitical will to be somebody and show up everyone as nothing. Their own art, aimed at Everyman, stands in the way of satisfying Everyman. The escape they offer from being nobody is the flight into nonbeing.

Socrates' ostensible argument against Homer for having had no effect on education has a foolish air, for if that criticism were justified, the expurgation of his poetry would have been unnecessary. His imitations of virtue are imitations of the phantoms (*eidōla*) of virtue (600e5), and the phantoms of virtue should correspond to the work of the legislators. Socrates does not say who made virtue itself. In the best city, true virtue, as the right order of soul, was philosophy and characterized the philosopher-king; phantoms of true virtue were to be the result of the original music education. It seems, then, that the members of the artisan-commercial class should be the recipients of poetry's semblances of the phantom virtue. Socrates certainly had not provided that class with anything to replace poetry; its obedience to the law and deference to its rulers were all that concerned him. If we now assign tragic poetry to the demos and say that like the demos its proper function is to serve and obey, what are we to make of the gods it represents who are as much phantoms as Achilles and Odysseus? Poetry seems to be inferior and superior to any actual legislation. It supports the law through its gods who urge mortals to think mortal thoughts; and it subverts the law through its gods whom it serves up as beings to be emulated. Poetry duplicates with its double message the twofold character of justice; but it undermines both morality and what transcends morality, for the poetic mode of each is an illusion. Poetry stands outside the city but not outside the cave.

The threefold scheme of god, couchmaker and painter is replaced by the threefold scheme of the art of use, the art of making and the art of painting. If the second scheme is superimposed on the first, all of us and especially Glaucon would be the users of couches without having any knowledge of their use. Glaucon did not know anything about couches and tables; he knew only that he was hungry and uncomfortable sitting for so long. If the couchmaker god had not saved him, he would have directly confronted the problem behind

Socrates' counterexample to Cephalus—knowledge of use alone makes for right. As it was, Socrates had indulged him in speech until Glaucon accepted the asceticism of the good city. The severity of that asceticism now emerges in Socrates' stating that the excellence, beauty, and rightness of any artifact, animal, or action consists solely in its use (601d4–6), but that the painter of flutes will adjust their appearance to the opinion the many have about the beautiful (602b2–4). In the first scheme, the painter was allowed to paint the couch in the same perspective as we would see it, and it was assumed that that perspective was neutral. Now, however, each artifact is not just a something, but good or bad as it conforms or not to the specifications of the user. The failure of the painter consists in not associating with the user (whereas the maker is obliged to do so), and in freeing himself from the user's guidance, attending instead to the common view of the independence of the beautiful from the good. Socrates implies that if the painter were compelled to heed the user, the picture of good flutes could exhibit an apparitional likeness of their goodness. Since the painter would still not know how to make good flutes, he could bypass the flutes as made and present an apparitional likeness that would not have to match the appearance which the flutemaker, with his correct opinion, would recognize as a true likeness. If, then, the user could have two sets of instructions, one for the maker and one for the painter, the ruler of the good city too could inform the soldiers with one kind of education and have the poets represent to the demos something else. The effect would be to induce in the demos a set of opinions compatible with those of the soldiers but without the love of the beautiful. In view of their own chrematistic function, the demos would probably have an exaggerated belief in the guardians' selflessness.

Poetry in principle has no concern for the good. Tragedy in particular suspends the good, since its concern is the just and the beautiful. The sensible Ismene is the foil to the noble criminality of Antigone. Socrates asks, What makes us go along with poetry's rejection of the good? The question is particularly acute for him, for he had said that every soul divines that the good is something, and poetry can have its effect only if reality vanishes along with the good. Poetry, then, is the opponent to the central thesis of the *Republic*: nothing can wholly shut off the cave from the light. Socrates has already accounted for the political conditions under which tragedy thrives; but that to which it appeals in the soul still remains unexplicated. Socrates first works out an elaborate comparison between measurement and appearance, on the one hand, and reason and experience, on the other, in order to show that poetry crosses appearances with experiences. We do not trust appearances, and often law, habit, and reason combine to make us distrust our experiences. What we do trust, however, are the appearances of experiences. We trust the poets who put at a distance everything we experience near at hand. When a decent man loses his son, he puts up with his loss more easily than anyone else; and though complete equanimity is impossible, he will strain to preserve the measure of the mean in his pain. This measure in turn will hold more in public when he is seen by his peers than in private when he is alone, and he is no longer ashamed to say and do what he would prefer no one to hear and see (603e3–604a8). Such a man realizes that he has not incorporated fully the injunction of the law, and that he is more dependent on public opinion then he imagined previously. The poets, in depicting this hidden grief, make this self-realization known to everyone (Sophocles *Ajax* 317–22; *Trachiniae* 1070–74). No one is really noble. The poets thus serve notice that nothing can be hidden from them. They are the true communists, who, in exposing the limits of the law, determine the character of what is beyond those limits. The publication of the private alters the private; it imposes on the private its interpretation. The law's indifference to whatever it cannot regulate does not prevent the supervention of shame and guilt in the case of the law-abiding: they are to rejoice at the victory of their city, yet cannot but mourn beyond what the law prescribes at the loss of their own (Aeschylus *Agamemnon* 636–49). Suffering breaks the illusion that one's country is one's own; and though no one but the tyrant will proscribe tears (Tacitus *Annals* 6.10, 19; 12.47), the poets make sure that the criminality of the heart is not a secret.

Socrates isolates this criminal element from that which strains against it and is prepared to obey the law; and he asserts, by the principle he had invoked to distinguish between the rational and the desiderative, that they must be two (604a10–b7). The rational here shows up in four maxims of the law, any one of which might be thought to be adequate to check the indulgence in grief: (1) the good and evil of the misfortune are not plain; (2) there is no going forward if one takes it hard; (3) nothing human is worthy of great concern; and (4) pain is an impediment to deliberation (604b9–d1). The first and third belong together, as do the second and fourth; but they are not quite consistent with one another. The first implies that in human affairs, which do not admit of deliberation, there might be a mysterious providence, and the third that in the larger scheme of things misfortune is necessary. The fourth alone argues that the misfortune was an evil and a matter of chance, and that one should pick oneself up and go on, for one can determine on one's own what is best. In comprehending these maxims under law, Socrates blurs the difference between the thumoeidetic and the rational, so that the nothingness of man and the good for man are presented as if the sobriety in behavior they severally promote proves their cooperation. It is therefore uncertain whether what he now calls *to aganaktēton* and *to thrēnōdes* (604e2, 606b1), the irritable and the dirgelike, has been falsely separated from that which would find the first and third maxims persuasive. The acceptance of the view that the good and evil of a loss cannot be made out falls together with grief as the experience of purposelessness. The painting of a flute represents one as easily as the other, for the painted flute is incapable of functioning and certainly makes it unclear whether a flute is any good. There are no flutemakers or flautists in the good city (399d3–5). Grief is the natural correlate of radical individuality, or our being nothing without the good. In the fifth ode of Bacchylides, Heracles weeps for the first and only time; he says, "Not to be born is best," but at once adds, "There is no doing (*prēxis*) for those who lament" (160–63). The realization that grief disengages one from life does not in itself contradict the retroactive wish not to have been.

The characteristic of *to aganaktēton* is rehearsal, the transposition of the original experience into a form that is repeatable. The refusal to let go of one's grief in the face of the irreparability of one's loss leads to the experience of insatiety (604d8–10). *To aganaktēton* thus teams up with imitation, whose re-presentation renders useless whatever it recalls. Tragic poetry is in a sense itself the tragic. It makes us suspend our own good and look upon alien things. We sympathize but do not identify, and we can do so because we believe that its images are not of ourselves. It pulls us out of ourselves and blinds us to ourselves. We rejoice and praise on seeing a man such as we would be ashamed to be, but we are not disgusted:

> That which has been forcibly repressed in one's own misfortunes and is starved for tears, lamentations, and satiation, being naturally of the sort to desire them, is that which is then filled up and made to rejoice by the poets; but that which is the best of us, because it has been educated inadequately by reason as well as habit, lets up its guard on the dirgelike, because it is beholding the experiences of

another and it is not shameful to it if another who says he is a good man grieves inopportunely; rather, it praises and pities him, and believes that it is a profit, the pleasure, and would not choose to be deprived of it out of contempt for the whole poem. It is, I suspect, given to few to calculate that necessarily one transfers the enjoyment from the things of another to one's own, and by the cherishing of pity in this case it is not easy to hold it down in one's own experiences. (606a3–b8)

The rational in us believes that the pleasure belongs to itself as spectator (*theōroun*); it cannot believe that it is the pleasure of weeping, for the tragic figure grieves in a form that is free of pleasure. He has pure pain and we have pure pleasure. The spectator pities the tragic figure because he believes he is his superior: there is nothing he is aware of in himself that has been under constraint. The spectator thus looks at and fails to know himself (cf. 606c8). He mistakes the pleasure of self-pity for the pleasure of contemplation. In his self-delusion he is a theoretical man. The alien is the mask of what is his own.

The family resemblance between the experience of tragedy and the Leontius story suggests that poetry tends to establish the spurious alliance between reason and spiritedness. Imitation transforms the cannibalistic eye of Leontius into the innocent eye of the spectator, so that he believes he is taking in through reason what he is absorbing into his heart. His heart is the place of his unitary experience, but he himself has split it between his pity for the protagonist and his pleasure in the poem. It is in light of this spurious distancing that the ancient quarrel between poetry and philosophy is to be understood. In Socrates' presentation, the defenders of poetry are the poetic and poetry herself as well as the lovers of poetry; but philosophy does not speak on her own behalf, and the only outspoken partisans are the philosophers. There are no wise men or even sophists who come to her defense. The lovers of poetry do not become poets, the lovers of philosophy are the philosophers. The lovers of poetry are enchanted by the poetry and praise the poet. They split the pleasant from the good (cf. 607e1–2). Through this disassociation they believe they are with the poet and are with the poem. Philosophy does not disassociate; there is for it no artifact apart from the artificer. Socrates tells his own story. Philosophy is not an *idea* to which one looks and in light of which one makes oneself. No god can be the maker of the idea of philosophy. The poets, on the other hand, induce in us an admiration for themselves without emulation and all the while turn us into their inventions. While we despise the reality whose images we delight in, we become that reality whose makers we praise. The poets are the *unacknowledged* legislators of mankind.

38

SOUL

(608c1–612b6)

In the course of the argument for the soul's immortality, Glaucon says that injustice, lack of self-control, cowardice, and folly make the soul bad (609b9–c1). He thus acknowledges that Socrates has proved what he wanted, that injustice is not good for soul regardless of whether one gets away with it; but this proof does not exhilarate Glaucon. When Socrates, in preparing the way for his description of the greatest rewards of virtue, asks, "What could be great in a short time?," and goes on to explain—"All this time at least from childhood to old age would doubtless be small relative to all time"—Glaucon corrects him and says, "No, not small, it's nothing" (608c5–8). Glaucon gets what he wants and despairs. The reminding of the eternal reduces human life to nothing. Socrates cannot but be just if he can get Glaucon to recover from his sense of the heterogeneity of human time and all of time and accept the possibility of establishing some ratio between them (608d7, 613e5). Socrates' proof of the soul's immortality, however, is inadequate. Either his proof requires a premise that contradicts that of the *Republic*—the soul must be noncomposite—or, contrary to his proof, the vices of soul are fatal to soul (611b5–7), and the perfectly ordered soul of the philosopher is alone deathless. Socrates further admits that his proof argues for the assignment of a quality to a something whose true nature has not been established in the *Republic* (611b9–612c5). He distinguishes between the true nature of soul and its monoeidetic or polyeidetic structure, all of which they are ignorant of, and their discovery that justice itself is best for soul itself. The *idea* of justice goes along with the *idea* of soul, and neither conforms with the truth. The thumoeidetic determination of soul is inseparable from whatever truth the *Republic* has displayed about political things. For the sake of the argument (*tou logou heneka*), the issue of the real separability of seeming from being had to be suspended; its suspension did not hinder, indeed, it is coincident with the affirmation of "justice itself" and "injustice itself" (612c7–d1). Socrates' justice, then, in combating Glaucon's despair, consists in suggesting to him that his despair is due to the centrality of the thumoeidetic in the *Republic* and in himself. A precise understanding of soul could indeed dissipate his despair, but only at the price of his failure to understand. Glaucon needs the immortality of the soul because he needs injustice to be altogether terrifying (610d5–e4).

The pivotal claim in Socrates' argument for the soul's immortality is that everything has its own vice or evil, and evil is that which makes it cease to be. The soul, he wants to argue, does not admit of soul-rust. There is no evil of soul that destroys soul. Socrates implies that soul is the only being whose being entails necessarily its goodness. Soul, then, is that which links the first argument against poetry with the second. Poetry denies that the soul in being something must be constituted at the same time by a divination of the good; but Socrates says one cannot speak of soul apart from the good. The souls in Hades which flit about like shadows are so many emblems of poetry's separation of being and being good.

Poetry's deepest expression of that separation is in Achilles' words after Odysseus has praised him for his rule over the dead: "Don't try to console me for my death, Odysseus, I would rather be tied to the soil as a slave to a stranger, who himself was needy and whose livelihood not much, than to rule over all the dead" (*Odyssey* 11.488–91). Socrates has cited these words twice, once in excising them from the music education of the soldiers, and once in putting them into the mouth of an ex-prisoner of the cave; but Achilles is conspicuously absent from the myth of Er. There is no lot labeled "Life" in the myth. To choose life is to choose a good life, however specious it might be. Achilles' words are the utterance of an impossible wish. They issue forth from the Beggar who lurks in the thumoeidetic and who alternates within it with pride. The ghost of Achilles, as soon as he heard from Odysseus about the glorious exploits of his son, "departed in joy with long strides across the meadow of asphodel" (11.539–540).

Socrates proves that no vice of soul destroys it; but he does not prove that the same holds true for every constituent of soul. Glaucon's correction of Socrates, that relative to all time mortal time is not small but nothing, suggests that time might be such an element. Could the awareness of time be incompatible with deathlessness? Such an awareness is tied in experientially with *erōs*, for it is in the experience of *erōs* that one's own death comes home to oneself. The issue therefore would be whether soul and eros are bound together in such a way that the soul's immortality is precluded. It is striking in any case that in the *Symposium*, in the dialogue devoted to eros, Diotima, though she defines a kind of eros as a desire for deathlessness, does not ascribe deathlessness to soul. A precise understanding of soul, then, would seem to require a confrontation between *erōs* and *thumos*, particularly as to how each experiences time *sub specie aeternitatis*. In lieu of such an account, Socrates' "small" and Glaucon's "nothing" can be taken as expressing the difference in our dual experience of time. Socrates now argues implicitly that the tragic will not to be is impotent, but he does not take up the question of whether soul ceases to be soul if it becomes what it aspires to be. The truth inherent in the parallel between city and soul might well be that what makes each good makes each imperfect and fortunately liable to destruction.

39

THE MYTH OF ER

(612b7–621d3)

The myth of Er is in eleven sections:

225

Socrates seems to complicate the myth needlessly. If there were no column of light, the place of judgment and the weaving of the Fates would fit more easily together. The column of light, which passes around the outside and through the center of the celestial sphere, makes heaven and earth into a single cosmos; but the spindle of Necessity seems to require that the sky be a hemisphere and its bottom the plane of the concentric circles of the planetary system. By deliberately putting a jog in his account, Socrates seems to acknowledge his failure to connect his ontology with a cosmological psychology. The column of light stands between heaven and earth as a vast system of reward and punishment, on the one hand, and the realm of conditional freedom, on the other. The journey of five days that Er and his fellow souls undertake, from the place where one's past is judged to the center of the cosmos where one chooses a future, seems to symbolize the eccentricity of justice to the good, and to imply that the good is linked more closely than the just with the notion of a cosmic whole. Among the lives there is none labeled "The just life"; and however unjust a life might be, no one chooses it because it is unjust. Everyone chooses a life on the basis of the nonidentity of just and good.

The fit between the just and the good is managed awkwardly through the Fates. Clotho, the Weaver, makes the outer whorl revolve, and she represents the present; Atropos, the Irrevocable, makes the planetary whorls revolve in the opposite direction, and she represents the future; and Lachesis, the Allotter, makes both revolve in turn when the others let go for a time, and she represents the past. The three forms of time out of which human life is woven are the daughters of Necessity, whose spindle is attached in a mysterious manner to the extremities of the bonds from heaven. Socrates is silent about the bonds from below. The strands on the spindle of Necessity, as they come off the bonds of heaven, seem to represent time before the Fates differentiate it into human time; but since the bonds of heaven must be the same as the column of light (616c2), the column of light seems as if it in turn must be time. Time, however, cannot simply be undifferentiated, for Er reports that the column of light resembled the rainbow, and a noncolorless time seems to point again to soul. What binds together the cosmos both inside and out would be soul (*Timaeus* 34b3–8). The manifold of essential soul-types would be so many strands of colored light continually being spun by Clotho into their present manifestations. While the spindle twists them tighter, Atropos would unravel them so as to give the illusion of freedom as they are picked up in front of the platform of Lachesis. If this picture is to be consistent, however, the spindle of Necessity would have to be linked with the lower extremities of the columnar bonds as well and make the condemned souls too part of the ordered cosmos. Injustice would thus be an ingredient in the good; and the spindle would compel good and bad to work together through their inversion in time. Most of the souls whose past has assigned them to the heavenly journey choose lives the next time around that assign them to a subterranean journey; whereas souls who emerge from the punishment underground are more sober the next time and gain a heavenly reward (619d1–d7). There is nothing worse than to gain such a reward without philosophy, for justice rewarded is then cloistered virtue and equivalent to self-ignorance.

Neither the just nor the unjust know anything about the thousand-year journey of the others except through hearsay. When they meet in the meadow, those from heaven report what they saw and experienced without either laughter or joy; but those from under the earth recall in tears and sorrow their punishment. Neither group puts much stock in what they hear. No one is punished or rewarded in terms of the soul itself, for otherwise the citizen of the best city who chose tyranny would have been punished. No one therefore is rewarded for having a just soul (in Socrates' sense of not injuring anyone), for such justice is certainly compatible with not benefiting anyone. Justice and injustice are judged solely in terms of actions and not in terms of circumstances. One chooses one's own circumstances and is judged by one's actions. There are no degrees of culpability; otherwise the exaction of a tenfold penalty for every injustice would be unjust. Although the future tyrant regrets his life before he is born and presumably will express remorse afterwards, his punishment is not altered. The myth of Er is wholly nontragic, for the equivalent to the removal of pity is the discounting of remorse. Only Er finds the sight of the choice of lives pitiable (620a1). The myth is designed to replace tragedy, for it puts lamentations off into the afterlife; but the consequences of this postponement, which destroys the possibility of pity, carries with it the total ignorance of

227

wickedness. The just come to the lottery with an exaggerated sense of their own goodness and resistance to temptation. The unjust, moreover, are without conscience, for the fear that they will not be allowed to pass up through the mouth of the chasm would otherwise not grip everyone alike. The placard that lists their crimes is behind them.

While Socrates seems to concede to Glaucon that his just man if given the ring of Gyges would choose injustice, he denies something that Glaucon had simply assumed, that what one can be is independent of what one was. Habit limits one's freedom; it puts blinkers on possibility. One's prospects are always restrospective. The principle that no one is willingly bad turns out to mean that one chooses to be oneself at the expense of both goodness and justice. The *daimōn* which each soul chooses is the couchmaker god of the first argument against poetry. The self one chooses, however, is a perfect version of oneself. It is individuality thoroughly penetrated by some opinion of one's own excellence. It is, in political terms, the city with some semblance of a regime. Orpheus, out of hatred of women, refuses to be born a man, but he does not choose to be a worm so as to avoid injustice. To escape from one's past is not to shake off one's own good. Odysseus gives up the political life, but he does not give up anything else. Socrates, in correcting Glaucon, seems to side with the poets. We know of the swan Orpheus, the lion Ajax, and the eagle Agamemnon from the poets. Their similes are the truth of each hero's good. The poets thus deprive the heroes of their own essence and claim it as their invention. They alienate the makeup of the character from the character and call it poetry. They conceal the source of their similes. Socrates gets rid of poetry. The images of things are the truth of things.

Socrates seems to grant as much to the poets as to Glaucon. How, then, does Thyestes differ from the citizen of Socrates' best city who chooses tyranny? Tragic poetry does not make the best city the setting for the possibility of Thyestes. It cannot imagine the kind of innocence Socrates has imagined. Socrates therefore implies that the poets invented human monsters who cannot be held accountable precisely because they could only come to be in a state of innocence; but the poets condemn these monsters as if they were responsible. Poetry, like Glaucon, exaggerates human freedom. It does not do what Socrates recommends to Glaucon as the one thing needful, to neglect all other disciplines and investigate one alone, "how to choose the better life on the basis of the feasible everywhere and always" (618c5–6). Socrates' recommendation amounts to a figuring out of all the relations that can possibly obtain between the just and the good in light of the nature of soul and all the circumstances of life (618c6–619b1; *Phaedrus* 277b5–c6). The *Republic* itself is but a fragment of the enterprise Socrates has in mind; indeed, all the dialogues of Plato together are but a fragment. Socrates inserts this recommendation between the two parts of the speech the spokesman of Lachesis gives (617d6–e5, 619b2–6). In the first part he says that the responsibility belongs exclusively to the elector; in the second he says that if the last to choose chooses with mind, he need not despair. Socrates' insertion splits apart freedom and rationality. Without rationality there is no freedom, for without the continual practice of dialectics there are only the snares of innocence and experience. To figure out the best life is the best life.

In the course of the *Republic*, Socrates identified the just life with the life of philosophy. In the myth of Er, no one chooses either of them. Each soul either perfects or compensates for its past to such a degree that the possibility of freeing oneself from habit seems precluded. Only the experiences of Odysseus might give him a chance; but Socrates himself seems never to have been Odysseus. His *daimonion*, he said, was probably unique (496c4–5). Perhaps, then, philosophy is a rare strand in the bond of the cosmos, and when babies who die at birth choose a life at random, they sometimes get lucky.

GENERAL INDEX

Achilles, 66, 224

Adimantus: ambiguous answer of, 49:
complements Glaucon, 40; on degeneration of city, 82

Aeschylus, 220

Agamemnon, Socrates' version of
speech of, 70

Alienation, 104

Anaxagoras, 1–4, 146

Ancestors, 172

Anger: syntax of, 100; See also Thumoeidetic

Animation, 99

Aphrodite and Ares, 123

Appearances, 216

Argument: and action, 164–65; displacement in, 44; kinds of, 4, 27

Aristophanes, 127 n

Aristotle, 63, 69, 73, 117, 151, 162

Art: development of, 150; division of,
113; as perfect, 24; teaching of, 19.
See also Knowledge

Ascent from cave, 176

Asceticism, 110, 219

Astronomy, 191. See also Cosmology

Athena, 62

Athens, 3, 124, 190

Bacchylides, 221

Beautiful, The, 72; and good, 115; and
law, 214

Beggar and Thief, 197, 206

Being (*ousia*), 139, 169; double meaning of, 162

Bestiality, 20

Body, 175; needs of, 25; privacy of, 117.
See also City

Caesar, 197

Cave, 138, 154; ascent from, 161; echoes
in, 173; as intentional imagination,
172; and noble lie, 171; poets and
gods of, 70. *See also* Line, Sun

Cephalus, 100, 202, 219; account of
old age by, 12; as impersonator, 71

Chance, 119, 148

Charmides (Plato's), 118

Cicero, 9

City: citizen in, 130; classes in, 91; core
of, 95; dialogic, 47, 123; doubled,
50, 54; as *eidos,* 103; expansion of,
53; feasibility of, 123; founding of,
44; inside and outside of, 46; in
speech, 47, 49, 170, 185; and knowledge, 50; love of, 76; and lying, 16;
nearer than individual, 45; nonsacred, 82; not by nature, 36; order
of, 104; of pigs, 51; sacred, 150; simulacrum of good in, 77

Class: analysis of justice, 94; formation
of, 135, 183; membership, 89, 93;
structure, 111, 202. *See also* Eidetic
analysis, Species

Classlessness, 203

Clitophon, 23, 68

Communism. goodness of, 118; and
ring of Gyges, 37; reasons for, 111

Comparison-test, 36-38

Conscience, 41

Consent, 87

Consumption and production, 51-52

Conversion, 179

Corpses, 121

INDEX OF *REPUBLIC* PASSAGES DISCUSSED

Passages cited from the section under discussion are not indexed.